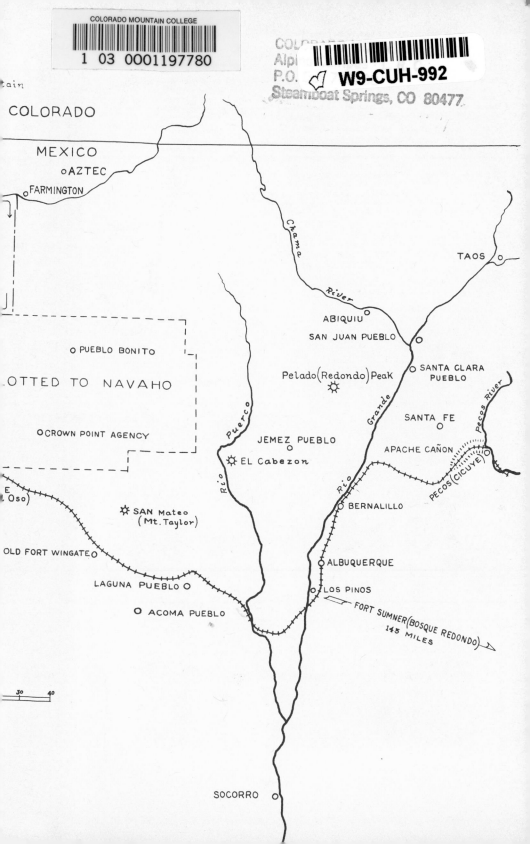

tain

COLORADO

MEXICO

o AZTEC

o FARMINGTON

Chama

River

TAOS o

ABIQUIU

SAN JUAN PUEBLO   o

o PUEBLO BONITO

SANTA CLARA
PUEBLO

Pecos River

Pelado (Redondo) Peak

LOTTED TO NAVAHO

o CROWN POINT AGENCY

Rio Puerco

JEMEZ PUEBLO

Grande

SANTA FE
o

APACHE CAÑON

☼ EL Cabezon

PECOS (CICUYE)

E
l Oso)

Rio

☼ SAN Mateo
(Mt. Taylor)

o BERNALILLO

OLD FORT WINGATE o

LAGUNA PUEBLO O

o ALBUQUERQUE

O ACOMA PUEBLO

o LOS PINOS

FORT SUMNER (BOSQUE REDONDO)
145 MILES

30   40

SOCORRO o

DATE DUE

5 ✓ or ✓'s to 2008		

INDIANS OF THE ENCHANTED DESERT

LITHO BY WALSWORTH PUB. CO., INC., MARCELINE, MO.

INDIANS OF THE ENCHANTED DESERT

BY

LEO CRANE

WITH ILLUSTRATIONS

The Rio Grande Press, Inc.

GLORIETA, NEW MEXICO · 87535

1972
© The Rio Grande Press, Inc.,
Glorieta, N. M.

First edition from which this edition was
reproduced was supplied by

INTERNATIONAL BOOKFINDERS, INC.,
P. O. Box 1
Pacific Palisades, Calif. 90272

A RIO GRANDE CLASSIC
First published in 1925

LIBRARY OF CONGRESS CARD CATALOG
73-188659

I.S.B.N. 87380-086-9

First Printing 1972

The Rio Grande Press, Inc.

GLORIETA, NEW MEXICO · 87535

Publisher's Preface

　* When we consider whether or not to reprint a book, one of our criteria is: how well does the book read? Is it an interesting book? Does it read easily? Does the development and narration hold the reader's interest? There are many books well worth reprinting for research purposes, but which are difficult if not impossible to read from beginning to end. We think we are an average reader—one who finds truth stranger, and far more interesting, than fiction. We therefore believe that if we read and like a book, then it would be equally interesting to other average readers. We hasten to add that we are aiming at a sweeping generalization, here, not a specific.

　So, we found Leo Crane's *Indians of the Enchanted Desert* totally absorbing. We read the book the first time years ago, in high school not knowing then where was Keams Canon or the great Indian reservations of the Navajo and the Hopi—indeed, that or little else about the American Southwest. It was fascinating to us in the 1930's; it was overwhelmingly so when we returned to it again a few weeks ago. We think it is a great book to read, especially so since we now have a pretty good perspective ourselves on the Indians of the Enchanted Desert.

We like the book especially, now, for its pure and unadulterated honesty. It is, from cover to cover, an honest book.

Author Leo Crane was born February 27, 1881, in Baltimore, Md., son of William Joseph and Mary Kailer Crane. He was educated in the public schools of Baltimore, but to what extent we have been unable to determine. The clarity and precision of his writing suggests a most excellent education, but it may have been obtained in his own way and his own time. Apparently he started to work at the age of 15. His biography sketch in *Who's Who in America* for 1940-1941 reports that he performed "commercial" work for five years and "newspaper" work for two, which brings him to 1903 when he joined what was then called the Indian Bureau of the Department of the Interior in Washington, D. C. Mr. Crane gives some fleeting glimpses of his career in the first few pages of this book, relating with dry humor how he came to relocate in the Southwest in 1910. He describes how it happened that he became the Indian Agent for the "Bureau" in 1911, thus embarking him on the remarkable and eventful years he describes so vividly thereafter. His tenure at Keams Cañon ended in 1919, when he was transferred to become the Indian Agent at Albuquerque for the Pueblo Indians of the Rio Grande Valley.

From 1919 to 1922, he was stationed thus in New Mexico. In the latter year, he again transferred to become the Indian Agent for the Lower Yankton Sioux of South Dakota. Apparently, his health prohibited the northern climate, so he returned to his beloved desert. Between the latter part of 1922 and 1925, he worked with the Mohave and Chemchuevi Indians along the lower Colorado River—in the area to be reclaimed by the then-projected Boulder (Hoover) Dam project. His biographical sketch does not say whether here he was "Agent" or not. In any event, after serving the Indian Bureau (now the Bureau of Indian Affairs) for 22 years, he resigned to work with various Indian tribes in a civil capacity. He is last mentioned in *Who's Who in America* in the 1940-1941 (Volume 21) edition, where he reported that he was an employee of the U. S. Bureau of Reclamation as a guide at the now-completed Boulder Dam. His home at the time was listed as Boulder City, Nev.

We attempted the nearly-impossible task of finding out what happened to Leo Crane. Mrs. Merpa J. Nickel, Librarian of the Boulder City Public Library, told us she heard he passed away in Tucson about 1959 or 1960. Mr. Sears, director of personnel at the Boulder Dam Project, found no records for Mr. Crane but he did locate one old timer who remembered that Crane had retired about 1942 and removed himself to Greaterville, Arizona. Greaterville still exists, after a fashion. Our telephone inquiries eventually reached Mr. Harold B. Thurber, of Sonoita (south by east of Tucson about 50 miles or so). Mr. Thurber is one of the valley old timers who did, indeed, remember meeting and knowing Leo Crane perhaps 30 years ago. What happened to him? Golly, Mr. Thurber didn't know. No one knew. We wrote to the Tucson Public Library to inquire of our good friend there, Mrs. Dorothy Hensley. She didn't know. The Arizona Historical Society didn't know, either, having in its voluminous files only a fleeting reference to this particular book. As is so often the case, we will publish Mr. Crane's books and then—too late to include here—we will receive all kinds of information about Leo

Crane from people who knew him or knew of him but didn't know we wanted to know about him.

For those interested in geography, Greaterville was "founded" in 1874, the site of a gold camp. By 1881, the gold played out and the camp was deserted. According to *Arizona Place Names* (Univ. of Ariz. Press, Tucson, 1960), the mines had a brief revival in the early 1900's, but subsequently died once again. Nothing much of Greaterville is left, now, Mr. Thurber reports, but some shacks occupied by Mexican families living in the United States.

Leo Crane married Mrs. Walbridge Padgett, a mining woman and journalist of Arizona, on March 18, 1922. Like Mr. Crane himself, we have been unable to discover any further reference to her.

We tried.

Author Crane wrote this book in 1925, and another, entitled *Desert Drums,* in 1927. We reprinted the latter simultaneously with this title. He authored more than 165 articles on various aspects of Indian life and culture and other aspects of the Great Southwest. However, there is no indication as to where the articles were published, or, indeed, if they were published at all. Considering the skill with which he wrote, we cannot see an editor refusing his manuscripts, so undoubtedly, somewhere, the Crane articles exist.

Neither *Indians of the Enchanted Desert* nor *Desert Drums* had an index or a frame-of-reference map. As we have so often in the past, we turned to that Greatest Indexer of All Time, our friend William (Bill) Farrington of Santa Fe. He not only indexed the books methodically and effectively, he was so intrigued with author Crane's evocative and vivid narrative that he (Farrington) wrote an introduction to each book as well. What indexer Farrington wrote follows these words; we are, as always, most grateful for his perceptive notes.

Years ago, when The Rio Grande Press was just beginning its not very meteoric rise into the publishing firmament, we reprinted books just about as was the edition we reproduced from (that is grammar?). Our friends in the book reviewing fraternity thereupon publicly took us to task and irascibly scolded our lack of "improvements" or "updating", by providing such as an index or a frame-of-reference map, or the like. Smarting under the lash, we began including such things. One thing we started to include besides indexes, new maps and new photographs, was a "Publisher's Preface", such as this one. As we have here, we outlined what we knew or could learn about the book and the author. Sometimes, since we were paying the bill, we felt at liberty to express a conservative viewpoint about this, that or the other; this seemed to be our right, under the First Amendment to the Constitution. Now, we find—all too often—that some reviewers get so outraged that we should dare to express an opinion different from theirs that they pay no attention whatever to, and say nothing at all about, our added new material.

We think any book reviewer, addressing himself earnestly to the task of evaluating the book at hand— any book—ought first to use his precious review space to mention the important things, such as a new index, new scholarly introduction, new frame-of-reference map, new photographs, or whatever. These things are important. So far as we are concerned, any reviewer mentioning our important additions first may thereupon castigate us or consign us to the nethermost regions to his heart's content. While on this subject, we think especially that the "liberal" reviewer quivering with outraged indignation at our expression of a conservative viewpoint should learn some word other than "reactionary" to describe us. That term has become so gauché, so odiously trite and hackneyed, so much a part of the Communist jargon, that the use of it almost always (in our opinion) identifies the user as one of the Comrades—and if not that, a writer whose paucity of lexicon deserves a refresher course somewhere. An educated, intelligent American book reviewer capable of independent thought should easily be able to come up with a fresh word equally denigrating, but more accurate, and certainly more literate, as well.

For the sake of clarity, let us observe now that this new edition of this title differs from the first edition used to reproduce it in these ways:

1. We have added a new Publisher's Preface, with some biographical data about the author.
2. We have added a new Introduction, scholarly in intent if not according to Hoyle.
3. We have added a new index.
4. We have added a frame-of-reference map, printed on the endpapers.

Some of our friends in the bookselling business have not been wild about our reprinting this title and *Desert Drums,* saying that neither is precisely a rare book in the first edition. Well, we know that, but we do not reprint rare books only because they are rare books. We reprint books that may not be rare from the antiquarian bookman's viewpoint, but which are not known to the contemporary generations. Thus this title, and *Desert Drums.* Both are excellent books; neither are well known today. We bring them back not because their first editions are rare books, but because each title is a solid source book of American history—and a readable and interesting one, at that. These are books much too fine, by every measure, to let lapse forever into bibliographic oblivion. Many libraries have first editions of these titles on circulating shelves, and we think that is too bad. If we were a librarian with a circulating first edition, we would stash it away as a book treasure for generations to come, and use the Rio Grande Press utility edition for circulation. In any case, it is our perfect conviction that this title and *Desert Drums* are books just simply *worth* reprinting. More than that, both books have a message for these turbulent times, for those readers with the compassion and wisdom to perceive it.

The first edition from which this edition was reproduced was supplied, as usual, by our peripatetic friend Richard (Dick) Mohr, President of International Bookfinders, Inc., of Pacific Palisades, California. Some weeks ago, we determined to reprint a marvelous work in two volumes entitled *Indian Biography, or, An Historical Account of Those Individuals Who Have Been Distinguished Among the North American Natives as Orators, Warriors, Statesmen and Other Remarkable Characters,* by B. B. Thatcher, Esq., first published in 1836. The book is almost totally unknown, not being listed in any of the standard bibliographic reference works. We had at hand a reprint published in 1900, but we wanted a first edition. A whisper wafted from us across the country to Mr. Mohr, and in a trice, we possessed not a first edition, but the 1840 edition—which is much better, as it contains important revisions from the first edition. It has always been so; a note or a call to International Bookfinders produces a veritable tornado of action on the West Coast, and out of that activity comes the book we want. Mr. Mohr is very good for locating hard-to-find books; we appreciate his service and his invariable courtesy.

Of the beautiful Rio Grande Classics, this is the

84th title. It is a book we consider of distinguished literary quality, and its subject commands much public interest these days. It is, although not terribly old as books go, a fine source book of American history, for it is an account of one man's experiences. We think this book should be a *must* for the Southwestern or the Indian history *aficionado*. We are certain the reader will find it well worth reading.

Robert B. McCoy

John T. Strachan

La Casa Escuela
Glorieta, New Mexico
March 1972

Introduction

This is a very difficult book to write about because it is a very difficult book to classify. It is easy to read (the author has, as we used to say, a neat turn of phrase), the facts are clear, the subject of current and continuing interest. The problem is the author. He won't stand still long enough to be labeled. How thoughtless of him. If he were a raging racist or a crusading champion of the downtrodden, the ever-vigilant enemy of bureaucracy or a stereotyped civil servant we'd all feel a lot better about it. But he isn't. He's a little of all and not much of either.

Crane's life reads like a novel of the period. He spent several years in the Washington offices of the Indian Service in the early part of the century. He had some success as a short story writer in his spare time (more than 160 published) and apparently did an adequate job for the government. However, illness or breakdown (he's vague on this point), sent him to the desert to recuperate. He stayed to become agent at Keams

Cañon and later held the same position at the New Mexico Pueblos and the Sioux Agency. He weighed, by his own account, 118 pounds. He ruled, by General Scott's account, an empire comprising several thousand square miles and several thousand 'ignorant savages.'

Now, here's where the trouble begins in the labeling process. Crane had no misty-eyed vision of the noble savage, in fact, he had only contempt for those who did. For the most part Indians were, in his book, ignorant, dirty, untrustworthy, immoral children of nature. Beings, perhaps human, who had to be driven, cajoled, threatened, lectured and dictated to in order that their heathen ways might be mended.

And yet, no man ever fought the BIA with such fervor. He hated the bureaucrats in Washington. He hated the politics, the bungling, the inefficiency, the utter stupidity of federal Indian policy. He blamed most of the 'Indian problems' on that policy and very little on the Indians.[1]

On the other hand, he defended the Indian Agents' hopeless struggle against Washington and a sometimes apathetic, sometimes hostile public. He said:

"But not a word has been printed, and few spoken without a sneer, regarding those of the United States Indian Service who keep watch and ward in the remote places: those who govern and protect, educate and guide; those who have kept the Indian living, that he may be sketched and analyzed and gaped at. This work extends beyond the dude season, through the lonely, bitter winters, embracing at times contagion - camps among an unreasoning, often unappreciative, and occasionally defiant population."[2]

1. see Fayette Robinson's *History of the United States Army,* Rio Grande Press, 1972
2. Crane. *Indians of the Enchanted Desert.* p. 18.

Not words calculated to please the 'new' Indian of our day. But they weren't written in our day. They were written at a time when Indians weren't even *second* class citizens. By 1925 women had the vote, Negroes had the vote, any immigrant who satisfied the rules had the vote, but the Indian did not have the vote. What they did have was a history of broken treaties, a paternalistic government that was one hell of a parent and a few agents who tried to apply Washington-made rules that were a nuisance at best, a disaster at worst.

This was a time when Indian money was held by the agency; when children were taken from their homes by force and sent to 'Indian' schools, which were really 'white' schools for Indians. This was a time when an enlightened man such as Crane could write, with a feeling of complete justification, about the removal of children from their parents in these words:

"He protested against the removal of (his) children, and grasped the axe as if to use it. The men with me promptly removed the implement, and threw him into a corner."[3]

Crane saw nothing wrong in legal kidnapping, when it was for the Indian's own good. But he was bitter about government policy toward certain Indian ceremonials and dances. He didn't always approve of these dances (he didn't approve of jazz and the Charleston, either) but felt they did have a place in Indian life. "Never," he says with heavy irony, "permit them to be happy in their own way. Teach them to be happy in our way."[4]

A lot of people aren't going to like this book. Sometimes it places the Indian in a bad light. It will probably be as revolting to some of the "new" Indians as Amos

3. *Ibid.,* p. 173.
4. *Ibid.,* p. 245.

and Andy is to the Negro. But this is not a book about how it should be. This is a book about how it was. A black period in Indian history, perhaps, but a period nevertheless and it will not disappear by simply ignoring it.

And there is always that possibility, that very slight possibility, that men like Leo Crane are in some small way responsible for the modern, emerging Indian. Maybe those generations at Carlisle did learn something more than personal hygiene and home economics. Maybe Leo Crane's constant war with the BIA taught them something about fighting City Hall.

This book is very difficult to classify. Therefore, I suggest you read it and leave the classification to a librarian. A description of how it *was* may help us understand how it *is*. If it does, that is enough.

Wm. H. Farrington, Santa Fe, N.M.

Photo. by W. C. Wilson

ANNOUNCING THE SNAKE DANCE
Priest at sunset removing kiva signal

INDIANS OF
THE ENCHANTED
DESERT

BY

LEO CRANE

WITH ILLUSTRATIONS

BOSTON
LITTLE, BROWN, AND COMPANY
1925

THE ATLANTIC MONTHLY PRESS PUBLICATIONS
ARE PUBLISHED BY
LITTLE, BROWN, AND COMPANY
IN ASSOCIATION WITH
THE ATLANTIC MONTHLY COMPANY

PRINTED IN THE UNITED STATES OF AMERICA

CONTENTS

PAGE

I Nolens Volens 3

II Across the Plains 11

III Into "Indian Country" 22

IV Old Trails and Desert Fare 30

V Desert Life and Literature 44

VI A Northern Wonderland 54

VII The First Ball of the Season 65

VIII Old Oraibi 78

IX The Making and Breaking of Chiefs . . . 94

X The Provinces of the "Mohoce or Mohoqui" 101

XI The Law of the Realm 113

XII Comments and Complaints 122

XIII A Desert Vendée 142

XIV Soldiers, Indians, and Schools 157

XV An Echo of the Dawn-Men 181

XVI Fiddles and Drums 191

XVII Service Tradition 210

XVIII Buttons and Bonds 224

XIX Our Friends, the Tourists 240

XX The Great Snake-Ceremony 260

CONTENTS

XXI Desert Belascos 275

XXII On the Heels of Adventure 287

XXIII The Red Bootleggers 297

XXIV Held for Ransom 312

XXV Wanted at Court 325

XXVI Hopi Annals 336

XXVII L'Envoi 361

ILLUSTRATIONS

ANNOUNCING THE SNAKE DANCE . . . . . . *Frontispiece*

WALPI, THE PUEBLO OF THE CLOUDS 12
THE VALLEY AND ITS HEADLANDS

A NAVAJO FLOCK AND ITS SHEPHERDS 16
CAÑON DE CHELLY, SEEN FROM THE RIM

CROSSING THE DESERT BELOW CHIMNEY BUTTE 58
THE ORAIBI WASH IN FLOOD-TIME

NAVAJO ON THEIR WAY TO A DANCE 70
A NAVAJO HOGAN AND ITS BLANKET LOOM

OUTFIT OF A WELL-DIGGER, THE DESERT "WATER-WITCH" . 84
DRYING BED OF THE LITTLE COLORADO RIVER

THE HOPI CEREMONIAL CORN-PLANTING 92
HOPI GARDENS IN A SPRING-FED NOOK OF THE DESERT . .

HOPI INDIAN AGENCY AT KEAMS CAÑON 106
HOPI INDIAN HOSPITAL AT KEAMS CAÑON

A BUSY DAY AT THE TRADING-POST, KEAMS CAÑON . . . 118
READY FOR THE 105-MILE TREK TO THE RAILROAD

HOSTIN NEZ, NAVAJO CHIEF AND MEDICINE MAN . . . 124

JUDGE HOOKER HONGAVE OF THE INDIAN COURT 132

YOUKEOMA, ANTELOPE PRIEST AND PROPHET 162

A MESA ROAD — OLD TRAIL TO HOTEVILLA 170
A PRETENTIOUS HOME AT HOTEVILLA

A HOPI SCHOOLGIRL 178
A HOPI YOUTH WHO IS PREPARING FOR COLLEGE

THE WALPI HEADLAND, SEEN FROM THE ORCHARDS . . . 196

THE WALPI STAIRWAY, A ROCK-LADDER TO THE SKY . . . 202

The Author, in the Enchanted Desert 230
Old Glory and the Bond Flag at the Agency

Albert Yava: Interpreter 234
Tom Pavatea: Hopi Merchant and Patriot

The Corn Rock, an Ancient Bartering-place . . . 238 ·

Opening the Walpi Snake Dance. 250
Dramatic Entry of the Snake Priests

The Gatherer, Handling a Rattlesnake 266
A Patriarch of Snakes

The Chief Snake-Priest 272

The Enchanted Desert and the Moqui Buttes . . . 282

In the Twin-Butte Country 294
Silversmith Jim: a Typical Navajo

Billa Chezzi: Chief of the Northern Navajo. . . . 316
Nelson Oyaping: Tewa Chief of Police

A Navajo Boy Who Has Never Been to Any School. . . 322

A Hopi Range-Rider 336
Blue Cañon: A Study in Blue-and-White

A Hopi Shrine 338
A Hopi Weaver of Ceremonial Robes
A Katchina Dance

Hopi Mother in Gala Dress, with Her Child. . . . 340
Navajo Mother with Child in Cradle

A New Son of the Desert 344
Hopi Girls Arrayed for a Dance

Hopi Wedding Costume 352

A Hopi Beauty 358

INDIANS OF THE ENCHANTED DESERT

I

NOLENS VOLENS

It is well for a man to respect his own vocation, whatever
it is, and to think himself bound to uphold it and to claim
for it the respect it deserves.— CHARLES DICKENS

THEY were good fellows, cordial, modest, although somewhat shy in manner, the sort that would have been more
at home perhaps among fewer men. They came out of the
West, at infrequent intervals, to visit the Chief, who in
those days did not keep them waiting. The course of business, filtering down through the red-taped labyrinth,
brought some of them to my desk and within my survey.
I wonder now what they thought of me, especially as I
am about to relate how I viewed them.

Imbued as I was then with the rare efficiency of bureaucracy, I sympathized with their apparent helplessness in
the transaction of Departmental business. They were
always wanting to do promptly things that were n't
done. Aside from that, I found them interesting, they
being from what an Easterner would term the "hinter-
land," had he vision enough to know that his country has
one. I thought they would have tales to tell — a hope
that never materialized.

When one came to know them better, as I sometimes
did, they would relate their problems in a constrained,
half pathetic manner, as if, seeking something and finding
it not, they were confused. The idea came to me that they
were awed, if not actually bewildered, by their uncommon

experiences in the big city. I did not dream that they were struggling manfully, as indeed they could, to restrain a just wrath; that their seeming pathos was a sort of crude pity, inspired by the artificialities and cheap bluff that they saw around them. Their manner of ill-at-ease, I know now, was a mighty urge to get away from that which distressed them, and to return whence they came — into the broader, franker places.

I knew that they were "out of the West," and this meant — of course it did — beyond — well, beyond the Mississippi. "The West" is a general term, and brings to mind the buffalo days, an unpolished period of a dim past. Therefore I did not know that this one's bailiwick contained five troublesome barriers across a coveted valley, where men of three different races met and snarled at each other, as they had for nearly four hundred years; that another's domain included six thousand square miles of God's most wonderful creation, having the Marble Cañon of the Colorado for its western fence; that four States met in a third's territory, while a treacherous river gave it a name and, at times, breaking the harness he had constructed, rolled its hissing flood through his very dooryard; that grizzlies and wild turkey tracked the solitudes of mountain parks within sight of this one's home; that still another had explored a dozen dead cities, lost, forgotten, in the silence of uncharted cañons.

No. I did not meet these men in the Smithsonian offices at Washington; nor were they lecturers before the National Geographic Society. They were Indian Agents.

They came to Washington, hoping for additional allotments of funds with which to construct roads and bridges, to harness torrents, build mills and housing, equip and maintain schools, and, what is more important, establish hospitals. Their general talk was of cement and queer machinery, when it did not turn on gasoline and blasting-powder. They wanted things necessary to fix civilization on the last of the frontiers.

Indian Agents! a much-maligned class of officials, al-though recognized as part of the National Government since 1796, clouded somewhat in their efforts by the memory — fact and fiction — of the "ration" days. They might have spoken proudly of the traditions of their Ser-vice, a Service that has had little recognition and possesses no chronicle other than a dry-as-dust Annual Report compiled by unknowing clerks. The reason for these officials' existence has produced much sound and fury. The very title seems to have infuriated the ablest writers of the past, and still causes some of the present to see red. When sentimentalists — and God knows the ignorance of them is astounding — take pen in hand to picture the fabled glories and the believed miseries of the savage, they usually begin by attacking those very men I met and have in mind. They forget, if indeed they have ever known, that they are privileged to view the savage be-cause of these men; that the miserable actualities of the "glorious past" would long since have engulfed the ideal-ized protégé but for them. Indian Agents may not vie with painters and poets; but tubes of color, Strathmore board, dreams, and rhyming dictionaries produce small knowledge of tuberculosis, trachoma, smallpox, measles, syphilis — scourges of the Indian people, whose long train of evils reach grimly down through the generations of an ignorant and devitalized race. No one feels this so keenly as the official who daily faces the unromantic task, charged with the duty of alleviating the miseries of the present. Unlike the Spanish explorers, these men have no historian, and but for prejudice and libel would probably be unknown.

Yet this one had succeeded to the task Custer left unfinished among the unrelenting, sullen Sioux; had checked a second rebellion; had faced and quelled and buried Sitting Bull, the last of the great savage charlatans. That one had built a city in the pines to shelter the children of murderer Geronimo; a third had tracked and mapped a region few civilized men had known. Now came one who had chained a river without an appropriation; now came another who had fought pestilence in winter, among a superstitious people, crippled by distances and lack of transport, without sufficient health-officers, to learn in the end that his mortality records were lower than those of enlightened civilization. Occasionally a fancied uprising brought one to unpleasant notice; occasionally, too, one was killed.

These unromantic facts, having no camouflage of feathers and war paint, nothing in them of the beating of tomtoms or the chanting of legends, do not invite a sentimental record; and, it is true, few such things occur in the "dude season," when sentimentality, accompanied by its handmaiden ignorance, takes its neurasthenic outing in the wild.

One of them, a man whose dress spoke rather of the club and office, invited me thus: —

"Come out with me for a leave. There are deer, and trout streams, and a hunting-lodge up in the hills." He was the chap who claimed to have a census of the grizzlies. "It'll do you good, and you look as if you needed a bit of the outside."

I thanked him casually, and turned aside his invitation with —

"What's this I hear about the Chief offering you an

inspectorship? That would give you some travel too,
and — "

"An inspectorship! Travel!" he snorted. "Why, good
God, man! I am the boss of the Switzerland of America.
I would n't trade my post for a seat in the Cabinet."

That is the way they talked, and a few of them undoubtedly meant it.

A large bulky man, with a face like a piece of granite,
twisted a crude silver ring on his finger as he extended a
similar invitation in an entirely different way. He was a
slow-speaking fellow, of few words and those of a definite,
precise character.

"You'd like it," he finished, sighing. "The Navajo
country is a great place — a great place — "

He seemed at loss for words to picture his meaning, and
I know now why language failed him.

Said a third, for whom I had unraveled the genealogy
of a much intermarried Indian family, and who was
grateful: —

"Why, you're just the lad for me. All you'll have to
do is ride fences, armed with a hammer and a pocketful
of staples" (I think he really said "steeples,") " — and
there's quarters for you; twelve hundred a year too.
You'll get a lot of dope for stories. That place fairly drips
'em. What say? I can fix it with the Chief?"

After having had the courtesy to thank them one and
all, I leaned back in the swivel-chair and laughed. While
they were present I good-humoredly laughed with them,
and later, at them. You see, in the Office I was known
as the Scribe, ever since that time when the boss of Indian
Territory had rushed in, mad as a hornet, waving a copy
of *Harper's Weekly*, and declaring that the essential guts
of an article therein had been stolen from his confidential

files. And while I had purloined them with the Chief's permission, I realized it was a fine thing for me not to have lived in the Indian Territory.

While I might spend odd time writing stories of heroic unwashed cowpunchers battling Dante-nosed cayuses across the vasty early-morning range, with the frost nipping down the alkali dust, and a pale-rose tone on the distant range of hills, I knew also that they did it for forty dollars the month and grub off the wheel. I was then and am to this day aware that cowmen give little thought to either the vasty sweep of the broad spaces or to the rose tones. And I was perfectly able to fake the western landscape, where a man's a man an' a' that, without removing myself more than five blocks from a café and a steak à la Bordelaise. I had placed one hundred stories in New York, and a hundred more on the stocks, without smelling an Indian camp or subjecting myself to the grave and anxious possibility of getting — well, inhabited, to say the least of it. I assumed that the dapper fellow was more of a clerk than a ranger; that the slow-moving granite-faced individual truly reflected the somber aridity of his monotonous desert; and the fact that the third had said "steeples" proved to me that I could never respect him as chief.

"No!" I decided, with a grin. "The Borax mule-team could n't drag me into that life." And I too meant it.

But — I was brutally launched out of this effete complacency and pitched into the great Navajo Desert country without disturbing a single mule. I scrapped for money to purchase the once-despised "critters" to enable my existence therein. And I have been proud of my mules since.

Without seeming to be missed by those to whom I had

thought my going would be tragedy, without causing a ripple among those few with whom I found myself, the Wheel turned over, and the vast immutable Desert received me with as much inscrutable kindness as it offers anyone. I had prepared the chute myself, and having greased it thoroughly, slipped and plunged down it, as has many a better man without sliding any further than his grave.

"See the Chief, and get a berth in the West. Live out o' doors, rough it, live on milk and eggs, and don't come home until I agree to it. You are two leaps ahead of the lion, and you'll beat him yet."

It was the cruel frankness of friendship. I had romped the city streets with the doctor, attended the same schools, appeared on the same stage as promoter of histrionic wares; in short, he had been the leader of my gang. I could recall the local excitement aroused by his first cane, and had carried his messages to his first girl. He knew how many times I had been thrashed, and had once turned the trick himself. There was no need for professional bluff between us.

Next day, perhaps a trifle groggy, I got to my feet in a more determined spirit, to prepare for the six-months' battle. The Chief was very kind.

"Why not take a superintendency?" he suggested. "There's one vacant, down in Rainbow Cañon. That's the Grand Cañon country, you know. Wonderful place, one of the rarest spots on earth."

I thanked him for the confidence, knowing that Rainbow Cañon was no place for an invalid. That Agency is nearly always vacant. New superintendents negotiate the trail but twice — ignorantly, going in, and wisely, coming out for ever. Even sure-footed mules have been known to miscalculate at Suicide Corner, and it is claimed that the bones of one such beast, entangled in the wires of his last burden, — a cottage piano, — still furnish a mystic Æolian effect when the wind sweeps below the place where he faltered. The last superintendent had spent forty-eight hours in a tree, evading flood-waters that threatened to carry him on a personally conducted tour through the Grand Cañon itself. I had arranged his relief by telegraphing the nearest offices adjacent to his tree, a mere matter of miles, up and down; and I had no great confidence that anyone would so rapidly arrange mine in similar circumstances. No! Rainbow Cañon sounded good, quite poetical, indeed; but none of it for one who required rest and as little exercise as possible.

So, in accord with my request and at my own valuation, based on my inexperience, I was formally transferred as a clerk to an Indian Agency that sits astride the Santa Fe trail — the modern trail connecting the ancient city of Santa Fe with the Pacific, along which pioneers wended in the forties.

One week later I had left Washington to make the trek of two thousand five hundred miles to the Painted Desert and — to me — a most desolate siding on the banks of the Little Colorado River in Arizona.

II

ACROSS THE PLAINS

Yet one could not but reflect upon the weariness of those who passed by there in old days at the foot's pace of oxen, painfully urging their teams, and with no landmark but that unattainable evening sun for which they steered, and which daily fled them by an equal stride. They had nothing, it would seem, to overtake; nothing by which to reckon their advance; no sight for repose or encouragement; but, stage after stage, only the dead green waste under foot and the mocking, fugitive horizon. — STEVENSON: *Across the Plains*

In the early days, those adventurous times when men pulled out of St. Louis of an early morning, and the dust of a long train of wagons and outriders arose; when they followed the Arkansas across to the Cimarron and Wagon Mound; when they warily entered the Indian country and somehow existed through the long dusty days and the longer nervous nights before sighting Santa Fe and safety in a foreign land, I suppose most of them felt the extraordinary vastness of the West. Certainly they knew its sterile immensity after a few weeks on that perilous road. Later, when they began seeking the Coast and the Pacific, leaving Santa Fe to plunge down La Bajada trail to follow the valley of the Rio Grande, to skirt the fields of the mysterious Pueblos, to risk thirst and ambush in the arid lands of the Navajo and Apache, to dare the flooded rivers and that brazen furnace, the Mohave Desert, all to reach the painted paradise of golden California, they surely became alive to the wonderful expanse of that southwestern empire first called New Spain — the Land of the Conquistadores!

A magic stage having magic scenes, bathed in glorious sunshine; a place of enchantment, where the rainbow colors linger on the cliffs and never leave the skies; an ancient garden of the gods, dreamily expecting that the gods will yet return; presenting ever its sphinx-like riddle; promising everything and yielding nothing but its lure. Once you have felt its sorcery, the spell is never broken.

Speaks the old-timer, "The Desert'll get yeh"; and he does n't add anything about watching-out. The pioneers eluded or fought off wandering war-parties, but the Desert got them nevertheless.

There is one point in Arizona where, between the Santa Fe Railway and central Utah, three hundred miles as the crow flies and a weary five hundred by the trails, there is nothing of civilization other than a few isolated trading-posts and a solitary Indian Agency, set in a terraced cañon, eighty miles from a telegraph key. As my train passed this point in 1910, I did not dream that for more than eight years I should direct that Indian Agency and its chain of scattered desert stations, supplying all of progress that the country had, maintaining all of law and order that its half-wild people knew, isolated, lonely, well-nigh forgotten.

Only one who has lived thus removed from the turmoil and petty vanity of cities, apart from careless crowds, unreached by artificiality, can fully realize the brooding mystery, the savage beauty, the power and cruelty of the Desert. One must penetrate its solitudes, stand atop the world to view dead or enchanted cities, pause on the naked brink of chasms leaning over faery valleys, to know

WALPI, THE PUEBLO OF THE CLOUDS

THE VALLEY AND ITS HEADLANDS

the grandeur of this silent country. One must grow weary on its heavy trails, feel its hunger, shrink in its bitter cold, and thirst for the water of the precious hidden springs. Fairly to hear its ominous hush at blazing noontime, to view the scarlet glory of its sunsets, to stand under its velvet dome at night, lighted by the burning stars, is to have caught a secret from the universe. To have watched Orion's flaming signal through that crystal atmosphere, to have loved the placid jewels of the Pleiades, is to have received the Desert's blessing, which is contentment — if not peace. One must spend whole days crossing its sun-baked emptiness, carry-on through the chill of twilight, feel the menace of its dark, and see its wondrous moon burst from black cedars on a mesa edge. One must have known the sigh of the night wind in the brush, heard the chatter of jackals in the snow, felt the sandstorm's acid lash, and stopped, spellbound, at the sibilant warning of its gliding Indian god. Then to have seen the drifting red-bellied rain-clouds that the Snake priests pray for, the crisp rending lightning at their pouches, the wild strength of arroyos after cloud-bursts, and the deluge of the swift midsummer rains, ending in the soft radiance of double rainbows! One must live as a hermit in the Desert to find its heart.

And only one who has done this may somehow feebly understand those bronzed people of whom the desert genii have made fatalists — the solemn, dreaming Indian of the waste lands, whether the Hopi of the mesa heights and kivas, the Pueblo in his mediæval towns, or the Navajo, chanting in his lonely, hidden camp. These know all the splendors, feel all the menace and the mystery, and call the Desert home. Timid, yet uncaring, ever bent on placating some unseen demon, trusting in songs and sorceries, they go their Oriental ways on a vast Occidental stage. The desert spell has touched them, every one.

That which is normal elsewhere cannot find its kindred in the Desert. Here the scale was made by giants. Nothing is small save those who enter it without respect. Left to it, crumbling, dust-covered, ancient, are the massive properties of splendid prehistoric plays. Its geology, a mosaic of the mesas, an open book in the shattered cañons, speaks of the twilight before Babylon. The shepherds on Chaldean hills were like its people of to-day. In this land, so strangely similar to His, one thinks of Christ in Judæa, at a time when cliff-dwellers, curious half-human pygmies, fought over this unknown continent and honeycombed its enormous cañon walls, as unmindful of their Divine contemporary as their descendants are. Here one may view the remnants of a civilization still in decadent being, clinging to the pueblos that have little changed since the thirteenth century, when Genghis Khan dominated their Mongol brothers, and rude gentlemen of England gathered at Runnymede to sign the Charter, the spirit of which now rules them too.

One comes, like Crusoe, upon historic footprints, younger signs, — not quite four hundred years old, — the first white man's record in the valley of the Rio Grande, and may trace them across the Desert and through the cañons to the Crossing of the Fathers. The dramatic entry of the Spanish marks a page as colorful and as stirring as any in history. Seeking new lands and treasure, they came from the South. One can picture their departure from Compostela in February 1540, a long train of adventurers making a new crusade. Romancists and friars, mercenaries, captains, Spanish braves. At their head, the great Conquistador. Swords and crosses beat against the savage desert shields; litanies sounded above the savage desert chants. Their gestures were of bravado, yet upon their lips were the *Ave* and the *Sanctus*. They struggled for a legend, found Cibola but a fable, yet were not discouraged. Supermen these, not to have feared the desert gods, not to have quailed before the sinister welcome of the empty desert spaces. From the Sangre de Christos to that awesome Cañon of the West they marched and countermarched, they prayed and fought, leaving their record deep in great El Morro, on the King's Road to Acoma.

Then the days of the Mission Fathers; the revolt of 1680; the massacre of the padres; the red calendar of the now drowsy pueblos along the Rio Grande. After that, a long silence in the Desert, broken only by sound of tom-toms and wild exultant chants, until the coming of De Vargas to reclaim this empire for his king. Then the Mission bells were hung, those very bells that sound at Acoma and San Felipe to this day.

But De Vargas waived the kingdom of the Farther West. Until the treaty with the Navajo in 1868, little more than solitude or bitter foray touched the heart of the Enchanted Empire of which I write. Three hundred years of Spanish steel and ritual were drifted down into sand and silence. One marks this chapter but a desert dream. Later civilization and progress moved north and south around it. The building of the frontier posts assured a pathway to the Coast and nothing more. "Fort Defiance" explains this desert challenge. And while the great Civil War was crashing in the East, Kit Carson made his desert raids, carried ruthless war into the cañon strongholds, to break the nomads who, desert-trained, keep their secrets still.

To have been thrust, a sickly tenderfoot, into this environment, to have observed the aftermath of these periods, to have known the desert people intimately, to have followed Coronado's trails, and to have had in charge quite nearly all that Spain controlled in 1600, perhaps will serve as a reason for this notebook.

Just as the early Spanish found it necessary to dominate and rule this kingdom of the Desert clans, so do the Indian Agents who govern it to-day. A Government post here, another one hundred miles away, mark all of civilization that one can find, held against the obliterating fingers of the hungry, unchanging Desert. Here is the last frontier, an area of fifty thousand square miles, having fifty thousand Indian inhabitants and few indeed of other men.

For the most part the native people are pagan barbarians, having savage customs, jealously guarding their secret mysteries, slow to obey, but quick to resent interference, feeling all the power of their isolation.

As late as 1911 a troop of United States cavalry was breaking camp at a point in Keams Cañon, of the Moqui Reservation, not a mile from where Kit Carson, with his New Mexican volunteers, made his camp in August 1863, during that famous march to Cañon de Chelly. Ostensibly this modern troop had acted as an escort to another famous Colonel of the older frontier Army — that gentleman who has out-talked so many Indian tribes, with his sign-weaving fingers if his words sound strange to them, with men of the plainest diction when all else fails. Actually it had served as a show of force, trooping in frontier fashion against a band of unreconstructed rebels of the hills. A bloodless campaign of thirty days was ending. Washington orders, irrevocable, called to other troubles on the

A NAVAJO FLOCK AND ITS SHEPHERDS

CAÑON DE CHELLY, SEEN FROM THE RIM
Where the Navajo retreated before Kit Carson in 1863. The earliest records mention
it as a Navajo stronghold. The cliff-dwellers held it before them. There
are places where its rock walls tower 1000 feet.

Border. The support lent to the Indian Agent, still a pallid tenderfoot, was about to be withdrawn. He ventured to remark that the serenity of the moment might be followed by untoward proceedings, once the uncombed native learned that the soldiers had departed. He asked for military advice, knowing full well that he would get no civil consolation.

Until then there had been a great show of tactful diplomacy between the two Governmental representatives; the one of war counseling peace, and the supposed civilian who had ventured close to war. The Colonel spoke, for the first time without regard to the gentle traditions of the Interior Department:—

"Young man, you have no empire to control. Either rule it, or part your hair."

And there is another reason for the telling. Probably no other section of Indian country is more visited than is the Painted Desert, where the snake gods have such influence. From June to October comes a host, packing cameras and notebooks and sketching-blocks, attired in weird garments, big with questions, and expecting to find hotels. Most of them wish to rough it smoothly, and are easily annoyed. They seek the natural wonders of the Empire, and especially the religious "dances" of the Indian people, chief of which is the annual Hopi Snake Dance. A strange crowd, having more of enthusiasm than sense, staggering under theories, swelled with importance and criticism, generously stuffed by guides.

A library has been written and vocabularies have been exhausted in their efforts to explain the beauties and the thrills. Canvas sufficient to tent a city has been spoiled by those who would capture the delicate and elusive Desert charm. Historians and ethnologists have recorded

Border. The support lent to the Indian Agent, still a
pallid tenderfoot, was about to be withdrawn. He ventured to remark that the serenity of the moment might
be followed by untoward proceedings, once the uncombed
native learned that the soldiers had departed. He asked
for military advice, knowing full well that he would get
no civil consolation.

Until then there had been a great show of tactful
diplomacy between the two Governmental representatives; the one of war counseling peace, and the supposed
civilian who had ventured close to war. The Colonel
spoke, for the first time without regard to the gentle
traditions of the Interior Department: —

*"Young man! you have an empire to control. Either rule
it, or pack your trunk!"*

And there is another reason for the telling. Probably
no other section of Indian country is more visited than is
the Painted Desert, where the Snake gods have such influence. From June to October comes a host, packing cameras and notebooks and sketching-blocks, attired in weird
garments, big with questions, and expecting to find hotels.
Most of them wish to rough it smoothly, and are easily
annoyed. They seek the natural wonders of the Empire,
and especially the religious "dances" of the Indian people,
chief of which is the annual Hopi Snake Dance. A strange
crowd, having more of enthusiasm than sense, staggering
under theories, swelled with importance and criticism,
generously stuffed by guides.

A library has been written and vocabularies have been
exhausted in their efforts to explain the beauties and the
thrills. Canvas sufficient to tent a city has been spoiled
by those who would capture the delicate and elusive
Desert charm. Historians and ethnologists have recorded

and traced; antiquaries have uncovered and restored. The museums of the East are filled with looted treasure, while the files at Washington drip complaints. ("Oblige me by referring to the files.") And the Indian as a savage — and a little-understood savage at that — has been idealized. And those who do not observe this view — berated.

But not a word has been printed, and few spoken without a sneer, regarding those of the United States Indian Service who keep watch and ward in the remote places: those who govern and protect, educate and guide; those who have kept the Indian living, that he may be sketched and analyzed and gaped at. This work extends beyond the dude season, through the lonely, bitter winters, embracing at times contagion-camps among an unreasoning, often unappreciative, and occasionally defiant population.

To further education among those who do not want it, to advance medication among fatalists, to attain some show of morals among an insensible and unmoral people, to demand respect and win affection from suspicious aliens, to rule absolutely without an army, and, above all, to keep sane and just without society, call for all of any man's ingenuity and resourcefulness, and should arouse something other than blatant criticism from those who boast intelligence.

Having accomplished these things, every one, I am proud of the record; and I shall not fail to acknowledge my full indebtedness to those faithful men and women of the Service who made my efforts possible of success — employees, traders, missioners, not forgetting those few from among the heathen who gave their loyalty and confidence. They too have felt the sneers and insults of the multitude; and the grudging appreciation of an equally insensible Bureau nearly three thousand miles away is small reward. Many valued employees have grown old in this Service without a syllable of commendation from Washington. And I have prompted at least one Commissioner of Indian Affairs to acknowledge his feeble debt to a dying physician — dying on his feet, still nobly making the rounds.

When I left Washington, in 1910, I had no idea that such a future work would extend my little vacation into the years. Six months out o' doors, and either I should be reëstablished at the old stand, pounding the old typewriter, or I should have attended a ceremony that is final but not interesting to the subject thereof. A simple calendar; not the first, however, to stand revision.

Morning brought Chicago, to me a grim and sinister city, and a day spent in its galleries and clubs; then the train again, and its long crawl across level, heated Kansas. Excellent living on a diner, and came the thought that wherever this railroad wended would follow good food, which I required, and service of the best. Vain and soon-to-be-exploded vision! The railroad carries food and service; the West sees it go by. In the Desert one has desert fare.

The contrast was outside the windows; on the third morning this contrast became acute. Instead of hamlets, farms, and country lanes, there was now the grayish-green of the sage, broken by stunted cedars on the slopes, with an overtone of brown as the soil reflected light. There was no indication of complete aridity, so one could not think of this as a desert. Scant vegetation lived from the brush of the foreground to the timbered blue of the distant ranges. They did not appear as lofty mountains, although many peaks lifted against a calm blue sky. Beyond the little telegraph points, the occasional adobes of section crews, and water tanks, the landscape held not a sign of habitation. In the middle distance were strange formations of crumbling shale, banded with the spectral white of gypsum: queer piles such as might have been designed by some sardonic humorist. Now straying cattle, gaunt as the hills, blanket Indians idling at a station, or a ranger on a shabby mount, were the only things of life. Over all the golden haze of New Mexico, moistened by the mists of the Rio Grande.

But later in the day this blue-toned view began to change. The sky grew clearer, the distance more intimate and revealing. Everything snapped into the brilliancy of sharp relief. Where had been isolated buttes, now ran barricades of rock, wind-worn, pinnacled, and domed, while the cold tones — blue and silver — of the river country warmed to the dry saffrons and parched reds of sun-baked Arizona, the Land of Little Rain. One could, as the old-timer sings, "see farther and see less" than on any other stage of the world.

Just at sunset the train slowed into a weather-browned, dust-covered town, its main street along the tracks and little else in sight. It was Sunday and the season of the wind. A swirling fog screened everything as the cars stopped. There is nothing more forlorn than a Southwest town of a Sunday in the windy season. A long rank of stores and saloons displayed false fronts, innocent of paint. A few starved trees waved crippled branches, and were most piteous. Flapping awnings, flying leaves, waste paper, sand, and cinders filled the air. When the wind ceased howling for a moment, there fell a deadly silence. It seemed to me as if that place must have been as it was for a thousand years, drowsing in the red-gold sunset, abandoned, overlaid by the itinerant dust of all the ages. A clatter of hoofs, a shot, a crash of glass, and a man or two by Remington would have completed the picture.

A little to the north of it was Poverty Flat. To the east was the drying bed of the Little Colorado, a mile in width, lined by withered cottonwoods, and possessing scarcely enough liquid to demand a foot-bridge. In the west, a thing of splendor, reared the beautiful San Francisco range, snow-crowned, radiant, the sun searing down into its ancient craters. Elsewhere, everywhere, stretched the Desert, sterile, barren, robing now in the purplish-brown shades of early dusk. Its unlimited expanse, silent, desolate, suggested something of foreboding, something of waiting menace.

Thank God! there was one of those splendid railroad hotels at hand. I hurried into it, a little of civilization such as I knew, glad to shut out the night that advanced across that empty plain, swallowing as it came the masses of the Moqui Buttes and all the strange upland country that a year later I was to call home.

III

INTO "INDIAN COUNTRY"

"Indian country" applies to all lands to which the Indian
title has not been extinguished, even when not within a reservation expressly set apart for the exclusive occupancy of
Indians. "Indian country" includes reservations set apart
for Indian tribes by treaty, Executive order, or Act of
Congress. — MERITT: *The Legal Status of the Indian*

THE next next morning was another day, as I have often
heard remarked since; and whatever the terrors of the
night, the crisp, cheerful Arizona morning brings with it
renewed hope and assurance.

The town waked-up; the air held the tonic thrill that
comes only from pine-clad peaks; the yellow dust of yesterday now kept its place. At this season in Arizona one
may expect the wind to rise about noon and continue its
nerve-racking tyranny until sunset. The blessed sunlight
prevents one from remaining depressed, however, and
there is always an end to the windy season, whatever the
nerves meantime. When the last shriek has died away
in early summer, it seems there lives a vacuum, a strange
stillness, like that which follows the stopping of a clock.

I found the station platform quite busy that morning.
Trains discharged their hungry freight, and the hotel
kitchens fed them in battalions. A well-stocked news-
stand promised that I would not lack for entertainment.
The general spirit of moving life and activity caused one
to forget that the Desert lurked beyond, that these rails

were simply a tiny causeway spanning it for many miles, desolation on either side.

Chance acquaintance is made easily in the Southwest, and it was not long before I answered the query of a young man as to where I headed. I replied that there was a long journey to make, out into the Desert, among the Indians perhaps. He seemed not to be aware that Indians were of the immediate locality, and asked: "How far?"

"Oh — about thirty miles."

"Humph!" he commented, drily; "people in this country go that far to water a horse."

The pastime and humor of Arizona is exaggeration. I know now that the ranchers of the Southwest, and the so-called nomadic Indians, for that matter, are people of definite localities. An Indian of the Desert will name and locate his hogan or home camp as specifically as the man of a city street. Indians are born, live, and frequently die within a very small area of the Desert. That is why Indians — and you may scoff — are likely to be lost at night during storms. Their distant travels are well planned, by daylight, much the same as anyone breaks monotony with a holiday or business trip. Only those of the most remote desert places make long journeys as a part of daily routine, and then when need compels. I have yet to see the man who lived miles from water. Water decides where any man *may* live in the Desert — and his animals too.

It was a different story when I aroused a very fat individual who dozed complacently with his chair propped back against a livery barn. I inquired about a team for the immense hike I had to make. There were no automobiles then to traverse the desert, and few were in the little towns. To-day gasoline and tires, coupled with much swearing, grease, and shoveling of sand, have conquered

most of the desert distances, and the last time I covered
that road was in one of those striped metallic potato-bugs
hatched by that Detroit genius who could not place
Benedict Arnold in his country's history, but who has
made possible thirty miles the hour as against a former
five. Then, or once upon a time, the horse — or his superior relative, the mule — was indispensable, and the
keeper of a stable was a king of transportation, something
akin to Jim Hill. This one acted just that way. Evidently
he had not lost anything out back.

"Well — " he hummed, doubtfully, "that's a longish
trip, that is. I've made it — " giving me the impression
that it had been an unusual effort, fraught with courage.
"I went out there once, but it was two days' hard travel,
'cause yeh have to rest the horses over night, returnin'
next day. That spoils two good days for me, and I have
to charge yeh accordin'. It'll be thirty dollars. When do
yeh want to start?"

"Never, at that rate!" I declared very promptly.

So I went back to the hotel and sent a telegram up the
line stating that I would there remain in comfort until
some reasonable means of travel came in sight. The answer indicated that I had been heard from. Several days
after a rather rough-looking individual called for me and
introduced himself as the Boss.

"I was coming to town anyway," he said, "but usually
I don't freight my employees." Waiving this little matter
of custom, I inquired: "How far is it to the Agency?"

"Twenty-five miles. We'll make it in less than four
hours."

And we did, for he drove an excellent team of mares,
and his reputation as a driver was like unto that of Jehu.

On the way I explained the purpose and definite length

of my visit. He seemed relieved, for it had been his original suspicion that I, being from Washington direct, came seeking his job. Having worked in a newspaper office long enough to learn that one must build absolute loyalty to the chief, I assured him that his interests were mine, and thereafter we got along famously. He was a lovable fellow when one had punctured the sun-dried skin of him, under which there was much to admire; and not the least was that he felt his tight little Agency to be the finest spot on earth. And why should he not?

Some few years before this he had drifted into that loop of the Little Colorado River, a place that for sterile barrenness could not be matched and that justified few visions. Armed with a single letter of authority, he had taken charge of the empty landscape. He pitched his tent beneath an old spreading cottonwood tree. I can imagine his lonely vigils and his planning under the brilliant desert stars. First, the well to tap the subcurrent of the river; then, one by one, the Government buildings, of rough rock quarried from the near-by mesas, meanwhile engaging and lodging and feeding rougher laborers, and disputing with contractors, and keeping them all from liquor, until a little town grew in this river-angle that for centuries had known only the withered trees, the cooing of many doves, and driftwood. The grounds were marked and leveled and drained. In springtime the river flooded the place, but he was not dismayed. An office, warehouses, shops, and barns were built. Then arose a well-appointed school, with dormitories for the Indian children, queer desert gamins that for a time were as frightened rabbits and wept for their smoky camps. There were kitchens, baths, a laundry, a plant to furnish light and ice and heat; for while the summer may be broiling,

the winter brings its snow and bitter wind in that unpro-
tected waste. He saw the sick and built a hospital. There
were quarters for his staff of employees. He planted trees
along cement walks; he broke ground for a farm, and
planned an irrigation system with its pumping-plant. His
barns held feed against the winter, and his commissaries
flour and clothing. A trader came for license, and then
another; and a grant was made to a little mission church.
Last, but not the least necessary to his desert kingdom,
was a guardhouse for those who disputed his sage counsels.
High above it all floated the Flag, stoutly whipping in the
desert wind.

One day he folded up his tent and walked into his capital. The town was not finished — true; it was not perfect
— true. Already he could see the mistakes of a pioneer
hand, similar to those of the Mormons who had settled
in that country generations before, and whose record was
a graveyard. It is not finished to-day, and several succes-
sors have added their work to his. It may eventually be
a folly and a failure in the sense of profits, for where the
Mormons failed in those early days of zealotry who can
hope to succeed? Ah! in the sense of material profits —
Yes! But where had been nothing but the blind Desert
and the savage river, nothing but the blow-sand and the
horned toad, he had created an outpost of civilization to
reach and serve and protect a helpless people who, theretofore, had only their desert demons.

As far as he could see to the north, where the red-toned
mesas raised their twisted shoulders above the desert rim,
where the dim blue crowns of monster lava-buttes loomed
against the sky, to the edge of the world, it seemed, the
domain was his kingdom. Twelve hundred human beings
hailed him "Nahtahni," which is Chief, and listened to

his advice. His was the only voice they heeded without
suspicion, for had they not been driven from this land in
midwinter, by armed men, packing their few possessions
through the snow? And had it not required a fighting
President of the United States to restore to them this
pitiful inheritance? No less, indeed!

But to them, people of no contrasts, was it not a wonderful inheritance — that all-embracing stage, from the
Red Mesa where the tumbled rocks stood in rings, "Children at Play"; from the Sapphire Lakes and the restless
river to the country of the Moqui, guarded by the lava
buttes, those somber blue-clad gods of the northern sky?
And was it not the Desert!

Perhaps — no doubt of it — that Great White Father
had sent this curious Nahtahni from his own household.
The world has four corner-posts, one the Desert and one
that is Washington. They could remember those nights
when they first gathered around his tent under the gnarled
old cottonwood, the surly river's murmur in their ears,
their glowing fires matching his against the stars. He had
told them of his mission. And he was not afraid of white
men — had sent some of them briskly about their business.
His commission read — they knew it by his action —
that all pertaining to their peace and welfare devolved
on him; that he was responsible for their best interests.
His mark upon a "nultsose" was the money of the land.
His police wore the eagle button. Truly this was a man
to be respected; and he was their Chief.

So at his command they brought children to the school,
for it seemed he had a peculiar fondness for children; and
yet he had no sheep to herd. A strange fellow! They came
in from their corrals and patches to work for implements
and livestock; they hauled the stores and coal from the

railroad, herding their wiry ponies with many a wild cry; they found that his queer blue papers could be exchanged for the hard silver dollars of the West.

And to this Chief they came too with foolish complaints and childish misfortunes; to him they came when ill and trembling, and him they sought when old and hungry, shivering against the desert wind, forsaken by their own cruel kindred, fearing that the jackals would pick their bones. In all that trading country they knew him as the one who would not barter.

His real title was — no matter; there must be tags and labels; actually, by law and practice, he was a desert czar, distributing his bounty, holding his courts of justice. Of course he was, and so are they all, each and every one. What came you out to see? A jurist splitting hairs and fearing to say too much, a ferret of accounts, a listening politician, a sutler and his bales? How many such can boast that they have constructed anything? This man had built a sanctuary, and he ruled a kingdom. He was the "Nahtahni!" That was enough, and what is needed, in the Desert.

When they did not call him that, affectionately they dubbed him "Sack-hair," because he wore a wig, and since one day, to their general consternation, his scalp had blown off into a bush. From Beck-a-shay Thlani, the man of many cattle, to the blind old woman of the tribe, he was counselor and friend. The curious, animal-like children loved him. They would scramble down the walks to take his hand and toddle by his side. He was justly proud of his work and of his industrious alien people; perhaps, in their silent desert way, they were proud of him.

A little of this he told me modestly as we rolled over the road along the river. The greater part I learned in

my own time, as did the Indians before me. He enlivened
the recital by a few choice Southwest legends, made for
and kept alive by greenhorns like myself. He showed
me where the last great flood had eaten away huge sections of the lower flat and spread all over. The river
was now a wide desolation of sand, glowing, sullen in
the sun. In flood time this was no plaything of a stream.
Its mark was on the country, a mile wide. I could have
walked across it dry-shod, and since that time I have
crossed it swimming a horse, and wondering when I should
go off to tow at his tail. Tangled masses of matted greasewood, like shingle of the beaches, and trunks of cottonwoods, picked clean of bark and twig, white as bleaching
bones, were piled on the bars. Over at one side remained
a shallow pool, holding dull fish as captives; and several
lean ponies came to suck eagerly at the turgid water.
Away off in the flat, he pointed out my first mirage: the
pretty view of a marshy place bordered by reeds, cool,
inviting — yet a dusty desert falsehood. Suddenly it
faded, vanished in thin air, to reveal nothing but brilliant
sunlight on a baking floor. Drifting clouds cast long
shadows on the sand. A tiny whirlwind twirled its dust-
spout higher and higher and glided across the plain.

Then, from a little rise, he waved his whip toward a
distant object, black against the western sun. It was very
far away, and looked like a bird-house on a pole.

"That's the Agency," he said.

And indeed it was, for without it existence there was
impossible. It was the stand-tank, most necessary thing
in that land of precious water. Just at dark we swung
through the gates. I had reached my first desert camp,
on the edge of the Enchanted Empire.

IV

OLD TRAILS AND DESERT FARE

We may live without poetry, music and art;
We may live without conscience, and live without heart;
We may live without friends; we may live without books;
But civilized men cannot live without cooks.
                                    — MEREDITH: *Lucile*

WHEN I crossed the border of the Enchanted Empire, in
the dusk of that entry to the Agency, I re-lived fancies
caught out of *Nicholas Nickleby*, his winter journey into
Yorkshire, coaching in company with the incomparable
Squeers; his arrival at the bleak and cheerless Dothe-
boys Hall, and the atmosphere of that strange institution;
and while there was something forlorn about them, there
was also enough of their humor to keep me alive.

Considering what I have written concerning "the Boss,"
who would have to be Squeers, this may seem a sorry and
unkind reflection. But really, forgetting for the moment
his generous heart and his earnest pride in the little desert
kingdom, there was a superficial resemblance to old
Squeers — the odd cock of the head, a certain quaint
expression, a quizzical look after some solemn pronounce-
ment, the rough exterior, — which in this case belied the
man, — and that rare touch of the grotesque given by
his wig: "Sack-hair." The atmosphere of the Agency
supported these impressions.

The ensemble of an Indian school, the cast of characters, their point of view, their quarters and customs — is

something unique and quite beyond comparison with normal things. One is often first conscious of odors; and the Navajo have many sheep. Once a desert station is given over to Indian school purposes, where a number of children and their mentors must be fed, it acquires the fragrance of boiled mutton for its very own. There is nothing else like it. Even an abandoned school retains this poignant atmosphere for years.

Bare — stark naked — calcimined walls, grim in their poverty and unashamed; bare pine floors; cheap pine trimmings covered with hideous varnish, the gloss of which seemed an uncaring grin; the whole sparsely strewn with Government-contract furniture, feeble in the beginning and now in the last stages of pathetic senility. This was the quarters for unmarried employees. And when you take such a scene and thoroughly impregnate it with the clinging atmosphere of yesterday's, and last week's, and last year's boiled mutton; animate it with characters gathered by the grab-bag method from the forty-eight States, persons warped and narrowed by their monotonous duties, impressed by the savage rather than impressing him, fulsome with petty gossip and radiating a cheap evangelical virtue, you have the indescribable — and invariable — locale of an isolated desert school. Dickens would have made it immortal, and his gallery of portraits would have gained many varieties of Bumbles and Mr. Chucksters and Sairey Gamps. I have walked in the Desert with Dick Swiveller and Mr. Cheggs; Mark Tapley I have known intimately; and I have dined several times with Pecksniff in the flesh, he lacking only a large shirt-collar to complete the picture. Hugh Walpole has glimpsed something similar to this in *The Gods and Mr. Perrin*. "It will be all right next term" is the fiscal cry of the restless, unsatisfied, and for the most part misfitted employees of the Indian Service. And the Indian stands mute, inarticulate, unable to express his confused amazement at this bizarre and ever-changing exhibition.

A strong sense of humor may keep one from going mad, but even the keenest humor grows blunted after a few months of such stolid association. If one has no relief in other mental pursuits, he succumbs finally to a moroseness that is not good in the unchanging, uncaring Desert.

We sat at a belated meal in the dining-hall. The drive of twenty odd miles and the tang of the desert air had given me an unusual appetite that promised the making of weight, when behold! in the doorway giving on to the kitchen appeared a vision, perhaps I should say an apparition, the cook! The expression turned on me was intended, I have no doubt, to be one of welcome; but whatever it was supposed to register, I have never forgotten the sardonic leer of that unkempt individual, promising worse to come. And it arrived. Leathery mutton, cold; baking-powder biscuit, lacking character; coffee, luke-warm, weakly concocted from the Arbuckle blend that retreated westward after the Civil War; milk, fresh from tin-plate Holsteins, mixed with water from an alkali pump; and last, but not least for a sick man's stomach, the "bull butter," innocent of ice, slimy, having the flavor of kerosene.

Farewell! a long farewell to Maryland cooking!

I remember having been snowed-in, on a time, back in the farthest Arizona hills, with a Government physician recently from the East. He had sought Arizona to stimulate a lagging constitution that threatened to initiate him as one of the Club. He had traveled westward, visioning the tropic palms, the date trees, the pomegranate hedges of Phœnix; and there we were at an altitude of 7000 feet above sea-level, with the snow two feet deep, and a frigid blast coming straight off the range. He had been lost that night and nearly frozen on the desert where the roads were obliterated, and only the sense of his team had brought him to this haven. We tore the harness from them first, and an engineer helped me to warm him into amiability after the horses were cared for. The time came for retiring, and I recall his diving between dank sheets in an unheated room at this little hill station, his teeth chattering, his lips blue, and the fervid expression of him: —

"*Blank!* And blankety-double-blank the damned Philadelphia fool who told me Arizona was warm!"

And as I surveyed that tempting array of victuals, I had the same feeling toward those kindly disposed men of Washington who, out of a crass ignorance, had assured me that their desert stations possessed food.

Later, a couple of obliging employees carried my trunk upstairs to a room that would have been a credit to a penitentiary. It welcomed one with four walls and possessed a window. There were also a ceiling and a floor. These necessary ornaments, together with a bed and a decrepit chair, which had crashed under many disconsolate employees and had been skillfully and maliciously fitted together again to lure me, comprised the generous list of fittings. All and several extras thought to be necessary to comfort could be supplied by the employee from his salary, the proportions of which had been established during the administration of Carl Schurz, and have changed but little since, despite wars and rumors of wars and the coming of the income tax, "which includes the quarters as part of the compensation."

Next morning I was aroused about dawn, or a little before, by the business of breaking stove-wood, a bombardment of mishandled crockery, and the hiss of vicious cooking. A thick wave of reanimated mutton-grease fogged upward and invaded my boudoir, which I sought to vacate as quickly as possible. I encountered the cook at the foot of the stairs, and she had not improved during the night.

"Good morning," I tried to say cheerfully, which caused her to notice me. "Who cares for the rooms?" I asked. She bent on me a sinister eye, as if divining my thought.

"You mean, who cleans 'em, an' all that?"

"Just so," I admitted.

"Well — you'll care for your own."

And that was that. It was final, with the wall-eyed finality that had become unwritten law in all properly conducted Agencies.

At table I met an Irrigation Service man who had just returned from a survey of farther desert conditions. He expressed great joy in having accomplished his journey without accident or delay, and in successfully returning to this oasis. He said he was always sure of decent meals at this place, whereas, at that post from which he had arrived, life was unbearable because of the atrocious and altogether impossible menu. I requested that he repeat this statement. There could not be *two* such places. But he was certain of his facts, and his wife confirmed the story. They cautioned me never to go to that other post — an entirely superfluous piece of advice.

Then I learned that at each of the Government establishments was maintained a Thing (as Carlyle would have phrased it), a fixture, an Institution Horrible, that dominated the people and to which they suffered allegiance.

It was termed "a Mess." And such had been its ascendancy and its acquired power, that they were more or less proud of its traditional horrors in due proportion to the misery produced. I learned that Washington recognized this thing, and actually advertised it to innocent incoming employees, suppressing with a cautious diplomacy its evils, and sounding aloud the one thing to be praised — the small cost per individual. The nomenclature is good. Never before was an hideous evil so briefly and so thoroughly described.

Having been deceived as to nearly everything concerning this Vale of Sharon, with the exception of the climate, — there it was before one, three hundred square miles of it in sight, unlimited, free and untaxed as yet; I learned of the altitude when I went to purchase a pair of shoes, — I dispatched a telegram for a case of prepared food, the kind that has everything from soup to nuts in one bottle, and began to debate whether it would be braver to die unflinchingly silent or to carry my views to the chief. The bottled food came in, and I tightened my belt on it for seven days, learning meantime that there was no dairy herd other than the kind that comes nested forty-eight tin cows to the case; that only the chief was rich enough to afford poultry, and therefore there were no eggs; there was no fruit save the oranges that dried at the trading-post, and an occasional wagonload of melons sold by the pound. One could buy a very fair sample of undernourished watermelon for a dollar.

The refrigerator freights, however, booming east from California, carrying fish and vegetables and fruit, passed that place twice a week and within thirteen miles. One could see the railroad water-tank from the mess-kitchen window. But it required three things to procure food from that refrigerator service, to wit: desire, energy and money; and they were all noticeably absent from these people. I decided to protest.

The Chief had wearied of such complaints, as indeed I did later when I faced the same problem. But it was his duty, nay his very safety, to settle everything. The skipper of this desert ship had no first-officer to take the deck with pride and responsibility, to smother complaints, and to avoid or crush mutinies. He must do it himself. Quelling revolts was one of his regular tasks; and he had become unusually — not to say cunningly — proficient in the various methods. Some he roared down, and others he trapped into submission.

"What's the trouble?" he asked, sourly.

"Well, sir, I came here to keep alive, and aside from my natural intelligence, several physicians of the East urged me to absorb food — *food* — as little of it tinned as possible. Now I have been out to survey the can-pile, and have arrived at the conclusion that your employees must consume several tons of embalmed materials each year. And too, my food must be cooked. My ancestors quit eating ac ns several centuries ago. The true state of your pe e is that of slow starvation. They have somehow g used to it. I shall not last that long. Their tradition has it that they can maintain life on a meal-bill of elev 1 dollars per month — "

"Give 'em credit," he interrupted, darkly; "they got it down to nine once."

"Which recalls your Mormon's idea of luxury," I hurried on. "Remember that story you told me coming in? Said the tourist — 'What would you do if you had a million dollars?' 'A million dollars!' cried the Mormon, his eyes shining; 'I'd buy a six-mule team, pull freight, an' eat nothing but canned goods!' That Mormon was weaned at this mess."

The Chief rubbed his wig reflectively, and from his rueful smile I knew that he possessed the remnant of a starved sense of humor. He glanced furtively about his office, and when he spoke it was in a low, cautious tone.

"True," he said; "The mess would drive a goat to suicide. But what can I do? They like it. It is a dangerous thing, young man, to disturb anything the proletariat likes. Thank God! I am married and have separate quarters. It has been a mystery to me for years how they keep alive, and turn out each morning for work."

And where Squeers's face would have cracked into a malevolent leer, the countenance of the Boss suddenly bubbled over with a wholesome expression that announced the winning of my case. He slapped his hand on his knee. He had found a solution — a Machiavellian scheme calculated to strike down at one blow the system and its latest critic. He leveled his finger at me.

"I'll make you manager of the mess!" he cried, triumphantly. "That's the ticket. It'll be up to you to provide real food, cooked, an' all, an' — "

Evidently a very hopeful light came into v eyes. He paused, grinned somewhat shamefacedly, and i. tened to advise me.

"Don't accept too hastily." He avoided my gaz : "At best it is a thankless job, this nourishing those who would rather starve that they may pay installments to California land-boosters. You'll be no benefactor. You will find it depressing. You will be ostracized, and it may even be unsafe for you to stroll around unguarded at night."

Notwithstanding these perils, I accepted.

The unwritten law, like most futile and messy things

requiring the democratic knowledge of all and the wisdom of none, demanded that a solemn conclave of those
to be fed was necessary in any change of the routine of
it, and that a vote be taken, after devious discussion
and debate. Imagine convening a group of circus lions
to inform them that hereafter, at feeding time — and
so on!

The Chief knew that a popular vote would demonstrate
the usual popular row. There are only two kinds of
Indian Agents: those who compromise with everything
and have interminable hell on their weakling hands, to
the end that they are respected neither at home nor
abroad, and those who compromise with nothing. The
first sort is never defeated, and never resigns. He remains
continually in service, shifted from point to point, clut-
tering it with his inefficiency and indecision. Neglected
plants and chaotic systems are monuments, kept at national expense, to these amiable bench-warmers and trim-
mers. The second variety rides the waves for a season or
two, and crashes down finally, as all tyrants, however
benevolent, before the clamorous indignation of outraged
and inefficient democracy.

The Chief being one of the last sort, the electorate was
disfranchised. There was no session of Parliament. The
whole thing was done in much the same fashion as had
cost Charles the First his head.

BULLETIN

Beginning with the first of the c   .ng month, and until
further orders, the Chief Clerk will administer the affairs of
the Mess.

It was received in a grim, not to say stony, silence.
Like a tenderfoot, I rushed in where an angel would

have sought the cyclone cellar. Cooks were employed monthly, and it was midway in the month. That night I gave the cook her time.

Now, having ended one dynasty, it behooved me to create another. I went to the Chief.

"When can I have the transportation necessary to my duties as *maître d'hôtel* hereabouts? I'll drive in to the railroad town."

"Do you know the road?" the Boss asked, doubtfully.

"That does n't bother me. When do I get a team?"

"To-morrow," he replied, and left me to my fate.

Now I had traversed the road but once, when coming in a month before. The doubtful tone in his voice disturbed me. Perhaps the route-finding would not be so easy as a trick with cards. I sought out the pleasantest of the range men, and asked his advice concerning the matter.

"It's as plain as the nose on your face," he assured, and as this would have been very plain indeed, it heartened me. "Keep to the main-traveled road, and take all the turns to the right — going in."

This seemed a very simple matter, and I gave no thought to the turns I might encounter coming out. I was then, of course, — and because of some mental defect am yet, — notoriously the worst road-finder in all the Southwest. And when I departed next day, with "the old woman's team," there was no one to crowd additional information on me.

In the city, to lose one's way may be foolish without being unfortunate; but in the Desert one must arrive at his destination, or the results may be serious. And all the road directions from old-timers are similar. The Plains

Indian can be more definite. He may say, "Three hills and a look." The Arizona guide is a despair.

"You can't miss it," they invariably prelude. "Take the main road until you reach that little cornfield just beyond the hogan of Benally Bega's — remember that draw before you come to Black Mesa? That's it. Then the left trail until you reach that scraggy cedar; then head down across for that old corral, where the sheriff caught Bob Peterson; then — you know where we nooned in 1913? It's right east of that; and then, you can't miss it — it's right over from there — " the whole distance being sixty miles, and no water in the first five townships.

One plunges deeply on the optimism indicated by "you can't miss it," and starts. At midnight, with a tired team and no blankets, one suddenly realizes that he *has* missed it, and missed it bad. The sun sinks to rest, the desert grows black and threatening, he is off the main-traveled road, and no candle-lights are gleaming through the dark. There he remains until morning, when, cold and cramped, having kindled a fire to warm a can of beans that a more sensible man had slung under the seat, he finds that he has invited in the whole Navajo tribe. Five minutes after the wisp of smoke and the aroma of the burnt beans, comes an Indian, and another, and another, each looking earnestly for breakfast. It never fails. Between many signs and all the beans, not forgetting the passing of "thathli ibeso," which is one dollar in hard, bitable silver, he finds that he is only five miles off the road, and that his original destination *is* "right over from there."

On the cook-side of the board I played in luck. A row occurred in the short-order section of a Harvey House, and one first-class itinerant cook was flung headlong out of a job on the morning I reached town. It might never happen again. And knowing nothing of the back-country, and especially being ignorant of an Indian Service mess, he embraced the opportunity to sign up for a desert cruise. It was necessary for him to pack his belongings, the most precious of which were a trick dog and a phonograph, together with one record entitled: "She Is the Ideal of My Dreams"; and this he insisted would occupy him several days. I arranged for him to meet a team at the Agency freight-station, and next day he assisted me in the purchase of supplies for the coming month. We bought nearly a ton of foodstuffs. My vehicle was one of those light spring wagons, a "desert hack," rated to carry about one thousand pounds. Like an Indian freighter who loads pig lead, we never tallied the dead weight, but piled it in. The wagon groaned in its every joint under the load; and so I began the return trip.

One could not miss the right direction, for there were the distant mountains to point it, with the river as an eastern boundary. So long as one remained west of the river he must arrive somewhere. True. But for that river, and my sensible determination not to cross its half-dry bed, I might still be en route.

The roads of the desert are many, and all converge toward a settlement. Proceeding to town is very simple. But on leaving it the roads begin diverging in a most puzzling fashion, and there is a decision to be made at each departure. Of course the main-traveled road is usually plain and definite — usually. About half way to the Agency I was deceived by ten yards of bunch grass at a road juncture, and blithely accepted the branch leading to a river-ford. Nearing sunset, I had reached the river, — which was no place to be at that time.

"If alone, always tie the horses to the wheel."

There is n't anything else in the Desert to tie them to. So I did it, and started on foot for the nearest rise to make a reconnaissance. The scene of empty desolation, blurring in the first grays of twilight, was not inspiring. The scarlet and gold of the sunset behind the 'Frisco Range did not awaken poetry within me. I was thinking about something else, and joyfully I hailed a faint gleam on the far middle-distance, the last rays gilding the Agency tank-roof.

Between my position on the river, and that haven of rest, as the crow would negotiate it, stretched at least five miles of the Desert. So short a distance caused me to snort at my former fears. I went back to the wagon and found that the impatient horses had wound the lines around that wheel until they resembled a chariot pair reined in at the finish of an exciting race. With some difficulty I managed to release them, and climbed in as they plunged off seeking their feed.

The shortest distance between two given points is a straight line, or so the books have it. I followed my early schooling, and headed straight for the tank.

The shortest distance between two points in the Desert is not a straight line. I there and then learned this lesson. Between that river-ford and the main road, meandering somewhere to the left, were at least a thousand different obstructions, skillfully concealed by Nature, deceptive in the half dark, and treacherous traps when night came on: sand dunes that were as bogs; wide, shallow arroyos; scrubby slopes cut by wicked little gullies, all flanked and faced by other sand-meshes. In and through all this the team tugged wearily, at times stopping of themselves for breath, at times plunging desperately. A dozen times I lashed the horses to the wheel and went ahead to plot the way; a dozen times I returned to find them wound back on their haunches, in their efforts to free themselves from the overloaded wagon and the fool that had come out of the East. About midnight, after traveling to every point of the modern compass, I tried a last rise, determined, if this failed, to unharness and ride in, trusting to the horses to find their oats. And topping this little ridge was an old, half-hidden road. It angled away from the river toward the place where a real road ought to be. We swung down it, and an hour later, at an easy jog, the axles holding- and groaning-out to the last, we reached the Agency gate. The sleepy barn-man, an Indian, came out to meet me.

"Where you been?" he asked, with that innocent curiosity his tribe is noted for. "Have trouble findin' the road?"

"No," I told him, feeling a confidence born of relieved anxiety. "Nope! just started from town late."

There is nothing like assurance after a distressing evening. And too, had I not landed a cook? I could not spoil such a triumph by admitting that I had been lost.

V

DESERT LIFE AND LITERATURE

The reputation of those writings, which he probably expected
to be immortal, is every day fading; while those peculiarities
of manner and that careless table-talk the memory of which,
he probably thought, would die with him, are likely to be
remembered as long as the English language is spoken in any
quarter of the globe. — T. B. MACAULAY: *Johnson*

LIFE in the little stone house to which I had now removed
was filled with books and tobacco smoke and belated plans
in futures — that time when I should be strong again. I
had regretted the impossibility of my packing out a Washington library, but my old friend and bitter critic, the
now astonishing Mr. Mencken, kept my intelligence alive
by sending parcels of the latest publications, and these
arrived fresh and unscorched, though having passed beneath his searing eye and ruthless pen. Later, my faithful
typewriter, a relic of newspaper days, was sent forward
in defiance of medical advice, and I wrote a few stories
that, with their magazines and editors, are now forgotten.

Evenings, swung in a hammock, I studied sunsets
and their glories, masked and reflected by the magnificent
San Francisco Range, and gradually began to absorb the
desert peace. To know its moods, those swift and unexpected changes, having in them often a dream's stealthi-
ness and unreality, one must live for a year in a little house
built low against the brown bosom of the Desert.

I remember the peculiar silvern radiance of one evening.

The light came through dust-screens and, filtering across brown levels, limned patches of greasewood in a lemon pallor. The sentry cottonwoods of the riverbank were picked out as brilliant etchings of gray trunks and lacy branches in a glow of apple-green. Night swarmed out of the east in great blue clouds. Flying before it were cottony puffballs, white and twisting into the sunset, like masses of fleece, newly washed. But in the northwest swung a dun-colored curtain, lighted by the afterglow, suspended from the higher sky, a drifting, heavy drapery, its ragged edges trailing the tops of the blunted buttes with filmy rain-tresses. Between this curtain and the middle distance the mesa barricades had not yet darkened, and they were sharply outlined as gaunt shapes of red and saffron sandstone.

Now the peaks cooled and the great mountain-range lived in silhouette, its backbone etched with a line of electric blue. Early night swept overhead, and a few timid stars peeked out, as if fearing the thunder-mutter that came on the night wind, sullen herald of a desert storm. Now pale red flames reflected in the far-away dun-colored curtain. The storm rushed eastward across the northern heavens, while above me the night rolled west, bringing its stars into a brighter glow.

But this storm was fifty miles away and had its prescribed circle to complete. Soon its gathering vanguard began blotting out the stars. Now came a dusty shrieking wind; now the purple belly of the sky was rent by a white-hot wire, and like the crash of a thousand cannon followed the voices of the storm; now fell a few drops of cold rain, fanned on the wind into spray; and then — the deluge — a silvery curtain in the half-light, like a river turned over a new brink, drenching the Desert, beating all weak things into the sand. Parched as the ground was, the water could not be absorbed at once, and soon stood as lakes in the hollows.

It seldom rains in the Desert; but when it does! — One may drown in arroyos that carry tearing leaping torrents immediately after such cloud-bursts, and at the same point next day the sand will be steaming in the hot sunlight.

Within the space of three hours I have observed a beautiful sunset, an afterglow, twilight with a storm brewing, stars and night overhead; then the flood of water, lighted by crisp terrifying flashes and bringing the noise of Niagara; to be followed by calm night again, the stars returning to see their reflections in the desert pools. But the observer had the advantage of a view embracing one hundred miles between the mountain range and the country of the buttes. The wonders of the heavens passed around him in full circle.

And where could one find such another place for the sight? Probably nowhere else in this hemisphere, save with a slight advantage in height and atmosphere at the Lowell Observatory, about sixty miles away, where the astronomer may have viewed the same spectacle from his study, perched on a shoulder of the San Francisco Range, having below him that mystic world of the Indians, the dim, illimitable stretches of the Painted Desert.

The New England States, all of them, could be gently eased into Arizona, and there would remain room for Pennsylvania and little Delaware without crowding. The one reservation that I had charge of from 1911 to 1919 embraced 3863 square miles, a trifle smaller than Connecticut, and it was a postage stamp on the broad yellow face of Arizona, which is in area one twenty-seventh of the entire United States. One hundred thousand persons, or one fourth of the state's estimated population, live in eight of its towns, leaving much less than three persons per square mile, including Indians and Mexicans, to inhabit the remaining emptiness. One tenth of the population is Indian, and one fourth of Arizona's land area is "Indian country." The reservations have 1.5 persons per square mile. The fastest train of the Santa Fe system requires ten hours to cross Arizona from its eastern boundary to the Colorado River, a distance of 386 miles. Arizona has mountains that lift their crests more than 12,000 feet above the sea; and to present a perfect contrast, it has Yuma and Parker, towns of the Mohave Desert, cozy places in summer, close to sea level, with temperatures of 116° to 120° in the shade. Yes, you can eat oranges from the Phœnix trees while listening to the story of the Yuma man who found Hell chilly; and you can find snow in June on the upper levels of the Apache Indian Reserve without scaling a mountain peak. In the northern Navajo country I have twice experienced thirty degrees below zero in February, while there is no doubt the American Beauty roses were blooming in Phœnix gardens. Once I nearly froze to death on the nineteenth of May in Arizona, the place of palms, and figs, and pomegranates!

I had expected to be sadly bored, but the steady routine of each reservation working-day ate up the hours. Time does not hang on one's hands; a strange thing too, considering the silence and solitude and lack of action in the Desert. Some writer has sought to picture this bustling, speaking emptiness: — "It is a land where one always expects to find something just around the corner; and there is never anything around the corner." Quite so. Therefore, it is a magic place, an Enchanted Empire, filled ever with a wistful anticipation that lures without the bitterness of disappointment. There is always another corner, and another beautiful possibility.

A multitude of office duties caused the four morning-hours to seem as one. Lunch time, and a bit of gossip with a dozen strange beings, and the quaint humor that isolation creates. Then the afternoon, filled with the shrieking wind and the hiss of sand against the panes. A passing traveler would stop to ask about the river fords and roads to nowhere; and those employees coming to requisition supplies, whether engineer or school matron or farrier, would have their talk out. The warehouses always presented the fascinating search for something, just to learn if indeed it was there, as the account stated, and in the exact quantity as the Bureau minutely charged; and when not found, there would be ample time for the cursing-out of the fellow who had used it and failed to make the credit to protect the Chief.

"That fencing!" wrathfully declared the Boss. "That wire was issued five years ago. I remember old Becode Bega got the last spool of it. It has rusted out by now in the Corn Creek. Hawkins was clerk then, and damn his eyes, he never expended anything. He had rheumatism, and sang hymns, and was always telling me that Congressman Floyd Witherspoon, of Spokane Flats, had married his wife's second cousin. Send a policeman up to Becode's camp, and have that old sinner ride in thirty miles to sign for that wire. It's a shame to do it, but who cares in Washington! They sent Hawkins out, and have him still, somewhere else, twisting somebody else's accounts. What's the next item?"

And so it went. Because under the accounting system then in vogue — a relic of the War Department days, and which ate up oodles of time and thousands of dollars in checking and balancing — everything from a quart of shoe pegs to a locomotive-type of stationary boiler had to be located and tested and receipted for by the Chief every three months, come Hades or come high-water!

Without this intense supervision by mail and blue pencil, through exceptions to accounts submitted, and silly questions, and equally silly answers, the Chief might have eaten either the shoe-pegs or the boiler during that odd time when he should have been making brick for lack of something to occupy him. The state of the Indians themselves, physically or mentally; the state of their holdings in stock, implements or gardens; the actual efficiency of the employee corps; the quality of supplies, and whether on hand or not in sufficient amount to insure a standard system — no one of these things particularly interested any Eastern authority to the point of correction; but the property accounts and the cash accounts were checked until the paper wore out, and until the Chief neglected everything else to satisfy them.

And dear old careful Uncle, who has wasted more cold cash in archaic systems than any other organization known to ancient or modern history, checked the spigot drainings every three months, unmindful of the bung, and scrupulously filed away the results in the catacombs of Washington, unaware of the negligence of Hawkins, the clerk, but always decidedly mindful of that worthy's relationship to the elected genius of Spokane Flats. One may now remark that the accounting systems have changed. They have — after years of travail. But Hawkins and his benevolent influence have not changed; Uncle has not changed; and the Chief's time is still spent checking inefficiency at home and reporting to ignorance abroad.

Three times a week, in late afternoon, a solitary horseman, jouncing above his laden saddlebags, would appear
over the slight rise beyond the trading-post, coming from
the railroad; and a cry would go up from the campus: —
"The mail!"

That call would cause a stir. What a thing of interest
is a newspaper five days old, a fresh magazine or catalogue,
in those waste places! And a letter from a friend or loved
one is a thing golden. Scarcely would the distribution
have ended, with joy or disappointment, when it would
be sunset, and the Desert cooling and browning into dusk
as the red ball plunged downward into the caverns of the
range, trailing behind it a glory that often compensated
for the trials and little evils of the day.

Sunday brought a pause that seemed unreal, an enforced
halt, a marking of time. For those who did not sing
"Beulah Land," it was a long-drawn-out monotony. A
thousand miles from anywhere inviting a visit, often
without the solace of a kindred spirit, the silence and
loneliness settled into one. The clanking pump was
hushed, the boiler no longer hissed steam, the whistle did
not summon, the mail did not arrive. Everyone arrayed
himself in latest fashion, as mail-order catalogues decreed,
and sat around in great discomfort. Where to go? There
was no hunting, fishing — nothing. One had photographed
everything above ground five thousand times. The nearest town was twenty-six miles off, and on Sunday as dead
as Julius Cæsar.

On such a day I became acquainted with the post trader,
a half-breed Navajo, handsome and smiling. I found this
lovable fellow in his quarters off the store. The place was
bare enough of comforts, but along one wall ran shelves,
piled with books and magazines — and such books and

magazines! There I found the famous five-foot shelf extended many feet. And old files of *Harper's Monthly*, the *Atlantic*, and *Scribner's*. Among the books my hand touched Boswell's *Johnson*, and I knew that the volumes I had left behind would be no longer missed. And Dickens, and Irving, and Macaulay, and Spencer, and Huxley, and Darwin.

"Why, I had not expected to find such books — here — "

He thanked me with a smile.

"Help yourself when you're lonely," he said. "Most of the employees lack reading matter only when Montgomery Ward's bible fails to come in." He noted the book in my hand. "Now that Johnson — he was a great old guy, was n't he?"

Criticism, à la Navajo!

Years before, he had been a student at Hampton Institute, that excellent institution of the South where Negroes and a few Indians were trained. The books were his prizes, won in scholastic debates, and they had returned with him to the edge of the Enchanted Empire. Here he could feel the white man's presence, enjoy a little of his society, read his books, and still be within call of his desert people. I have known Indian athletes who bartered their trophies when they returned to the old life. This strange Indian had kept his treasures, and at night, those long desert winter nights, when he tired of the *Alhambra* he could talk with Doctor Johnson ("a great old guy"); he could follow Macaulay down the ages to visit London in the days of Charles the Second; and sometimes he permitted Darwin to tell him of his beginnings. He knew the books, each and every one. He had stepped from paganism into a gentle skepticism, and his armor was not dented by snatches of the Scriptures. The good missionary people sighed about it; but they could be defeated by a quotation, and were.

His comments on those novelists who treat the Desert as a stage and people it with costumes tricking out traditional characters, were acrid and amusing. A certain very popular writer would have been humbled after a short session with this half-savage critic. What he left of that writer's Navajo picture was very little, and that little in shreds.

As for his own people, their customs and superstitions, he had an equally sane view of them, and would explain many things that, farcical to the alien's first thought, were no stranger when resolved than our own wives' tales. He pictured for me the actual worthlessness of native policemen, a system that Washington is devoted to, while admitting all their skill as trackers and go-betweens. As an interpreter at trials, he was invaluable, and his knowledge of what a Navajo would do under given conditions was almost uncanny.

Occupying the position of field-interpreter and chief of range police, this man would have been worth a very creditable salary, because he was undeniably honest, progressive, and without deceit. I urged him to accept such a position with me in later years, and when he gave his reasons for declining, one of them was the analysis of the superstitious native who would have to serve under him, and the other was the abject parsimony of the United States Government.

I shall always remember and be grateful to that Navajo gentleman. He is dead. I do not know how he died. Perhaps he relented, and for his pagan jests begged forgiveness; perhaps he died to the Medicine Man's chanting

— counting, counting, as they always die in the Desert — calling on his tribal gods.

But I know that he met the answer with a smile. For so he would have joined the long shadowy line of weaving plumes and tossing lances as the tribe sought new and happier hunting-grounds; or would have entered the council ring of the chiefs, to advise in reviewing their material errors, when they saw the white man as a conqueror, rather than as a friend, and matched his evils with their savage ingenuity.

VI

A NORTHERN WONDERLAND

To those unaccustomed to desert lands the Navajo country presents in form and color and grouping of topographic features a surprising and fascinating variety; and those familiar with arid regions will find here erosion features of unusual grandeur and beauty." — GREGORY: *The Navajo Country*

THE nearest place of change was the town, with a dinner at the Harvey House. I planned to make this trip each month, to have a food spree, quite as on a time rude gentlemen of the cattle days came in from the ranges, hungry for sights and pleasures, and devoted themselves to the swift consumption of raw liquors. But four hours of dragging through heated sand and sunlight, from one lonely landmark to another, with nothing of interest between, destroyed much of the anticipated satisfaction. I recall a bit of Washington advice.

"You will find that country," said the well-meaning fellow, "covered with black gramma grass. Buy a pinto pony the very first thing you do. Its keep will be negligible. A saddle will cost but a few dollars. Thus you will have transportation at all times. It will be a pleasure to ride into town after office hours. You'll enjoy riding above all things."

Twenty-six miles — fifty-two miles there and back!

Now I had read Western stories, written by O. Henry and others who knew less about the subject. Playing the sedulous ape, I had written a few myself. These epics all mentioned areas of black gramma grass, and made much of swift-footed cayuses that were camouflaged by Nature and possessed Dante-like noses and broom tails. There is a wondrous lot of this in the movies, too, and the joyous bounding of the aforesaid animals, from prairie rise to prairie rise, pressing the miles behind them, and the care-free demeanor of their riders, surrounded as they are by creaking leather, wide-barred shirts, and jingling spurs, appeals to one.

But when you learn that a cayuse-bronk in northern Arizona eats imported hay at forty and sometimes sixty dollars the ton, the black gramma grass and pastures all being three hundred miles to the south; and when you find that the devil is not to be trusted for an instant, and that he has to be flayed constantly to produce even an amble; and when you feel — "feel" is the word — the misery twitching completely throughout the human system from pounding on the wooden anatomy of the brute, a large part of this paper-and-film appeal vanishes. More-over, dusty shirts, alkali-impregnated handkerchiefs, and the smell of a harness shop do not combine to flavor one's meals delicately. Big Bill Hart may have my share of this, and he is welcome.

But there does come a longing "for to admire and for to see" what is actually out back. That adventure and romance are not to be found in the beautiful desert dis-tances seems impossible. The dim blue buttes of the north, mysterious altars of the gods, promised to yield some-thing from the land they guarded. And when an Agency mechanic told me that he had orders to visit the Castle Butte station, a far-away outpost, I recommended my-self as a standard camp-cook, recalling the early mornings of newspaper days when I fried eggs on a gas-stove. We did not go to the horse-corral and lay our ropes over two spirited steeds, but at an early hour wended to the barn and harnessed two sturdy old plugs to a twelve-hundred-pound farm wagon. They were capable of making four miles an hour, and the wagon had capacity for a grub-box, for blankets, shovels, rope, and all the things necessary — perhaps — to our getting there first, and to accomplishing something afterward.

Have you never wondered how those adventurous fellows of the yarns, outfitted with nothing but a handkerchief, a saddle, and a lariat, manage to cover leagues upon leagues with the one horse, and never stop overnight? A Navajo Indian can do with one blanket and a sheepskin lashed behind his saddle; but even he contrives to find the trading-posts of the Desert for his grub, and he always reaches a friendly camp at nightfall.

Smith cautioned me to take a heavy coat, which I would not have thought of. Right at the start I committed a serious blunder, one that caused me to suffer bitterly, and one that I have not repeated since. Expecting to return next day, I persuaded myself that two sacks of beck-a-shay nahto, or genuine "cattle" tobacco, would be sufficient for the trip. But desert plans are subject to change, and desert wisdom is painfully acquired. I now have drilled myself never to forget matches and a filled canteen, baling-wire, — otherwise "Arizona silk," — repair parts for the lizard, a piece of rope, tools, and a heavy coat of sheepskin, plus a tobacco factory unless the route is marked by trading-posts every thirty miles. I arrange these things automatically, because on that trip I tried to smoke powdered alfalfa in a cob pipe.

Northward we wended all day, one rugged mesa slope

and huge flat succeeding another, always rising. After passing Lone Cottonwood Spring, where the water was an excellent imitation of thick gray pea-soup that the horses disdained, we lunched at a delightful place known as Coyote Springs, one of the ten thousand Southwest waterholes so named. In the naming of springs and precious water it would seem that the vocabulary of the pioneers was decidedly limited. But it would have been the same by any other name. A hole scooped in a soft rock and sand hill, fenced with crooked and cracking cottonwood branches, as the Navajo build their corrals, with not a vestige of relieving green within miles of it. All around the sand was packed hard by the flocks of sheep that came to water. Overhead was a broiling sun, and this barren area reflected every bit of the glare and heat that it did not hold as a stove. The air was heavy with the aroma of sheep, and alkali showed ghastly white in the spring's overflow. Nevertheless, it was an oasis and held water. Here and there were picked and bleaching bones. The coyotes knew its name.

Many buttes not to be seen from the Agency were now in sight. One lumpy mound resembled a coiled snake — Rattlesnake Butte; another was shaped as a pyramid, although no one had heard of Cheops or Chephren; and a third, which had crumbled, was like a huge four-poster bed that some forgotten giant had wrecked.

A bite to eat, and on again, lumbering down the yielding banks of washes, and scrambling up and out of them. Truly a couple of sturdy plugs were required to drag the wagon up those heavy slopes. Providing the traveler has time and patience, and is built with a steel-riveted frame, the old-time farm wagon with three-inch tires is the surest method of making such a journey. It rolls and pitches as a squat lugger in a choppy sea, but it gets there.

While the Desert appears as a level sward, one soon finds that there is no sward to speak of, and that one million tangled hummocks fast follow the first million, each bunch of sparse grass, each growth of greasewood or salt-bush having its own protecting hillock of sand. A good road in those days was one that a stout wagon could get over without being wrecked.

It is quite an experience to travel for hours toward a given point marked by a solitary pinnacle, a veritable mountain having sheer sides, and fail to reduce the distance appreciably. The sun was nearly down when we crawled along a valley between two of these monsters. One, named Chimney Butte, a huge truncated cone resting on massive shoulders, was the highest in that country; and the other, Castle Butte, looked like a ruined mediæval stronghold, having a causeway flanked by towers, above which loomed dim embattlements and casements. In the brilliant daylight the height of Chimney Butte is dwarfed by desert distances; and Castle Butte is not al-ways robed in fancy; but it was now twilight, the time when the Desert is most sombre and fanciful, and it was my entrance to that garden of the vanished gods. These two gigantic piles were as the awesome portals of a ruined gateway, the pass to an unknown, mysterious country; and the whole setting, fading into night, gloomy with with the menace of silence, held something of the strange unreality of a dream. And came on suddenly the dark and cold.

How did Smith manage to follow the road? I could no longer see it, and had more than enough to do to cling to the pitching seat of the wagon. We headed straight

CROSSING THE DESERT BELOW CHIMNEY BUTTE

THE ORAIBI WASH IN FLOOD-TIME
Where quicksands are ready to engulf a stalled car

into the blackness. What yawning precipices might be awaiting us! I became chilled and cramped, and was thankful for that greatcoat, though it did not pad me against the rude shocks of the going.

"How much farther is it to this Agency?" I asked.

"Oh! over in the hills a bit — 'bout three miles furder to go yit. It ain't an agency, yeh know — nothin' but a missionary and a log hut."

And we plunged into another of the dark defiles. Then out of the black, on a bit of cold wind, came a desert welcome that one never forgets, a promise of rare comfort when one is hungry and cramped with cold, the pungent incense of burning cedar. Now from the deep shadow of a hillside arose a thin column of sparks, glinting, flying jewels of the night.

"There's it," he announced, as if somewhat relieved, himself.

It was a little house, built of boards, having but two rooms, one large enough for a bed and dresser, the other containing a cookstove, table, and two chairs. Its outside dimensions could not have been more than twelve by twenty feet. And when the stove was filled with dry cedar one was tempted, after a complete toasting on one side, to dispense with the table. But there was no complaint to make of this on our arrival. The fire had the cheering crackle of Yuletide, and soon coffee and bacon added their aroma. The hospitality of the good missionary and his wife was like all those welcomes extended in the solitary places, when the visitor is not touring with a notebook and a nose. The meal ended, and all news exchanged, we said good night and opened the door.

"'Ere's a go!" one might have exclaimed, without hurting the feelings of a preacher. It was snowing! And even a preacher would have remarked further, probably with adjectives, on seeing that Government house in which we were to spend the night. It was a log hut in truth, built corral-fashion, the poles set on end, the chinks originally plastered with adobe. There was but one room, containing a single bunk made of boards, an old cookstove, and a collection of broken tools and empty canned-goods cases. The floor was of packed earth. Without exaggeration, I may say that the roof and the floor were intact; but practically all the caulking had escaped from the log walls, and the wind felt its way inside with long icy fingers. The mechanic dropped into the bunk and was asleep almost instantly; and, after building a rushing fire in the stove, I rolled myself in Government blankets, and rolled again, this time under the stove, to pass the night.

But I did not rest in the poetry of the wild. The refulgent moon did not come up to spill its splendor through the open door, nor even through the extensive openings of the wall; the perfume of the growing pines did not soothe with healing balsam, the cry of the loon did not sound from across the lake, and so forth. The floor, however, was under that stove; and the floor had not been constructed along those scientific lines followed in the building of Ostermoor mattresses. Plastic as is my figure, it refused to conform.

And to add to my distress, someone in all that vast and lonely country owned an old gray horse. I know he was old, and I know he was gray, for he acted just like a silly old gray horse. And he was hobbled, and he was out in the snow, and he had a bell tied to his neck.

Clankety-clank-clank, cla*ng*, claaa*ngngng* — clankety, clang, *clank!*

Around and around and around the house he voyaged all that night, proceeding by hops and plunges as a hobbled horse must, his gait just enough hampered by the lashings of his two front feet to impart a syncopated tempo to the discords and jangles of that flat metallic bell. At times he would pause, as if for breath, and there would be quiet — deep silence — just sufficient for a doze; then — clankety, clang, clang, *clank!* he would break out again.

I have listened to jazz orchestras of various colors and degrees of crime, and other peace-destroying nuisances meriting death; but I have never heard anything equal to the nocturnal pilgrimage of that old gray horse. I would drop off to sleep, and suddenly wake as if feeling his hobbled feet squarely in the centre of my contracted chest; but he would be ten yards off, miserably clanking his way to another sector of the snow-covered terrain. And confused, I would lift my head to listen, knocking it of course against the bottom of the stove, when a long icicle would stab through a wall chink and take me fairly in the ear. Perhaps it was a pleasant night for Smith, who faithfully and harmoniously snored away the hours.

With the dawn I struggled up. No! I did not bound out joyously to gambol in the pure air of the stunted cedar-forest. It was a cold gray dawn with a foot of snow, and there was a dank rheumatic caress in it. With all speed I began smashing a packing case for kindling. Crash! down came the axe, and splinters flew wide, when Smith stirred in his bunk, awakening to duty and the dangers thereof. He blinked his eyes and spluttered: —

"Watch out for that dynamite."

"Dynamite?"

"Yes; it's right under my bunk. Chop your wood furder off."

I followed these directions to the letter. In fact, I gently carried all the wood outside and chopped it.

The getting of breakfast, a complete demonstration of my culinary ignorance, occupied me fully in the half-dark. I walked to and fro gingerly, fearing to wake the dynamite; and I wondered how that stupid fellow could have slept and have snored as he did, superimposed above a quiescent earthquake. Dynamite is a great friend to man in the rocky gorges of the West, but it should not be permitted to join the family circle.

When next I opened the door, what a transformation! I had come to this place in the cold grim darkness, heartened only by the perfume of burning cedar. Occupied with the wood and the wet-handled axe, I was dimly aware of a drowsy landscape in the clammy mist of dawn. But now the sun had lifted, and the scene was a snowy fairyland. The gnarled cedars of the foreground were laden with dripping snow, their branches picked out with gems. And where the snow lay in unbroken sheets, pure white, glistening, the shadows of the dwarfed trees formed rare patterns. Behind the house were cliffs, and each gaunt angle held its draping of snow. The time-worn bastions of those lava ledges stood as gaping at the winter's cheery Good-morning. It was a stage scene under the great amber light.

A long valley stretched away to the Biddahoche Plains and the Bad Lands with their honeycombed hills. Its dim recesses were now painted by the first plashes of sunshine. To left and right, overhanging the snowy meadows, reared great buttresses and crags of lava, and all down the valley ancient promontories loomed amid the fading veils of mist. Prehistoric ages had seen these as the shelving inner walls of some vast crater, when they had seared and glazed and baked and colored to form Nature's pottery. Now, broken and rent apart, they stood as fantastic separate monuments, lining that sunlit corridor to the outer plains.

Dominating the foreground was Squash Blossom Butte, an inverted bloom that the storms of æons had carved and a million rare sunsets tinted. The Indians reverence the squash blossom as a symbol of fruition, and perhaps — who knows — in its delicate bell-shaped flower they see more than the mere promise of a harvest. It is found in Navajo silver-work, strung into those massive necklaces of which they are so proud; and when one goes into Hopi land he finds it imitated in the dressing of their maidens' hair. So they named this altar.

It was commanding in the morning light; it was the last thing seen down the valley, a scarlet head thrust into a sober sky, as that second night came on. The sunset lavished all its rainbow shades on it. Richest gold and lavender above, purple tones and lava-green below; bands of saffron melting into slatey shades; emerald and crimson deepening into jetty blacks when the afterglow had vanished. An aged throne of the gods. And clearly sweet, as desert music, came the half-hushed sound of sheep moving among the cedars; and a young Navajo girl paused at the edge of a thicket to gaze shyly at our cabin, then to hurry away, the tiny bells at her belt tinkling, having all the romance of the gypsies.

There is no finer landscape in the Southwest than this seldom-visited country of the Moqui Buttes where, according to the Hopi, the one-time giants had their dwelling places. The wondrous piles and pinnacles of the Grand Cañon present a chaotic struggle that has ceased in all its awesome disorder and aged grandeur. It makes man gasp and wonder, but it does not invite the smile of reverie. This scene about the sunset throne had that serenity born of isolation. It was small enough to invite intimacy. Like the kingdom of a fairy tale, the tranquil valley encompassed its own world, dreaming, smiling in its sleep.

Many times since have I crossed the Butte country, seeing it frozen in winter and again broiling under a summer sun that scorched from the cedars their sweetest aromas. I have always found it a haven, full of peace.

Next day we returned to the Agency, an uneventful retreat, save for a jouncing box of dynamite that leaped like a thing fiendishly alive whenever the wheels slammed into a rut. My nerves were not in the best shape. I had been smoking powdered alfalfa in a pipe. And I would look back from the high seat, half fearing each time to catch that dynamite in the very act of going off. But luck was with us; we herded it safely into the Agency storehouse; and I rushed to the post for a can of real tobacco.

VII

THE FIRST BALL OF THE SEASON

> Of Harrison's barn, with its muster
> Of flags festooned over the wall,
> Of the candles that shed their soft lustre
> And tallow on headdress and shawl;
> Of the steps that we took to one fiddle,
> Of the dress of my queer vis-à-vis,
> And how I once went down the middle
> With the man who shot Sandy McGee.
> BRET HARTE: "Her Letter"

AMONG employees of the Desert Indian Service, the Mary-lander is a rarity. Back in Maryland the Indian Service is unknown, all readers of the *Sun*-paper believing that Indians were originally designed by Buffalo Bill.

So when a lad seated himself on my porch one night, and announced: "Why, Ah'm from Maheland too; yes, indeed!" it rather struck me where I ought to have lived. I was eating at the mess then.

He was out with an irrigation crew, surveying levels, and in a few months had become obsessed by all things Southwest Indian. He wore moccasins and a bracelet studded with turquoise, and he could chant like a cold Navajo on his way home from a Yabachai.

"Ah'm goin' to get me a gourd-drum, an' go in for 'singing,'" he told me, when we had become better acquainted, and he demonstrated the eerie half-croon-half-yodel of the Medicine Man. "Say, Nultsose! have yo' heard them? — Medicine 'sings'?"

This was my first intimation that a title attached to my position.

"Nultsose — "

He explained it as Navajo for paper or writing, hence; one who writes on or issues papers pertaining to the mysteries of white men's wholly unnecessary accounting. Nearly all clerks wear spectacles, as I did, and one would think that the Indian, naming his own so often because of infirmities, would have seized on this defect for a name. But not so; the check, order, issue-script, permit, or warrant, the paper, the "nultsose," is the important thing to him. It means money in hard dollars, authority perhaps, demand for goods, leave to go on a journey with recommendation or safe-conduct; or, if fortune has waned, summons to the Chief.

"And if yo' go to a 'sing,' Nultsose, remember to take change, an' don't give the squaws more'n two bits at a time. Yo'll have to dance with 'em, yeh know, an' instead of thankin' 'em, yo' pay 'em. Hand out a dollar, an' Good-night — they keep the change. Now old Beck-a-shay Thlani is inviting to one sometime soon. It'll be a reg'lar hoe-down, an' we'll go."

The doctor was present, and he grinned uncomfortably. The Nahtahni, stretched in his hammock, rubbed his wig and grunted.

"Ah! yo'-all come too," urged Roberts; "It'll be fun. They all know me, and I'll do the interpreting. Every old shemah with a dotter has her eye cast my way, anyhow. They pick out the handsome boys for the weddings at 'sings.' I'll have to get me a Piute wedding-basket, though, next pay-day. There's a trader over at Red Lake who's got my order for it."

The doctor cautioned me later not to be too hasty in

this matter, and I perceived that he had reason for timidity.

"They'll get you," he declared. "They never fail to land a fellow; and then he has to prance like a fool before five thousand Indians. That's all right for Roberts, 'cause he'll wind up a squaw man; but I'm advising you."

And one twilight, when we were again arranged on deck after supper, a half-dozen little Navajo boys from the school sidled up to the Chief, daring and timid by turns, their eyes snapping with the fire of hope. They hung around until he asked: —

"Ah-tish-ah?"

"Dence!" they exclaimed, breathlessly.

"Noki yisconga, epten," the Nahtahni severely decided. "Doe-yah-shaunta! She-no-be-hosen. E-yah-tay."

The Old Man was proud of his linguistic ability, and this was the complete extent of his Navajo on any topic. The last sentence but one he had made up, somehow, all by himself. It bore no semblance to anything any Navajo had ever enunciated; but he knew what it meant. A free — a very free — translation would run something like this: "Two days from now, nothing doing. Don't you dare to do it. It's bad for you. I know nothing about it. Yes; all right!"

The last was all the kids wanted. The scrub crackled as they disappeared into and through it, going as frightened rabbits.

Roberts spoke next.

"That's old Beck-a-shay Thlani's 'sing.' Say, boss, the Doc and young Nultsose here are both pinin' for to shake a toe in that soiree. Let us have a team, will yeh?"

The Nahtahni grunted.

"You know the horses have worked hard to-day — "

"Yes; let us have a team," said his stepdaughter, who afterward married the doctor; and that settled it, and also bound the medico to the adventures of the evening. There are a few things no different in the Desert. The Navajo woman of the hogan, the Hopi dowager of the household on the height, the Pueblo wife of the lower vineyards, all settle these questions in much the same manner. Man proposes and begins to make a noise with words, and immediately thereafter attends strictly to the holding of his peace. Roberts knew this, and without further parley disappeared in the direction of the barn. Shortly came a farm wagon, drawn by two solid animals, and a dozen of us piled into it, the doctor noticeably lagging.

"Don't forget your change, Nultsose," called Roberts.

It was no great distance to the river, and soon we were splashing through shallow waters. Mounting the high farther bank, the wagon began tossing and rolling over an old desert road. Then the dark laid down its thick blanket, and the stars burned through overhead. From the next rise we noticed a faint glow, away off, and this grew larger as we blundered along. Now a whiff of pungent smoke came on the thin desert wind. Now the deep shadows began to dissolve into a golden gloom, and now gleamed the white-hot flare of burning cottonwood. Then a furious challenge from the dogs, and we saw the camp. As feudal lords were once accompanied by retainers and shock-headed varlets, so the nomadic lord of the Desert is followed by a multitude of canines. It seemed that a thousand of them started up to greet us, a fearsome, throaty bedlam.

Wagons loomed up, their canvas tops lending a touch of the pioneer days; and in the spaces between the poles were the little cooking-fires, around which women and children huddled amid pots and pans, saddles and boxes and water-kegs and tangled harness — all the clutter of a desert camp. Beyond the huge central fire was a hogan, that queer house the Navajo builds of logs and plasters with adobe, domed like a beehive, and from its roof wreathed a thin column of smoke. There rested the sick man for whom all this preparation had been made, the cost of which would likely break old Beck-a-shay Thlani, or at least seriously strain his credit at the trading-posts.

Coarse Navajo rugs were spread close to the fire and, with grave salutations from the older men and smiles from mothers who convoyed a bevy of Navajo girls, we were invited to be seated in the place of honor. This would have impressed any blank-record Easterner, going about making notes, as rude but wholesome hospitality, and it was; but the courtesy also enabled the Navajo to indulge himself — and particularly herself — in a bit of fun. The doctor slipped away into the shadows; and I noticed that the young men of the Navajo, scores of them, sat their ponies, a long line of horsemen behind us. They eased in their saddles, reins hanging, their faces having the grave solemnity that marks a shy and diffident people.

That is, shy of strangers, before whom they draw on the mask of gravity, mistaken since the days of Fenimore Cooper for stoicism. But no one was shy of Roberts; and especially had he friends among the ladies. Every old shemah greeted him with a smile and exclamations of pleased surprise. He held the confidence of these people; and well he might, considering the pains he had been to in acquiring a working vocabulary of their language, which is probably as difficult to master as Chinese. And I felt somewhat reassured in having him for sponsor. We lolled comfortably on the rugs, and the fire burned our faces and lighted everything as at a play.

"The doc' has vamoosed," he said, grinning; "but that won't do him any good. They'll run him down in the scrub, and bring him in hog-tied. I've told a dozen old women that he is stingy with his dancing. Self-defense — otherwise you an' me'd have to do it all."

"Explain this dancing act," I requested.

"Don't worry," Robert replied. "The squaws will attend to everything for yeh. Just yield gracefully — an' pay 'em. Don't forget that."

Now from the hogan came a band of solemn-featured men, led by an old gentleman of the tribe who bore a strong resemblance to Rameses III, straight out of glass case No. 12, as you go down the east corridor, save that he was slightly animated. He bore a staff, to which a little gourd-drum was tied. The group formed a wedge behind him. Silently they swayed together, shoulders touching, for several seconds. Then the old one tapped the drum and intoned a howl, and with one accord they were off, like a flock of coon dogs on a cold night. In time with the curious rhythm they continued swaying, and occasionally did a hop-step without moving forward. The fire beat upon them and, as they warmed to the chanting, heads thrown back, mouths agape, and vocal chords never missing a note, the sweat beaded on their foreheads.

"This," said Roberts to me, in solemn appreciation, "this is some singing — I never heard better." And I agreed with him. It laid over anything I had ever heard, including a Mott Street theatre choir.

It is impossible to describe the nuances of the Navajo chants. At the farthest northern trading-post there lives a lady who can translate the Rain Song, the Prayer before

NAVAJO ON THEIR WAY TO A DANCE

A NAVAJO HOGAN AND ITS BLANKET LOOM

Day, and other of their invocations; and I know a white
man who had a "medicine sing" held over him to comfort
his Navajo wife; but until you meet up with Roberts,
properly chaperoned nowadays in the great Jedito Wash,
I pass giving any idea of that weird combination of
sounds. A long sustained note at times, now a crooning
melody, now a sad, half-wild cry, filled with minor effects
that would be the delight and the despair of any jazz
artist, it is indeed a song of the Desert.

And the most astounding thing of all was the endurance
of that aged vocalist, the old Medicine Man. The pitch
of his drum simply encouraged him in new effects. There
was an energy, a sustaining confidence in his efforts that
must have had a rare effect on the ailing one within the
hogan. And for two mortal hours the others of the singing
band followed his lead without once rivaling him. When
one hesitated, as might be seen but not heard, the clamor
of the pack smothered all defects; and the faltering one
would cough, spit straight upward into the air, uncaring,
and get a fresh start. But the old man was never headed;
not once did he waver, hesitate, or fail in the key. He had
begun with that first flat sounding of the drum, and he
continued faithfully unto the end. He was an artist. I
admired him. And when Roberts told me that the old
charlatan would receive at least twenty sheep and five
head of cows for his fee, I began to understand his unflag-
ging spirit. He had a reputation to sustain.

The Regulations of the Interior Department, issued to
Nahtahnis, state that all such interesting old comedians
should be in jail for this offense against medical ethics.
But, mark you! the Interior Department does not encourage
Nahtahni to put him in jail. There are too many of him.
The Navajo number between thirty and forty thousand

souls on the six Navajo reserves, and about every seventh man is a doctor of tribal medicine. While a lucrative calling, it is not always a desirable one for the neophyte, since failure to exorcise successfully the evil spirits enmeshed in the patient has been followed more than once by swift demise, and the blundering physician did not heal himself later, nor did he hear the singing.

Once to me came an Inspector from the Department, and he said: —

"Now you have been having trouble with these Indians, and I am surprised that you have dismissed all your Navajo policemen as unworthy. You must have a police force to keep the Navajo in line. We will call a council and select a new outfit to sustain you in this important work."

Which we did. There were flour and meat, coffee and sugar, together with the all-necessary beck-a-shay nahto, cattle tobacco provided for distribution, and the people came. As usual, the men were diffident and modest, and no one offered himself for appointment as an officer of the realm. The nominations were made by head-men, and discussion followed as to individual merits, influence, bravery, and all those virtues that are supposed to animate the warrior. The Inspector was finally satisfied with the selections.

An old-timer sat on the platform with us, acting as interpreter. Ed had skinned mules across the Zuni Mountains in 1889, and he could take an old single-action forty-five and keep a tin can moving as if it were alive. He could roll a saddle-blanket cigarette with one hand, sing a puncher song, and play the guitar. He was one of the post-traders, and perhaps the best Navajo interpreter alive. He knew the Navajo Indian, having had the advantage

of a living dictionary in his early days. But Ed knew
when to keep his mouth shut, and aside from faithfully
interpreting from English into Navajo and from Navajo
into English he said nothing at the time. But later: —

"It was n't for me, a mere uneducated Indian trader,
to give my advice to a wise guy from the East who was
pointing the trails out to a Nahtahni; *but* ... every
damned one of them new police has 'medicine turquoise'
in his ears."

It was true. Every one of them should have been in jail!

The Navajo are lithe and lean, for the most part, and
their dress is picturesque. One could see all sorts of costume at this "sing." There was the old fellow with trousers compiled of flour sacks, the brand having been
arranged as a bit of decoration, and where "OUR BEST"
would show to most advantage; and there was that one
satisfied with a pair of cast-off overalls. But the majority
were in rich-toned velveteen shirts, open at the neck,
and with sleeves vented under the armpits; and desert
trousers, loose and flapping garments, Spanish-style, split
below the knee, made of highly colored and figured calico.
One fellow's legs were a riot of gaudy parrots. The twisted
silk handkerchiefs worn about the head came from the
Spanish too, no doubt. Their hair was drawn back from
the forehead and corded in a long knot, a Mongol touch.
Their moccasins were of red-stained buckskin, half-shoe,
half-leggin, warm and noiseless. The young men wore
gay shirts and neckerchiefs, store-bought, and their ponies
showed more of decoration than themselves. Each had a
good saddle, most necessary to a desert Romeo, and the
headdresses of the ponies were heavy with silver bands
and rosettes.

Now a middle-aged dandy would strut about, proud

of a crimson shirt, and the firelight would paint him as a figure from old opera. He would shine whitely of silver — a huge necklace, with turquoise pendants and many strands of shell and coral; bracelets, and the khado that is still worn, though the wrist no longer needs protection from the bowstring; silver rings and silver buttons, all studded with turquoise chips. Not less than five hundred dollars in metal and workmanship would adorn these old beaux, and an Indian valuation would be enormous.

Silver and turquoise are the jeweled wealth of the Navajo, the white metal contrasting with their sunburnt skins and the stone holding the color of their matchless skies.

The women wore velveteen bodices and curiously full skirts. They too were weighted with silver ornaments, one having the more of beads and bandeaux being the favorite wife or daughter. Some of the smaller girls moved about accompanied by the tinkling of little bells strung to their moccasins and belts.

All this in the brilliant flare of the cottonwood fire, above which fanned a mist of sparks like another Milky Way; and there was the incense of the smoking logs; and the star-pinned dome overhead; and all around the dark maw of the great lonely Desert.

Suddenly came a halt in these "singing" proceedings. The choir withdrew somewhere, and the centre of the stage was taken by another old man, who led a little girl. Other and older girls began to hurry around the circle, darting here, darting there, as if running something down. At first the little one seemed a trifle confused and stood in wide-eyed hesitation; but with a bit of urging from the elder master of the ceremonies, she made for Roberts. He would lead this german. Grinning, he permitted her

to pull him into the ring, his partner maintaining a solemnity that was comical.

"Get ready for the next set," he called to me over his
shoulder.

The social features were on, and the girls were hunting
partners. Did the young men of the ponies vie with each
other? They did not. They sat their steeds as if cut from
granite. For it would seem that a young man would
likely lose half his finery, certainly all his change, if captured, and might find himself later up against a breach-
of-promise suit. On foot, he was at a disadvantage;
mounted, it was the more difficult to drag him down. I
cannot say that I noticed any chivalry among those young
Navajo fellows.

But Roberts — there was a fine accommodating chap
for you. One partner was not enough for him; he now had
two of the tiny ones.

The dance seemed simple enough. It consisted in one's
acting as a pivot, around which the little squaw, or several
of them, turned backward with rapid scuffling steps. Her
one hand tightly gripped the man's belt, the other held
as tightly her blanket. Her expression was as sober as a
Chinaman's. But she accomplished the purpose of the
business. After a few moments of that turning, the subject would be too dizzy to argue out of a donation. It
kept up until Roberts was weaving; but when they stopped
he protested that he was a poverty-stricken wretch —
and promptly, without cracking a smile, they began again.
He must shell out at least a quarter to each, which he did
finally, and they scuttled back to their chaperons, who
banked the money. And here he came unsteadily to the
blanket we shared, while I suspected several of the old
women casting menacing glances in my direction. There

sounded a scurry in the outer darkness, and a crashing of the greasewood.

"The doc' has beat it," said Roberts, dropping down. I raised to look around; and just then, from behind, I felt a very muscular hand grasping my belt. There was nothing to do but yield in the best humor possible. A wild shout from the Indians, men and women, even from the ungallant horsemen grouped in the rear, and I was thrust and pulled forward. They had appointed two of the small girls to me, and their hold on my belt was like grim death.

And now the shuffle began.

I endeavored to spin without entangling my feet, but there was something wrong with my action. I was no such success as friend Roberts had been. Now the master of ceremonies came forward, his wrinkled face having the benevolence of a grandfather, and with expressive gestures he explained his sorrow because of my inefficiency. He would give me a lesson. We used words that neither understood, and made signs at each other until wholesale laughter retired the teacher. But I was not retired. I was still in the ring.

The gold-and-orange flares of the fires dazzled one's eyes, and then one began to turn faster; the circle of bright figures in the full light lost outline, and then the wagons and horses and hogan and Roberts on his blanket blurred into and formed one jumbled merry-go-round of which I was the centre. A little more of this, and I cried "Enough!" and very nearly staggered into the fire. Solemnly my partners waited for and clutched at their two-bit pieces, and I weaved back to the blanket.

The doctor was not captured that night. Perhaps he managed to hide until we harnessed the team and started for home; perhaps he walked into the Agency, as several accused. But this was a "running dance," meaning a moving one. A second installment of it was held the next night at a point ten miles down the river. The doctor was compelled to go, and there they ran him down and forced his performance. His effort was not half bad, and I wondered if mine had been as funny.

Affairs of this sort taught me that the desert Navajo are a good-natured and interesting people, in many ways like our own country folk at quilting-bees and huskings. They have their renegades and black sheep, with which the white race is as fully endowed; and my ugly experiences of later days could not be charged to the tribe.

When a Navajo is ailing, they manage to combine exorcism of the evil spirits with the amusing dance, and whether or not old Beck-a-shay Thlani was improved physically, the girls had a good time. It often helps them to find a husband; and in this case, how were they to know that Roberts would desert them for an Albuquerque girl, or that in a few months I would be interested only in solemnizing the marriages of older sisters and the herding of the remainder into schools?

But I have often wondered, when on those trails leading down into Beck-a-shay Thlani's district, and coming suddenly on a shy Navajo maiden chivvying a band of sheep, if she were one I danced with that night on the Little Colorado River, when I was simply "Nultsose," and the worries and responsibilities of Nahtahni had not been clamped to my shoulders.

VIII

OLD ORAIBI

But still the drowsy pueblo hears
　　The voices of the Bells;
They speak as ghosts of other years,
　　Their message faintly swells
And sighs away above the town,
　　Echoing history;
The whisper of an old renown
　　That dwelt at Cochiti.
　　　　　　　　— "The Bells of Cochiti"

ONE day, when it was quiet in the office, the Chief became reminiscent. He spoke of his coming to this station; how he had pitched his tent under the old cottonwoods at the present well; of the length of time it had taken to interest Pesh-la-kai Etsetti, the silversmith, and Beck-a-shay Thlani, the man of many cattle, in his plans; and of the winter when a posse of whites, led by a county sheriff who is now a Senator of the United States, drove the Indians through the snow, packing their few belongings, and across the river, in order that a few cattlemen who owned everything else might also have this poor grazing-area. That was before Great Heart quit the Washington helm; and Great Heart, with characteristic strenuosity, very promptly — one might say, rudely — dispossessed the self-appointed white inheritors of the earth.

"I have not had a vacation in six years," he said, as a wind-up, "And do you know, I'm tired out, and think I'll just take one."

Well, I was not surprised at his being a trifle weary. He seldom had a moment to himself — except nights, when perhaps he slept. He had just returned from a long trip in the Butte country, had made numerous drives to town on business, had assisted in running down a band of horse-thieves, and only that morning had been on the range to locate and evict certain trespassers. When such work did not occupy him, there was the ruined boiler to dally with, a pumping-plant to construct, and reports to indite; to say nothing of the sessions of the Indian Court, long and involved and farcical, the dipping of sheep, and the never-ending complaints of employees — a garrulous, gossiping, complaining lot.

It was a great life, but he had momentarily weakened.

"Yes, I am tired," he said; "And I'll let you run this ranch for a brief spell, while I go off resting. I have never seen a snake dance, and the Moqui hold 'em over beyond those Buttes. To-morrow I start."

Now that is the Southwesterner's idea of a real vacation. He would travel about one hundred miles by team, toiling slowly through sand, probably in rain at this season and its aftermath of treacherous mud; struggle across arroyos and stream-beds where quicksand might ensnare his outfit and cause him days of labor; through broiling sunlight certainly, and general discomfort, to perch himself finally atop an overheated rock on the edge of a cliff and witness a score of well-meaning but deluded Hopi Indians juggling their precious rattlesnakes. Within two hours he could have had a berth on one of the finest trains in the world, and within twenty-four have reached the magnificently overadvertised and overgrown city of Los Angeles. Not so! Across the Desert called an unsatisfied lure, the sorcery of the unrelieved distances. "Out there somewhere" was something he had not seen. That was the excuse. Actually he longed to be free, and the unmapped Desert offered its splendid unbounded freedom.

At that time I had no conception that hard-going, with no cares other than those of keeping to trail, was the finest sort of rest for an active man whose routine had been filled with the pettiness of irritating and never-to-be-settled Governmental farces. I now know that the way to rest is to remove from telephones and telegraph-lines, from both superiors and subordinates who wish to pass the buck, from the hellish routine of menus and meals, from begging complaints and complaining beggars; to get away from everything, and so far into the back-country that in case of war, pestilence, or death those interested are staggered by the idea of reaching you.

One learns to act quickly. Delay half a day, and the incoming mail may present a dozen obstacles. Promptly at dawn next morning he started, his camp-outfit lashed to a light buckboard; and on the bulletin-post he left a notice that my commands would be as the law of the Medes and Persians during his absence.

I took him at his word, and one very necessary improvement was immediately set in motion. The place had become an asylum for stray desert dogs and forlorn disinherited cats. This livestock was promptly rounded up, and there were interment ceremonies over at the river. The succeeding nights were filled with a comforting peace.

But it was not all beer and skittles. The boiler did manage to burn out during his leave, thanks to the careful inattention of an underpaid and irresponsible Indian stoker; and without a boiler one does not run a steam-laundry, does not make ice, and most serious of all in the Desert, does not pump water. This last is the one thing that may not be done without. So for two days and nights the engineer and helpers labored with a loyalty that was revelation to me, rolling and re-rolling the crumbling tubes of that relic of the Dark Ages, while tank-wagons struggled in from the river with the drinking-supply.

The doctor and I sat in the office and talked of many things.

"When the Chief returns," he suggested, winking, "We'll go over there and have a look-see. How 'bout it?"

"Done!" I agreed. "But do they hold these snake dances every month?"

"Our good friends, the Moqui, hold some sort of shindig every day, from what I have heard of them, but not all are snake dances. Those are reserved for serious and important occasions, regulated by the sun, moon, and stars. They occur once a year at certain fixed points."

"Then — we must have an object; and — "

"Peaches," he said, cunningly. "We'll go to old Oraibi after peaches — succulent fruit, the gift of the Spanish padres."

Noting my blank amazement, he hurried into an explanation.

"One of the legal amusements at an Indian Agency is keeping the help occupied, on the theory that, as with horses, it can think of only one thing at a time. Now it has been discovered in this Service that a dozen women paring peaches for preserving not only are happy in the thought of reducing expenses, but the more easily talk of what ails 'em. We'll suggest peaches to them, they'll bring pressure on the Boss, and we'll go. Lots of rabbit in that country, and ducks at the Lakes. Oraibi is some place to visit, too. It was built about the time of Noah, and has n't been cleaned since. Flood did n't reach it."

All of which was very interesting to one who wanted to go somewhere, anywhere, after having been penned up for months. I had viewed the same draggled trees, the same cement walks, the same old trading-post, for so long that all judgment was leaving me, and I had begun to buy Navajo blankets. When one reaches this point, the inoculative powers of the subtle Desert are beginning to work.

Everything came about just as the doctor had prophesied. The Chief returned one day at dusk, encrusted with sand and a week's growth of beard. While he was shaving, I made a complete report against the stoker and the boiler, with comment on those in Washington responsible for both. Then the doctor heard of a terrifically sick Indian over beyond the Lakes, and the pressure of peaches-and-economy was brought by the other parties. Next morning, the medico and I made our get-away before the utter absence of dogs was discovered.

The only thing that tried to affect our escape was a little animal perched on my walk in the late moonlight. The doctor cautioned me not to disturb this visitor, and for once I did not neglect a physician's advice. The team being harnessed at the barn, we drove to within fair shooting-distance of this guest, and the doctor handed me the lines, saying: —

"When I shoot, let 'em go."

Which he did, and I did.

Later, we regretted this adventure, for the stupid ammoniacal creature proceeded to dive into the mess cellar, and all food in storage was strangely savored. A matter of this kind, begun in the innocent vacation spirit, may be far-reaching. When we returned with our cargo of peaches, the sewing-circle did not receive us with any fervent warmth. In fact, it was most broadly insinuated that we, having worked a leave, had performed this trick on purpose, to the utter horror and dismay of all unsuspecting persons.

Our going down to the river was through that mysterious half-luminous light that follows the darkness before dawn. Then the Desert has an ashen pallor, and a chill and silence that are like winter at whatever season of the year. The bare spaces seem to be covered with snow. There are no calls from birds. One moves in a dead world.

At the ford the wheels clattered ominously over flat slabs of rock, and then the horses splashed through shallow pools to the far bank. We turned westward, and the mountains showed their volcanic peaks, grim gray wings in the pallid dawn. They lifted, gaunt and rugged, from a ruff of pines. There had been a fall of snow on those higher levels between the timber and the crests, and the shoulders were draped in white. Now — the very tips of the range were seared with red-gold; and now — each snowbound crest began warming with a rosy glow, as if blood were stirring, pulsing, through the masses of icy lava and eroded stone. And the whole range warmed in a blaze of fresh rose and glinting gold as it turned to greet the sun.

Down by the river the cottonwoods were still veiled in colorless mist; above were those radiant wings of the morning; and the birds began calling, piping, rustling, as a band of crimson broadened across the gray lips of the east.

Soon we ascended a ridge of the orange-hued mesa I had so long viewed from the Agency grounds. It was my first close-up of the havoc wrought in clay and sandstone by the tearing, aging fingers of the Desert. There were no smooth planes in those tortured hills. They sprawled down to the river-bottoms in petrified agony, the worn death-mask of that time when Hell burst from the vol-canoes and flowed its molten masses over the plains.

Slowly we gained the topmost ridge of all, the back-bone dividing the river country from the beyond, and looked north over a vast plain, fresh in the morning light, holding the Tolani Lakes. Those wide splotches of bluish green, miles away, seemed as a mirage; but it was water, where one would least expect to find it, the over-flow of the great Oraibi Wash, trapped in a flat basin, drying until another flood. The shores were marshy, reed-lined, and invited the migratory birds. Ten thousand ducks wheeled above the Lakes that year.

And reflected in the greenish mirror were the dull red walls of Monument Point, the end of the great Red Mesa that stretched northward, rising hugely from the sand dunes and the Desert, flanked and buttressed as some Babylonian city. Perhaps it was a city of the ancients, snuffed out as Pompeii. One longed for time to explore its dead streets. There would be lions, no doubt, slinking down ruined terraces; and rutted pavements; and broken columns to cast long shadows under the autumn moon. And was it lifeless — or only enchanted? One paused and waited for a cry, a rumble of wheels, the far-off blare of a buccina, to wake its spearmen and send flashes along the walls.

This was my first impression, and eleven years after, not having seen it again, I went there over the old route to learn if first impressions fade. I found that the Desert and its visions do not change.

We "nooned" in a barren space that would have graced the Sahara. The sun burned down on us, but the air was quite stimulating. At these higher levels the skin browns,

OUTFIT OF A WELL-DIGGER, THE DESERT WATER-WITCH

THE DRYING BED OF THE LITTLE COLORADO RIVER
Showing how the river supplies are inadequate

but the appetite is not affected. The fire, a mere handful of chips and twigs, was kindled in the little shade afforded by the rig. The doctor gave me a lesson in Southwest camping, just prior to my upsetting the can of peeled potatoes, after which he considered me impossible. With my usual energy, I had gathered greasewood branches for the fire, and had brought them from some distance. They would have made an election-night blaze. The doctor selected a pitiful handful from this mountain of brush, and briefly commented: —

"'Just like a white man,' Injun says. 'White man build big fire, sit far off; Injun make little fire, sit close by.' You don't need a conflagration to boil coffee. I can make camp here with seven sticks five inches long. Where do you think you are? Up in Canada, hunting moose?"

All that afternoon we jogged on through the hot sunlight, shooting at and occasionally hitting a young jackrabbit. The place was alive with them. The shadows of the horses grew longer as the sun dipped toward the Red Mesa. And then came the gray evening, with us peering ahead for the sign of a well-rig derrick. There were drillers in the valley, patiently pounding down their drills in the hope of striking the underflow of the Oraibi Wash. We had helped them outfit at the Agency, and they were of the I. D. Service. Their location should be somewhere close to the pueblo of Oraibi, "the town on the high flat rock," a place long famous in the annals of the Tusayan provinces, first sighted by white men nearly four hundred years before.

We gave little thought to the ancient past of Oraibi, and certainly I did not dream that for more than eight years it would concern me personally. Pedro de Tovar, that adventurous lieutenant of the great conquistador

Coronado, reached it in 1540, the first year of the Spanish exploration north of the Rio Grande; and in 1629, or perhaps a trifle earlier, zealous friars of the Franciscan order built a mission there and, surrounded by an always suspicious population, far removed from Spanish head-quarters at Santa Fe, had worked and prayed and governed until the revolt of 1680, when they met martyrdom and the mission disappeared.

Until recently Oraibi had been the largest pueblo-community in North America, having had more than one thousand inhabitants, thus exceeding any of the pueblos of New Mexico. But its leading citizens, one Tewaquap-tewa and one Youkeoma, the first a politician and the second a natural prophet and witch-charmer, backed by devoted and fanatical adherents, had prophesied, conjured visions and interpretations of signs, wrangled among themselves, and defied the Government until carried into captivity. Their imprisonment had been brief, and they were now busy making new medicine.

Tewaquaptewa's portrait appears in that fine book of Indian chants, edited by Miss Natalie Curtis and published by the Harpers; and his singing countenance presents a rapt ecstatic expression as he yodels the Butterfly Song. The translation of his name is there given as "Sun-down-shining," and is imperfect as most translations, but just as good as any other, providing you do not have to consider him on a Governmental basis. I never dealt with him on a musical scale, and his undoubted genius in this respect made no appeal to me. As his Indian Agent, however, I tried for eight long years to make a sensible human being of him, and failed, for lack of material. After having tried him as an Indian judge, and then as an Indian police-man, in the hope of preserving his dignity and authority as hereditary chief, he was found to be the most negatively contentious savage and unreconstructed rebel remaining in the Oraibi community, so filled with malicious mischief-making to his benefit that a group of his own people petitioned me to exile him from the mesa settlement, in the hope that they might then exist in peace. Of course, this had little to do with his "Sun-down-shining" or his Butterfly chanting; but when the folks at home cannot get along with father, there is something wrong.

Youkeoma, a different type of Hopi, had been defeated by the Tewaquaptewa faction, and was now in the medicine-man and prophecy business about seven miles to the west, in his new and already odorous town of Hotevilla, whence, after the tribal troubles, like another Moses he had led his faithful. Tradition has it that there will always be jealousy and enmity among the Oraibans until the pretender to leadership is martyred; so when Youkeoma was thrown out, he accepted it as a manifestation of the rules. But that did not prevent both outfits from resisting the Government, an alien intruder, wholly unmindful of the sacred prophecies, who entered in to pacify a perfectly legitimate family scrap.

Kewanimptewa, a third Oraibi factionist, who headed the weakest band of all, had trekked in another direction, a second upheaval having resulted in his eviction and retirement from the political field. His allies went to a little-known cañon, Bacabi, where, but for the prompt assistance of the Government Agent, the whole lot of Ishmaelites would have perished. It was winter and they had no harvest. Aid in this case was gratefully accepted, and out of the truce grew a friendliness now unbroken. Those who followed Youkeoma, however, remained sullen and unreconstructed, accepting nothing, acknowledging nothing, rebels and defiant.

Therefore the original Oraibi, which had been the largest Indian community, was split into three parts, and the parent place has been still further reduced by emigration to Moencopi in the farther west. As will be related later, all this foolish dissension could have been avoided, and the Government might have saved many thousands of dollars by a firm and impartial policy toward these Indians. While the separation weakened them, they had to be followed with the means of control and education, sanitation, and medicines — a far more expensive job than a full Oraibi pueblo would have demanded.

This little expedition for peaches I thought would mark my whole acquaintance with the Hopitu, the "peaceful" wrangling ones. In 1907 I had written several stories for *Harper's Magazine*, one of which concerned these people. The ethnological facts I had exhumed from the library of the Indian Office at Washington, and the skeleton on which I strung these fancies was produced from that fearful thing known as the writer's imagination. God forgive me! I have always believed that I was given charge of the Hopitu as a punishment for that crime against the verities.

And then, when we were about to confess that the stupid team had taken the wrong road, to the end that we were strayed, lost, and would probably be stolen, the well-rig loomed up as a tall gallows at the roadside. There were calls and hearty greetings.

"Shorty," a minor water-witch of the Empire, had laid aside his wand for the day, which is one way of saying that the rig-tower no longer trembled, the cable no longer jerked, and the drill did not pound in its hole. Shorty was ready to receive visitors and to relate how he shot the mountain lion.

It matters not in that country how shabby the guest, how poor the host, or how wild the place of meeting, there is always a welcome and entertainment of the board, to be followed by talk of the Empire. A veteran of the garrison days told me that in his time, on reaching a post-trader's, it would be impossible to escape for a week. Every item of news from the outside would be demanded and paid for in a liquid coin that is no longer circulated. Then the bowl flowed freely when the pipes were lit, and the company gathered around a roaring fireplace in the evening.

"We would gossip and swap lies until we could not see, and then tumble into the nearest bed to sleep it off. Next day, if he had had enough, a fellow would call for his horse. Consternation would follow. Everyone would regret, with much language, that Bonehead Bill had left the corral-gate open last night, and now not a hoof in all that valley.

"'Fore Gad! pardner, they're clear t'hell an' gone over into Palisade Cañon by now. It'll take two wranglers to git 'em up. Make yourself t'homelike, 'cause to-morrow's another day.'"

So there would be no means of travel until the great exchange of ideas was exhausted, and the whiskey out, when they would speed him onward. Said the veteran, "Them was times!"

But in Indian country to-day one has to be content with the ensemble without the olden stimulus.

At this well-camp there were no extra beds, so for the first time I slept on the open range. We had packed a dozen thick blankets, six for the ground and three apiece for wrappings. By the time bed was made, the contrast between that day's noon and three hours after sunset was a trifle more than bitter. To remove one's clothing in that extraordinary boudoir of a thousand square, open, and draughty miles was a shrinking bit of business.

Several times during the night I awoke, convinced that I was slowly freezing; and on one of the occasions I was quite certain that I had died and reached a certain destination; for at the edge of the Wash a troop of coyotes had assembled, and they made night hideous. It was my first close-up of such a chorus, a bedlam of ghoulish chattering. Fiends might have been braver, but they could not have uttered cries more horribly depraved. The coyote is very low in the social scale of the Desert. While the orthodox Navajo will not kill one, even as the Hopi will seldom slay a snake, this does not mean that he rejoices in the vicinity of the beast. Notwithstanding the souls of ancestors that are believed to possess him, "Mi-he," the coyote, receives little welcome or respect. There is something so miserably unclean, so slinkingly evil, in Mi-he, the jackal of the Southwest, that I have yet to discover anything of sympathy for him under any conditions. He follows and preys on the sheep and calves, poor, stupid, defenseless creatures, and in a remote spot I have seen several of him circle a band of wild ponies, patiently waiting for a colt to drop behind. At night, when there are mysteries and fancies enough without him, his mournful howl, followed by ghoulish chattering like unearthly laughter or the mockery of lost souls, gives the Indian good cause to include him among the worthless members of a savage mythology.

But morning brought the radiant sun god, and all unclean things fled away. Warmed into amiability, we covered the last five miles to our goal. Oraibi occupies a projecting point of a huge tumbled mesa, one that has known the rack and twist of volcanic convulsion. Below it in the plain were a Government school, a trading-post, and quite a settlement of Indians who had been persuaded to remove from the unsanitary height. To reach the pueblo proper, we drove up a long, winding sand-road, using the drifts and dunes of centuries for a ladder. This connected with a rather perilous mesa-ledge road, overhanging the valley, around the edge of which we found the ancient town.

The newcomer to the Hopi desert always assumes that the Indian sought the heights because of view and scenic beauty, purest air, and freedom. Freedom had something to do with it, for there is no doubt he was driven to accept the mesa as a citadel. In order that he might have a chance to defend himself against marauding "Apaches du Navaju," who raided his camps and herds, killed his sons, and carried his women into captivity, he risked the scarcity of water, depending on pools during sieges, and fortified the mesas. There, with his house built for closer defense and his flocks under the ledges, he felt secure. The fields of the tribe, presenting assurance against famine, were of necessity at a distance from these strongholds, and this handicap trained the Hopi into the wonderful long-distance runner that he is to-day.

Old Oraibi is not a pretty picture, although its setting relieves much of squalor and debris. The narrow streets were filled with rubbish and worse; fowls scratched in the offal, burros herded in doorways, and lanky, half-starved dogs were legion. Many of the houses had crumbled and others were being demolished. These were the abandoned homes of the defeated factionists. There were short alleys and blind courts, while around a central plaza the dwellings arose to the height of three stories, reached by little ladders, where a few of the inhabitants were sunning. The roofs were piled with drying peaches. The place of the ceremonial kiva sloped away to the mesa edge, and from it one looked away, many miles, to the dimming river-country. The men were in the fields, the children at school; the place seemed abandoned, dead. Here was a perfect picture of the senility of a one-time civilization that had been decaying for many centuries, and in this our day had reached very nearly to utter devitalization.

From the edge of the great cliff one looked down on the immense stretches of the desert. Grazed-out long ago by flocks that were held too close to the pueblo, the land had become barren, a sea of drifting sand that stirred and lifted in the winds. But in this sand were the cornfields and bean patches of the stubborn race. The Hopi, whatever else he may be, is the greatest dry-farmer on earth. He tills the unirrigated sand, fighting the drought and the pests and the scorching winds according to his rituals, and from it produces the corn which is his staff of life.

A commanding promontory at some distance was the "Judgment Seat," or place of accounting, where the spirits of all save Hopi children must repair on leaving the earthly body. One had to walk but a little way to stumble on their tombs.

> Now here, now there, a broken bowl
>   Half buried in the sand,
> Marks where some pueblo chieftain dreams,
>   Forgotten by his band.
> Those shallow mounds, where age the toys,—
>   Weak spirits dwell not deep,—
> The Desert presses light on them;
>   The pueblo children sleep.

Our guide directed us to a sheltered angle of the mesa where, among boulders and sand-drifts, we found the one unperished gift of the padres, delicious peaches, not so

Photo. by A. H. Womack

THE HOPI CEREMONIAL CORN-PLANTING
The stick whose twirling prepares the hole
will some day be placed by the man's
head in his own grave

HOPI GARDENS IN A SPRING-FED NOOK OF THE DESERT

large as California fruit, but having all the flavor and quality of that grown in Maryland and Delaware. We bargained with a smiling Hopi, and loaded.

And then, like all wise travelers in the Desert, we started to make "a long step on the road" while the sun was high; we camped that night in the greasewood, with well-smoked jack-rabbit for supper, and trundled into the Agency next evening, tired and hungry, to be received with coldness and suspicion. Our offering of peaches did not discount this bitterness. So small a thing as the erratic flight of a confused mammal may thus strain friendship and affect the most sincere labors.

IX

THE MAKING AND BREAKING OF CHIEFS

"You'll have charge of the district till my successor comes.
I wish they would appoint you permanently; you know the
folk. I suppose it will be Bullows, though. Good man, but
too weak for frontier work; and he does n't understand the
priests. . . . Call the Khusru Kheyl men up; I'll hold
my last public audience." — KIPLING: "The Head of the
District."

A YEAR drifted by in this fashion. The November-December days were glorious. At a time when the effete East
was slopping about in goloshes, and taking cold and
quinine, and sniffling and having sick-leave, and generally hurrying toward the grave, we were reveling in sunshine.

January and February brought real crimping winter
nights. Spring came in early March, and quickly the
cottonwoods of the river-bank were all greening again.
Then suddenly, as if in a flare of anger, the springtime
wind cried its challenge to the moisture of the sand, and
began driving everything that was loose before it. Then
too, suddenly something happened: the Chief resigned.

A matter like this brings a dramatic pause to those in
isolated places. Something of unexplained dread crept
into everyone, from the Indian lad who curried the horses
to the chief Nultsose. A little company of people, knowing
each other thoroughly and marooned in a sense, would
lose the Skipper, the Old Man, the Chief who had attended

to most of their routine thinking, and made decisions, and was responsible, and caused them generally to exist comfortably whether they were capable of it or not.

Who would succeed him?

Whatever the faults and frailties of the Chief, they at least knew him, his humors and his moods. He had not been difficult to analyze. There had been a time to flatter, and a time to leave him alone; there had been moments on drives, in camps, and at little social affairs, when all that was left of the youth — one might say the "boy" — of him returned, when for a brief space he had ceased to be the Old Man. So they realized abruptly, forgetting petty differences, that something of affection had grown up unconsciously between them.

But why abandon a little kingdom? Why, indeed!

He had grown covetous. The pride that the Desert builds in those few who manage to command it had somehow got the better of his judgment. He had developed the astounding effrontery to think that he earned and was justified in demanding a salary of more than thirteen hundred dollars a year! Think of that — he had come to re-view the value of himself. It was not honor enough for him to have created a little centre of civilization. He actually felt that the laborer was worthy of his hire. It reminded one of a particular scene in *Oliver Twist*. It was stupefying. It was downright impudence in the man. Washington had never heard the like, and confessed itself painfully shocked; in fact, it became almost infuriated.

Had not a whole series of clerks, working at white heat between ball-games and vacations, checked his accounts and requested an explanation of his every action for years, just to keep him from this very state of mind — to prevent his fondly imagining that he had accomplished anything? Think of the man who had struggled, under orders, to that forlorn station in 1908, breasting the wind and the sand and a falling thermometer, just to demonstrate scientifically how concrete is mixed in New Jersey. Why, this advising concrete genius drew only two thousand and a per-diem, a man skilled in methods known to the Atlantic seaboard, and aside from his having political influence, was every ready, under orders, at this pitiful stipend, to place his all-embracing knowledge at the disposal of this non-comprehending desert roughneck, who — Words fail one!

As for the Indians to be affected by this change, they were inarticulate and did not count. Someone would be appointed to the vacancy, someone just as good — well, anyway, good enough for Indians.

Then came an experience such as a complacent court must suffer when an old monarch dies. It happens, no doubt, when there is a change of chiefs anywhere; but it is the more personal and grinding when one has to live next door to the chief, breakfast with him, lunch with him, dine with him, face him across a desk, or ride cheek-by-jowl with him from daylight to dark; in short, to serve him loyally twenty-four hours the day. Comparisons are not odious; they are hellish. Those so situated as to be thus dependent on one another for duty and society must have some bond of sympathy, something of confidence and regard, respect if nothing more, like unto that which takes the curse off marriage. The living conditions, the lack of society and amusement, the introspection that the Desert invites, these things make the casual word to be an insult and a chance sentence to produce tragedy. Unless it be aboard ship, I know of no relative situation in which one man can become so terrible a burden to others as at an isolated desert-station.

Suffice to relate that the period of reconstruction and change brought many disputes, all of them crushed and smothered by the turgid heaviness of forty years' experience. The new Chief was different, and aged, and sick, a misery to himself and to everyone else. As is invariably the case, the most valuable of the employees began to prepare to quit the ship. I have seen a great deal of loyalty in the West, and the man who is fair may count on men until they drop; but these same men speak their minds freely, and it is hard for them to change czars. Old traditions were restored; the cook quit in a flame of anger, leaving as his vengeance a last meal garnished with a defunct mouse. The pot boiled fifteen hours the day.

When the thing had become a trifle too thick for me, like a flash from the blue came an unsought, unexpected telegram: — "WILL YOU ACCEPT APPOINTMENT SUPERINTENDENT MOQUI SALARY EIGHTEEN HUNDRED BOND THIRTY THOUSAND WIRE."

A courteous expression that is now rare: "Will you accept." The mere transposition of a word makes all the difference. "You will accept" is the tone of recent orders — a reaction of the great war against Prussianism on those who reject with an unctuous civilian horror all idea of militarism.

And yet there is a certain fine discipline and training in the military atmosphere, even a copy of it, as practised at the properly conducted schools and agencies of the farther deserts. One learns to obey in unpleasant things, and feels something of duty and loyalty in acceding. Where there is nothing of civilization for one hundred miles in any direction, not even a telegraph wire, one comes to revere that refreshing bit of bravery, the Flag, whipping above trees, a symbol of authority and order; one thrills at the music of the band; and bugle-calls, in the wine of seven thousand feet above the sea, add a character-forming stimulation: reveille, mess, re-treat, or at the end of a long day's drive homeward in the dark, cramped and cold from fifty miles, to hear the sol-emn notes of "taps."

The night hush of the drowsy desert has succeeded all daylight bustle. The clatter of shops, the hum of machin-ery, the hiss of steam, have quieted. There are no more calls from children at play. One by one the lamps go out on campus and in quarters, and great Orion burns down the empty spaces to glimpse a scrap of feeble civilization gripped in the aged everlasting hills. Then, on the cold wind, stealthily, comes the eerie chant of a Navajo, riding across the mesa, calling on his gods.

"Will you accept . . . Moqui — "

That was the country of the Buttes and craggy mesas; of Old Oraibi; of the Second Mesa and its broad stairway to the dome-like pueblos; of ancient Walpi and its rocky ladder to the sky; the land of ruins dating from the misty dawn of history. Across it the Spaniards had marched, contemporaries of Columbus, their halberds gleaming in the sun; and there the early padres had ruled, their mis-sion bells now silent. The "provinces of the Mohoce or Mohoqui," as Coronado bade his poet-historian write it down. It was the very heart of the Enchanted Empire.

There were but two persons to give me a modern view of the situation. The Navajo interpreter at my present station was one of those half-educated, half-sullen re-turned students who would accept the meagre wage when the trader would not, a part of the economic system aimed at cheaply teaching grandfather through his unrespected grandson. He came from that northern country, and his immediate family composed a most insolent gang — a mere detail I discovered later in time of stress.

"Lots of Navajo up there," he said. "Those Black Mountain fellows — mean Indians, too. Down here, quiet, never any trouble, 'cause they liked the Chief; but up there, always something doing."

Having little confidence in the fellow, I discounted his words heavily. But that afternoon came the missionary from down-river.

"Hello!" he called to me. "What's this I hear? You going to Moqui? Well, well! I hope you handle that bunch of mean ones over beyond Oraibi — those Hotevillas. About every four years they flare up. The last was in 1906, so it's about due. The present Agent hasn't Christianized those Indians, and the one ahead of him was a bit mild. They need the fear of God put into them. Many Agents? Well, come to think of it, yes. I can recall several of them. One stayed four years; they average about two, as a rule. Let me hear from you sometime."

A combined Indian Agency, half Hopi, half Navajo, and the two ancient enemies who fraternized on the surface when the Agent was strong enough to compel it. Ninety miles back in the hills. No telephone and no telegraph. And agents averaged about two years each of service. What happened to them? I wondered. Were they buried there, quietly and without fuss, or did they depart between suns, seeking more peaceful climes? The padres were not an excellent vision, and the Spaniards had abandoned the country as hopeless, notwithstanding their usual methods of domination. True — there was such a thing as having a chap on for the good of his soul, after the manner of whimsical Arizona.

I debated the matter seriously before answering that

wire. My plans were changing. From six months, my exile had been extended into a year; and the year was now up. Acceptance would mean a longer stay, an habitation enforced, as I would be under bond and no longer free to come and go, with the added chance of failure in an unsought position of responsibility. I had not envied my old Chief. I do not envy any Indian Agent to-day.

And yet — the Desert called to me from over beyond those blue-toned Buttes to come and find that intangible something "just around the corner." So finally, like Kipling's Pagan, I decided: —

> And I think it will kill me or cure,
> So I think I will go there an' see.

X

THE PROVINCES OF THE "MOHOCE OR MOHOQUI"

It now remains for me to tell about this city and kingdom and province, of which the Father Provincial gave your Lordship an account. In brief, I can assure you in reality he has not told the truth in a single thing that he said, but everything is the reverse of what he said, except the name of the city and the large stone houses. — *Don Francisco Vasquez Coronado to Don Antonio de Mendoza, First Viceroy of New Spain, August 3,* 1540

I AM now glad that I went to the Painted Desert and entered Hopi-land before the advent of the automobile. The going then was a picturesque if toilsome journey. After two days in a farm-wagon loaded with my plunder, I reached the first back-country trading-post, and met the official I was to succeed. That old store at Indian Wells, with its back against the hills, seemed a fanciful place in the twilight of a summer's day. Across a wide plain lifted purple mesas gashed with red clays, and Rabbit-ear Butte stuck its two inquisitive peaks into the evening sky. There was something far removed in the atmosphere and setting of Indian Wells, something of true desert solitude.

Next day we wended northward across Hauke Mesa, passing the White Cone, a solitary bleached-out pyramid that marks the southeast corner of the Hopi Reservation. Two huge white horses drew us; not a very fast pace, but decidedly a sure one. The vehicle was a mountain spring-

wagon, and its one wide seat served three of us, the driver
and I simple figures in comparison with the gentleman I
was to relieve. He was a large, pompous man, who had
sought the Southwest for his health and had not found
all of it, principally because he had not arrived soon
enough, and also because he was continually fretted by
the vision of his former importance. He had come from
the East from a much larger Governmental position.
In fact, he had been quite within the shadow of the Cabinet, and was bulwarked with political tradition. He
knew the President personally, and immediately told one
so; and when he came into the Desert he wore — Suffering
Pioneers! — a top hat.

It takes a long time to make forty miles in a wagon of
that type, whatever the entertainment of political con-
ventions and presidential anecdotes.

In late afternoon we crossed the sandy waste of the
Jedito Wash, and passed out of it by a steep rocky road
that ascended a high mesa. A short distance to the left
were the ruins of Awatobi, that once important pueblo
of Tusayan, where Tovar had his first view of and encounter with the "Mohoce or Mohoqui" of the Spanish
chronicles. This meeting occurred twenty-five years before
the settlement of St. Augustine, and eighty years before
the gentlemen from Plymouth reached the historic New
England Rock. He was accompanied by that intrepid
soldier-priest, Fray Juan de Padilla, who later retraced
Coronado's trail into the mysterious and legendary country of Quivira, there to be martyred, the first white man
to meet death in the present State of Kansas.

After the conquest of Cibola, or Zuni, Tovar was dispatched by Coronado to locate the seven cities of the
Mohoqui. Notwithstanding the fighting in the Zuni prov-

inces, the coming of pale men who rode strange animals and carried sticks that discharged lightning, it would appear that the Hopi knew nothing of these happenings. Tovar, leading a company of calvary and footmen, crossed into their country without discovery, and encamped one night before a Hopi pueblo. It is recorded that they approached close enough to hear the people talking in their homes. Morning revealed the Spanish spears.

A little later came Cardenas, searching for the great cañon of the West; and Espejo in 1583; and then Onate in 1598, who was the first to make permanent settlements among the Pueblo Indians. It was Onate who established the missions, and one was built at Awatobi between 1621 and 1630, so Fray Alonzo de Benavides, the first custodian of missions in these provinces of New Spain, reported to his King.

Before the founding of Boston by Winthrop, when Charles I was King of England and Laud was Archbishop of Canterbury, a Franciscan friar named Porras ministered to the Hopi in the Tusayan provinces. In June 1633 he died there by poison. In this same year Galileo appeared before 'the Inquisition. Strange contrasts!

When the great Pueblo rebellion occurred in 1680, the mission at Awatobi was destroyed by the Hopi, and its friar, Fray Jose de Figueroa, was killed.[1] When came De Vargas, bent on reconquering the Pueblo people, he halted before Awatobi on November 19, 1692. The friars

[1] The Hopi joined their kinsmen in the Pueblo rebellion of 1680, and four Franciscan friars were killed at their missions in the Tusayan provinces: at Aguatobi (Awatobi), mission of San Bernardino, the Reverend Padre Fray Joseph de Figueroa, a native of Mexico; at Xongopavi (Chimopovi), mission of San Bartolome, the Reverend Padre Fray Joseph de Truxillo; at Oraibi, mission of San Francisco, the Reverend Padre Fray Joseph de Espeleta, a native of Estela in the Kingdom of Navarre, and the Reverend Padre Fray Agustin de Santa Maria, a native of Pasquaro. The pueblos of Machongnovi and Walpi were visitas.

planned a return to their duties among the Hopi, and it would appear that the Awatobans, or a part of them, received these advances. Because of this the pueblo of Awatobi was suddenly destroyed in the latter part of 1700 by pagan Hopi from the other mesas. It is said that many of the warriors were stifled in the ceremonial kivas, and the women and children were carried off as captives. During the early years of the eighteenth century, Spanish officials and priests still contemplated a return to this territory, but the efforts were abortive, although as late as 1748 friars visited the Second Mesa country to return fugitive Indians of the Pueblos proper to their homes in the valley of the Rio Grande. Most of these were Sandias, the remnant of this band now living close to Albuquerque, New Mexico; and when I took charge of the Pueblo Indians in 1919, the Sandias above all others evidenced characteristics that were not new to one who had sat in council with their ancient hosts.

In 1911 only a series of low walls, the pueblo foundations, were discernible at Awatobi. The place of the old Spanish mission could not be determined. The blowing desert sand had quite nearly reclaimed the site to solitude and unbroken sterility. But following the sacred customs of their forefathers, the Hopi were still making trouble for their guardians.

My predecessor told me how he had sought to quiet this antagonism. At great expense he had taken the old chief, Youkeoma, and several of his retainers, on a trip to and through the East. At Washington they were honored by an audience with President Taft. The power and the glory of the American nation, it was thought, would overwhelm the savage. He might as well have taken a piece of Oraibi sandrock to see the Pope. Not even the size of President Taft impressed the old spider-like Hopi prophet, as he afterward told me in diplomatic confidence. Youkeoma returned as sullen and determined as before, made some new medicine with corn meal and feathers, and then repudiated the whole hegira, including President Taft, telling his people that he had seen nothing of importance, received no counsel that contained wisdom, and that he sincerely doubted those men were chiefs of anything. Certainly they were not the mythical Bohannas that the Hopi — following their own version of the Messianic legend — expect to come and rule them. And then, having refused to do that which Washington had urbanely decreed, he sat down in his warren of a pueblo, amid the sand and the garbage, to await whatever the white man might see fit to do about it.

That was my inheritance.

Toward evening in the cañon country the sun grows a bit more burnishing. Ahead of us appeared a space in the cedars, and beyond that rift one could see a more distant desert, rising as a sunlit moor, but quite removed — as if one looked across a chasm. A little later the team tipped forward on a rocky ledge. With brakes applied, we began to grind downward — it seemed to me, straight down. On the left, walls of rock arose in sheer planefaces, and to the right I gathered that there was nothing at all: just an empty hole, beginning two feet from the outer wheels, and nicely garnished with huge boulders awaiting some driver's bad judgment.

I became more familiar with mesa trails thereafter, but this first one was a thrill. Sand had blown into the road, and the wheels crunched through it, and the brakes ground and screeched against the tires.

"When the troops were here last," said the driver cheerfully, "a pack-mule went over at this place, and he rolled until he fetched up against the bottom."

I silently wished he would attend to his driving.

"And there is your Agency," said the official, pointing. "You can see as far as you like from that place, if you look straight up."

Below in the great gash were the buildings of the plant, gray, lonely-looking, standing in barren grounds; but large as they were, the rocky walls of the cañon dwarfed them. So clear was the air that they appeared as toy houses, cut-outs pasted on a strip of pebbled cardboard. There was a straight line of them, for the cañon, generous enough in other dimensions, had not room for grouping at its bottom. It was a rough trough hewn by quake and flood. For centuries the waters had torn at it, until their bed was now far below the site of the buildings; and for centuries the sand had drifted in to form rounded domes that buttressed the walls. Each season's tremors disturbed the shattered rocks, sending some to the bottom in tearing, grinding slides and posing others at new angles.

It was disappointing — a lonely, dreary place. No trees or hedges relieved the starved-looking site. There was little to be proud of. As for the natural beauties, one must grow to feel the majesty of worn rocks, tinted in all the shades of weathering sandstone, from saffron through gold to ruddy brown, toned to a thousand delicate hues by the stunted cedars and diversified cacti that struggled from every crevice. In the springtime there would be flowers in the crannies, winsome purple and pink flowers, with here and there the blazing scarlet of the Indian paintbrush; and in springtime too would come the great flocks of migratory birds.

HOPI INDIAN AGENCY AT KEAMS CAÑON

HOPI INDIAN HOSPITAL AT KEAMS CAÑON
Capacity, 40 patients: Designed and constructed by employees of the Agency under
Superintendent Crane

Why build in such a place? The answer is that stereo-typed one affecting everything in the Desert — water. At the upper end of this cañon lived the springs. Water could be brought to the site without great expense. There was enough to furnish a small settlement, and more than could have been harnessed cheaply at any other point of the territory when the plant was built. Water in greater quantity has been discovered since; but there were no "water-witches" in the provinces of the Mohoqui prior to 1910.

All that day the thunder had muttered sullenly, and occasionally a few drops of rain had fallen on us. It was too early in the year to expect a shower of any conse-quence, so my guides told me. It was June, and the red-bellied clouds that the Snake priests watch for do not appear until late August, when they herald the Snake Dance and prove Hopi wisdom; then cloudbursts send torrents through these cañons, and flood the plains, and guarantee the harvest. But, just as we drove up the main road, came a sharp downpour that settled into a rare thing indeed — a steady summer rain.

A group of Indians stood close as we alighted. This was a delegation of welcome, for the tribes are very curious. A Navajo grunted, "Nahtahni." And a Hopi said some-thing that brought smiles to their faces; it was interpreted to me as we shook hands around. He said, "You must be a good Chief, for you bring the rain."

The Agency consisted of an office and quarters and shops for the clerks, farmers, and mechanics, and there was a school for about one hundred and fifty pupils of the grammar grades. This was a boarding-school and, in addition to teachers, it had a corps of cooks, matrons, laundress, and seamstress, all necessary to the work. In the field, close to the pueblos of the Indians, were five day-schools, serving from fifty to one hundred and twenty children each, and stations for physicians, field-nurses, and range men. Therefore the equipment, furniture, and stores of six small settlements had to be inventoried and receipted for at any change of directors.

The outgoing Agent was anxious to have his papers signed, that he might be off to his next post in further search of health. For two weeks we labored over those accounts, and it seemed that it would require another three months — as it did — to adjust and compare and reduce them to something approximating accuracy. So the major part of it was arranged conditionally between us, and I filed my official signature, together with bond for thirty thousand dollars, and we two shook hands as cordially as it was possible for men to do who had been debating for a fortnight.

In this manner I became Indian Agent for twenty-two hundred Hopi Indians of the Pueblo stock — maligned under a stupid Departmental label as "Moqui" — who would call me "Moungwi"; and for a trifle more of Navajo, the nomads of the desert, who would title me "Nahtahni," very likely Nahtahni Yezzi, meaning Little Chief. They had undoubtedly named my predecessor Nahtahni Tso, Fat Chief.

That time of inventory I recall as a bad dream. Every conceivable article of useless equipment had been dumped and carefully preserved at that post. The greatest care had been taken of the most useless. Once, when the tailors of Chicago were long on swatches, they presented them to the Indian Service, and to save storage the warehouse custodian had promptly shipped them to the most distant point, the Moqui Agency, in the hope and quite sure belief that they would never come back. Aside from transcontinental railroad charges, Indian wagoners had hauled such precious supplies from the receiving station, one hundred miles, at a cartage of one cent per pound. So it was with hundreds of lamp-chimneys that never fitted a lamp, clothing too small for infants or too large for giants, machetes that were needed in the Cuban cane-fields, tools that Noah would have spurned, and broadcast seeders for use where the Indians plant corn with ceremonial sticks. One warehouse was jammed with wagon-repair material, spokes, fellies, bolsters, and so on, of dimensions that must have been current in the period of the pioneers.

Some of this waste had been the result of stupid ordering, while much of it grew from the system of yearly contracts, neither of which has changed unto this day. Smith furnishes wagons one year, by virtue of being the lowest bidder, and one must have Smith's repair-parts. Next year Brown has the contract, again by virtue of being the lowest and therefore cheapest bidder; and part of Smith's material is a dead loss to the Service.

The method of checking stores was a grotesque science. Sewing-needles were counted, the unit being a single needle, whereas darning needles were accepted by the hundred. Anvils, log-chains, sledges, and mason-axes were known by weight, other tools by description; still other tools identified by sets. Each textbook, each library and reference volume, — and there were thousands, — was known by its more or less involved title, and so catalogued and counted and charged every three months.

The technical names that came across Kansas with our forefathers had not changed. "Eveners" and "whiffletrees" were recognized; but double and swingle-trees were taboo.

And there were things that even the Westerners' Bible could not define. Apparently no one ever wrote to Montgomery Ward for "crandalls" or "loop-sticks." Sometimes Funk and Wagnall's *New Standard Dictionary* helped to an explanation, and at other times the *Encyclopædia Britannica* shed light down the ages to identify an article. It was like examining and listing the contents of Tutankhamen's tomb, and we believed that the mummy of the original Indian Agent would be discovered in the depths of those cluttered warehouse-shrines.

> Of shoes — and ships — and sealing-wax —
> Of cabbages — and kings —

quite so — there were shoes, men's, women's, misses', boys', youths' and children's, each divided into two sorts: Sunday and everyday; twelve classifications, and all counted and all charged. There were boxes of sealing-wax, and cobblers' wax, and beeswax, in quantity; and in the attenuated garden, irrigated by the hand-bucket method, grew something resembling cabbages where free Congressional seeds had been planted. There were no ships of the keel variety; it was too dry — even the fish carried canteens; but there were burros, those pack-ships of the Desert, that cheerfully doubled as "Arizona nightingales." And there was one official king, who, if he did not find that crandall the smith had made in 1893, would have months of explaining to those who did not know then, and do not know now, what a crandall is.

At the same time the employees of the station were existing in pasteboard cottages designed for the climate of Southern California, and winter at that altitude —

6600 feet — would bring many nights below zero. One couple lived in a tent heated by a sheet-iron stove; the miner lodged in a cupboard, and the chief mechanic's family occupied a cellar. They were all, according to the Civil Service announcements, entitled to "quarters," and did they not have them?

The returns were received as well from all the field points. Election night in the editorial rooms is but one night. After thirty days of this, I felt myself going mad; so I started forth to view the domain.

Having had but little experience in the handling of horses, I selected one of my Indian interpreters for Jehu, and so he proved. My idea was that an Indian not only would be a thorough horseman, but would possess the rare faculty of driving equally well after dark. The Indian has the eye of the eagle, say the books, and so on; and those winding, narrow, switchback roads did not invite me after nightfall. Sure enough, my first return to the cañon was made in pitch blackness; but I lolled in the buggy, well wrapped-up, enjoying a feeling of perfect security. An excellent thing to have an eagle's eye, I thought — when suddenly the world tipped and heaved. There was a moment of crashing confusion and complete chaos. The lines and my Indian driver and I were all on the floor of the buggy together, hopelessly mixed and entangled in the blankets and foot-brake and nose-bags and halters. The vehicle had pitched forward, and seemed to have climbed on to the backs of the struggling horses. Jehu had driven over a six foot bank into an arroyo. Fortunately, the team had taken it straight over, without swerving and, fortunately too, those arroyo banks are of crumbling sand.

We scrambled out to catch the heads of the horses.

"What in the blankety-blank did you do that for?" I cried at the dazed Indian who, like myself, was very much numbed and scared. "Where were your eyes? Could n't you see the crossing to the left?"

"Did n't you see it?" he mumbled.

"I can't see in this dark — never pretended to; but you — you're an Indian, and — "

"Indian eyes no different from white man's!" he announced in his defense, and with complete composure. "I can't see in the dark, either."

Another precious ideal exploded.

XI

THE LAW OF THE REALM

Ko Ko. I want to consult you —
Pooh Bah. Certainly. In which of my capacities? As First
Lord of the Treasury, Lord Chamberlain, Attorney-General,
Chancellor of the Exchequer, Privy Purse, or Private
Secretary? — *The Mikado*

A NEW Agent at the Cañon headquarters, a greenhorn to
boot, and immediately a thousand questions were asked:
questions of Indians, of employees, of missionaries, of
traders, of traveling cattlemen and drummers, of tourists,
of everyone having an interest in that country, even if
ever so little. And the new Agent was to answer them all,
promptly, that they might go forth with instructions and
permits to do the things that they felt most necessary to
themselves. I had brought a little book of regulations
from Washington, and too, I thought of the commission.
It read: —

All the duties relating to the Moqui schools, Agency, and the
Indians contiguous thereto, are hereby devolved upon you
as Superintendent.

Rather a large order, depending of course on how sincerely
and conscientiously one would view the matter. Here
were close to four thousand square miles of territory,
having five thousand people of many conditions, three
fourths of them uncombed savages; and all their problems
devolved upon me.

I remember one particularly worthless Civil Service

employee who once said to me: "But, Mr. Crane, you take these matters too seriously."

It was necessary for me to cancel his engagement shortly thereafter. I did this abruptly, for he had shown a strong tendency to go off to sleep at the scales. He then emitted another philosophical remark, worthy of a Civil Service employee: —

"Well," he said, "I will get home just at watermelon time."

Now one does not have to take the thing seriously. I have followed several Agents who did not. But there is no traditional "George" in the Arizona Desert, and the Agent can always be found. He is the official goat, tagged, manacled, bonded. He may not leave his jurisdiction for longer than one week without having procured special permission; and when he goes, the work continues in the hands of irresponsibles under his responsibility and his bond. I spent several evenings with the little book of regulations, and answered my own queries.

What are the duties and responsibilities of an Indian Agent?

On a closed reservation, where the Indians are non-citizen wards:

1. He is the Disbursing Officer for all activities, and will expend $100,000 or more yearly, the reserve's allotment of funds, without including the moneys of individual Indians that may be deposited with him.
2. He directs a corps of employees, persons procured from the Civil Service grab-bag (persons he does not select), a gregarious and vagarious outfit, consisting of physicians, nurses, stockmen, farmers or rangemen, mechanics, teachers; and he often coöperates with the Irrigation or other services and their corps.

3. When there is construction work of any kind, from quarters and schools to roads and bridges, he often designs these things, always passes on the efficiency, and nearly always directs the actual work.

4. As Chief Health Officer, he should know enough to advise and support the physicians, who require more of direction and guidance than one would imagine; and among the Indians he is in great measure responsible for the legality of their actions. In times of epidemic he must lead.

5. He is the Chief of Indian Police.

6. He is a special deputy officer of the Liquor Service, a branch designed for the suppression of the liquor traffic among Indians.

7. He is Judge of the Indian Court, with the powers of a magistrate, unless there is an intelligent Indian who may be commissioned so to act. Such are not in the Arizona Desert. If there should be intelligent Indians to act, the Agent has appellate power.

8. He is the Game Warden.

9. He holds hearings, determines heirs, and probates estates.

10. He often makes allotment of lands to Indians and determines values.

11. He is Superintendent of Indian Trade, recommends those persons who seek Governmental license to trade with Indians at designated trading-posts, and is expected to regulate the prices of that trade in accordance with market conditions.

12. Should the Indians have moneys accruing from supervised activities, such as the leasing or sale of lands, or from stock-selling, and so on, the Agent first sets his approval on the leases or sales, and thereafter acts as banker of the money.

13. As banker again, he makes loans to Indians under the Government's reimbursable plan, whereby an

Indian may purchase of the Agent livestock, implements, materials, tools, or seed, with borrowed money, and repay such loans during a period of years.

14. In the Navajo country he guarantees the genuineness of the famous Navajo blanket before it goes to market.

15. He should encourage Indian agriculture, seek to improve their livestock holdings, and generally strengthen their industries.

16. Under an Act of the Legislature of Arizona, he issues marriage licenses as a clerk of the court, and may solemnize marriage.

17. He is to see that all Indian children between the ages of six and eighteen years attend school; to provide and equip properly the schools; and to improve if possible the sanitary and moral conditions of the Indian communities.

18. In some places, and the Moqui Reservation is one, he should police and protect Indian ceremonies, such as the Snake Dance.

19. He has authority to make minor regulations in good judgment for the government of Indian country of his jurisdiction; and in larger measures, if he is informed and possesses a backbone, he usually sways the policy of the Service as it affects his people.

20. The laws of the State do not apply directly to his territory, but serve as guides in those cases not specifically covered by Federal law, and through him as Agent.

21. Every war-time activity was carried out by Indian Agents, from the registration of whites and Indians, the observance of interned aliens, through the good regulations, to bond-selling and the application of the Income Tax.

Have you had enough?

If these are not sufficient in number to be convincing,

there are a few others in the two thousand amendments issued since 1904.

A white citizen of no responsibility toward others beyond his obeying the signals of the traffic officer, — the sort who used to quarrel with belated street-cars, — and who aims to be humorous, might say, "This is not the description of a Federal official. This is none other than Pooh Bah!" Exactly so. But the Indians title him "Nahtahni" among the Navajo, "Moungwi" among the Hopi, "Ah-hin-ti" among the Spanish-speaking Pueblos of New Mexico, "Mayoro" among the Mohave, "Ah-tay-ah-pe" among the Sioux, "Ta-ta" among the Apache; to wit: Chief, or Head-man, or Father. He is no less. His rule is quite feudal and absolute.

Seldom is his authority disputed by Indians; but it is challenged and criticized by everyone else on earth, including his superiors, who, after having commissioned him with these powers, live in mortal dread that he will prove the sort of man to make use of them.

The Agent's financial transactions are subject to audit by designated Governmental auditors, and his other official acts come under the occasional survey of inspectors. But neither of these officials has the power to take charge of affairs, or to give directions within the jurisdiction, without first having had the commissioned Agent suspended from his office.

Now here is a job sufficient in scope to occupy anyone, whatever the quality of mentality brought to bear upon it; and few who find themselves in the position go looking for a clay deposit that they may make brick in their spare time.

Naturally too, he who endeavors to meet these duties as they arise, and is surprised when he makes enemies, is one who will look stupidly for the millennium. By the very nature of things human he must expect to be viewed by some of those ruled among the Indians, by those seeking their favor or trade, by those who wish to play with them, paint them, model them, live with them, beg from them, steal from them — in short, all *those who wish to use Indians or their lands and resources*, as a Meddlesome Matty.

These were the late Colonel Roosevelt's words. He took a sincere interest in Indians and their problems as administered by honest Indian Agents, and he vigorously supported such officials without considering them either meddlesome or matties, and he personally respected their regulations when visiting the reserves.

Roosevelt was an exalted Indian Agent. He had no false ideas that the common people are filled with wisdom, that capitalism oozes virtue, that labor is sincere, that poverty is an assurance of honesty. But he did believe that the poor and helpless deserved fair dealing and protection from predatory interests of whatever kind; and that the mute required a fearless voice. It was his judgment that Indian country should be governed very much in line with those suggestions made by Colonel Kit Carson, who swept rebellion out of the Painted Desert and the Moqui cañons in 1863. He who follows Carson's advices in formulating his policy at an Agency may have trouble with his civil superiors, with politicians, with critics and tourists, and with a whole horde of people in office and out; but he will be respected by the Indians as their Chief, and in a brief time they will give him their confidence. In the end he will have their affection and loyalty.

In a report dated at Fort Lyon, Colorado Territory, August 1865, Carson replied to the questions of a Congres-

A BUSY DAY AT THE TRADING-POST, KEAMS CAÑON

READY FOR THE 105-MILE TREK TO THE RAILROAD
A trader's train

sional Committee that sought counsel concerning the
future management of the Indian: —

From a long-continued residence among or in the immediate
vicinity of Indians, and from a personal observation of their
manners, customs, and habits, acquired both in private life
and the transaction of official business as an Agent of the
Federal Government, I have been convinced that the only
rule to be successfully applied for their government is one
firm, yet just, consistent and unchangeable.

For the Indian, judging only by the effect of that which
appeals to his senses, as brought directly before his observation,
regards with contempt a weak and indecisive policy as the
result of hesitation, fear, and cowardice, whilst a changeable
and capricious one excites his apprehension and distrust.
Both of these courses should be carefully avoided.

The rule for the government of Indians should be strong
enough to inspire their respect and fear, yet protecting them
from both internal dissension and external aggression.

It is true that Carson thought this power should be
vested in the military, a view that has changed among
the elder statesmen without convincing anyone who knows
uneducated and remotely located Indians.

Carson was right. In a brief paragraph he advised
against the perfect picture of a civil Indian Service that
for years has worked its political capriciousness.

*It has seldom been firm; it has been most confused and
unjust; it has rarely been consistent; and it is always
changing.*

More and worse than this — it has at times been cowardly in the face of political and private buccaneering.

Each new administration, having to pay its pressing
political debts, — those debts that helped boost it into
office, — must deliver the hapless Indian over to a new

set of theorizing experimentalists who do not know a moccasin from a sabot. Men too small for the Cabinet, yet who have spent anxious years in log-rolling and who must be paid somehow, offer themselves eagerly to the job of guaranteeing the destiny of nations of aliens. Problems that puzzle the ethnologist and sociologist are approached without alarm, with a crude and vicious confidence, by a politician from Squawk Centre who once crossed an Indian reservation to shoot ducks.

Finding that methods current in doubtful precincts are of no avail in this work, and being forced to do something to make a showing, he proceeds to tear down the work of his predecessor, who had started in the same way but had learned a little during four years of fumbling; and when the whole works are fatuously gumbled, it must be done all over again to reach a point of normalcy, all Indians and their officers of the field marking time until the new Colonel has learned the traditions of the old barracks. Imagine John McGraw signing as pitcher some aspiring village quoit-champion! Conceive of Henry Ford halting his factories until a needy ward-heeler mastered the mysteries of a carburetor!

And the Indian, judging only by the effects of vacillation, springs to the suspicion of chicanery. The many inventions of stupid officials excite his apprehension and distrust. The Indian comprehends very little of first or political causes. When he distrusts his superiors he tends to throw himself on the hungry bosom of sentimentalists. He knows only the Agent on the ground, and too frequently finds in him a reflection of that which someone interested wants Washington to arrange. And no sooner does the Indian find an Agent who will fearlessly represent him, investigate his complaints, support his charges, and fight his just battles, and who will have nothing to do with intrigue, than he expects the removal of that uncompromising and foolish idealist to other scenes.

To-day the Hopi waits for a reasonably just settlement of his range problem, and he has been hoping for seventy-five years. He packed the trail to Santa Fe in 1850 to petition the first Indian Agent of the Americans, with the same evidence he brings patiently to his present one. The Navajo who troubles the Hopi in the west of the Empire, suffers similarly from whites on his eastern lines.

The point is that neither the Indian nor those who best know his actual condition have any direct voice in matters that affect his very existence.

XII

COMMENTS AND COMPLAINTS

The seven Moqui pueblos sent to me a deputation who presented themselves on the sixth day of this month. Their object, as announced, was to ascertain the purposes and views of the Government of the United States toward them. They complained, bitterly, of the depredations of the Navajos. — Report of James S. Calhoun, First Indian Agent at Santa Fe, October 12, 1850

Now the Indians drifted in to greet their new Chief. Although possessed by a great curiosity, they came shyly, diffidently, as is the Indian way. One would suppose that a grand council of braves would have been called to introduce a new Agent with some semblance of formality, a thing that impresses a primitive people. But not so. The old Agent, who was agent no longer, glad that someone else had succeeded to the petty headaches which are worse than the problems, packed his gear and departed. It was up to me to meet the savage in the course of business, and to make what impression I could. There were no individual records to guide one, and first impressions are not infallible; in fact, the most serious mistakes of Agents, things that long affect their gaining the confidence of the people, come about through the necessity of accepting the Indian at his face value — a slipshod method. The census, for example, was a string of names, having little accuracy, that had not been annotated in years.

The prominent men of the several districts were not at all backward in telling me how influential they were. The Navajo came first, and with reason, for they held five sixths of the range by right of might, and were eager to impress one that they should not be disturbed.

Came Hostin Nez, "Tall Man," a lean, shrewd genius, who could remember the captivity after Carson's campaigns. He stood proudly erect, and yet had an ingratiating manner that was part of his profession; for besides dominating a large faction of his people and being the hereditary chief of all the Navajo, he was a Medicine Man of high degree. Came from the north old Billa Chezzi, better known as "Crooked Fingers" because of a crippled hand, who had in him nothing that was sullen or criminal perhaps, but who pictured a bloodthirsty pirate on a desperate mission.

These two represented communities of Navajo, living and roaming north, south, east, and west of the Hopi mesa settlements, and by whom the Hopi have been throttled from the range. There were lesser men, headmen of groups or families. I remember Senegathe, "Wanderer," with his gray hair blowing in long snaky wisps; and Scar Chin, who resembled a good-natured friar, though a long rip in his face suggested a strenuous past; and Silversmith Jim, and Yellow-Horse, and Bitani, and Whispering Bill, each having something of distinction in his manner or personal eccentricity.

But for the most part, my Navajo business was with Hostin Nez. He was a Judge of the Indian Court, and carried a "pretty paper," a ragged commission, lithographed in bright colors. We had many a long and dispassionate argument, he rolling cigarettes in pieces of newspaper, which he evidently preferred to the "saddleblankets" that came in packages, and wiping his lips now and then with a Turkish towel that was draped about his neck — a fashion in neckcloths that he affected. I never knew Hostin Nez to lose patience, and he would return again and again to a point at issue in the hope of gaining advantage — in appearance a Tartar chieftain, in methods a Talleyrand.

"Think of it, Nahtahni," he said to me, very shortly after our first meeting, "I have never had a wagon. Here I am, an influential man among my people, and all the others have been favored. When the children first went to school, the Agents used to give each father a wagon; but that was years ago, and my children are men, and I never had a wagon."

Now this was hard lines, for a Navajo who did not possess a wagon was prevented from hauling freight, at that time a most lucrative occupation, and the camp need for a vehicle of some sort was great. The Navajo has to haul wood and water, and must somehow transport his products of wool and hides to the trader. So I promised him a wagon from the next lot received.

This would not be a present. The Indians of the Empire are independent and self-supporting; they do not receive rations, and the Nahtahnis do not make presents of implements or other necessary things. The Indians paid for such issues by laboring on the roads and at other constructive work of the jurisdiction, and were credited at current rates for laborers. The "wagon" meant the issue of a full freighting outfit — everything save the horses, of which the Navajo have a surplus. He would receive a stout farm-type wagon, having top-box, bows, and cover; also harness for four horses, all at Government cost-price, about one half the figure a trader would have quoted it. And at the appointed time he would assemble from ten to twenty of his clan to labor out the bill, his followers helping him as he would in turn help them.

HOSTIN NEZ, NAVAJO CHIEF AND MEDICINE MAN
Judge of the Indian Court

But Hostin Nez sent his son to sign the receipt for the issue. This was Hostin Nez Bega Number 4, indicating that there were other scions numbered one, two, and three, and perhaps even others bearing more fanciful Indian names. A great suspicion dawned on me. The issue-papers for several years back were examined, and lo! old Talleyrand had worked that game many times. *He* had never received a wagon; but each of his sons had received wagons after the father had made the plea for himself. When they went for freight the Nez outfit comprised a caravan, and at the scales their pay-checks totaled hundreds of dollars. Hostin Nez did not go for freight. He was the main guy, and procured the wagons!

When I taxed the Chief with this, he was not offended. He smiled benignly and repeated:

"But, Citcili" (my younger brother), "*I* have never had a wagon."

We let it go at that.

Now Billa Chezzi, chief of the northern steppes, was not so clever. He was a rougher, blustering type of Indian, and lacked finesse. Once I endeavored to make a census of the Navajo, a very difficult thing of accomplishment because of their nomadism. Two enumerators cornered old Billa and insisted that he give up the details of his private life. He named six wives living, and counted forty-seven sons in various parts of the Empire. Then he said he was tired, and getting old anyway, and that his memory did not serve him as once it did. Had he followed the system of Hostin Nez, he would have crowded the Studebaker wagon-works to full capacity.

And came Kewanimptewa, chief of that third and weakest faction of the Oraibi Hopi that had nearly perished in the hills. He was a stolid fellow, not at all like his name, which signifies Chameleon. He gave me the once-over, and then said frankly: —

"Well, you are a little man — a very little man. The last one was a big man — very big man. But — perhaps you will do."

Hardly had I moved the big desk to a place where I could see the Indians as they came in at the main door, in order that their pleas should not have to filter down through clerks, when the quiet of the summer afternoon was broken by cries of dismay and excited grief. A Navajo came running, weeping, his manner hysterical. He rushed into the office and stammered: —

"Charlie Bega, he dead — kill — Charlie Bega!"

For the moment I thought someone had been murdered; and a second thought did not lessen my dismay, for this man was a miner. His face was streaked where the tears had washed down through the smudges of coal-dust. The reservation has large deposits of soft coal, and fuel for the Government plants is mined by Indians under a skilled white miner. I had been down the mine that week, and had noted its sagging pillars under the pressure of that heavy mesa roof. It flashed through my mind that there had been a tragedy down the drift, and that other miners were either dead or entombed. But the Navajo interpreter quickly explained: —

"His son has just died. Their hogan is down the cañon near the mine, and he came to tell you of it, and he wants a coffin built and a grave dug."

The doctor came in to confirm this statement, and added: —

"The carpenter makes coffins for the people. The Navajo have a great fear of the dead, and they will not bury when it is possible to have the work done by someone else. We usually send a squad of men to prepare a grave, and the parson conducts a little service. If you say so, I will tell him."

It was late afternoon, and would soon be twilight.

"You may tell the carpenter," I said to the interpreter; "we will arrange this funeral for to-morrow morning."

"Pardon me, sir, but they have queer customs. No member of that family will eat until the body is disposed of; and they must purify themselves by sweat-baths and ceremonies. When one dies close to the Agency, we help them bury at once."

My first inclination was not to be ruled by such superstition; and then I thought how little four centuries of progress around them and fifty years of American influence had changed the Navajo. Like his Desert, he has remained untouched, unaffected. A hogan that has held the dead is never afterward occupied by the living. Its wood will not be used to make a fire, though they come to freezing.

"Very well," I said. "Have things made ready to-night."

And I shall never forget my first Indian funeral. At different times since, and among other tribes and circumstances, I have had more of excitement and not a little anxiety at funerals; but this was my first in the Desert.

The carpenter made a substantial box, much too large I thought; but when the body was placed in it, wrapped in new blankets, decked with silver ornaments, with the dead boy's saddle, bridle, and quirt at the foot, it was none too large. They could ill afford to part with those blankets and silver things, and especially that saddle. But he must be caparisoned and equipped for his new life in the ghostly land where he would go a-roaming.

A half-dozen of the employees climbed into the wagon that would carry the body to the grave. Among them was a visitor, a noted geologist who has made the Empire his study, and who took his share of labor along with the rest. The minister from the Baptist Mission met us at the gate. The burial ground was a desolate place across the arroyo, in a little hollow of those great drifted dunes, shunned by the Indians and not very inviting to anyone. By the time the grave was ready, it was quite dark and lanterns had been lighted.

"Do you wish a commitment service, sir?" asked the minister. I did not at once understand him, having to learn that the new Agent decides everything, and I had thought he would take his place as the man of prayer without request. He had a short ritual for pagans, and this was one of them. It was solemn and sufficient.

"Dust to dust . . . " and the tossing of earth on the box followed. Four of the men began filling in the grave. I had looked around for the relatives of the dead, but as yet none were in evidence, when out of the dusk came two strange Navajo, leading a pony. It was a very good animal as desert mounts go. And the missionary presented to me a serious problem.

"They wish to kill the horse. Will you permit that?"

And there was something in his tone of voice that indicated a hope I would deny something as an innovation. Again I called for an explanation.

"The Navajo always kill a horse at the grave," said the trader.

"It seems a merciless thing to do — that's a good pony."

The missionary brightened. He had little use for pagan customs and longed for an arbitrary decision.

"It is the custom of the people," said the trader, an honest man who advised me for many days thereafter. "You may not like it, and — you may be strong enough to stop it" — there was doubt in his voice; — "but it is their custom."

It went against the grain; but there stood the Indians with the animal, silent, waiting. This problem had been presented to many Agents, perhaps.

"If we do not kill it mercifully with a gun, they will only go away and beat it to death with rocks," said the trader. "It must be done to-night. I have brought a rifle."

The desert custom of the Navajo won its first round.

The two Indians led the pony to the head of the grave, and, seeming to understand that we had settled it, scuttled away in the shadows. The trader leveled his rifle and shot that very good pony through the brain. It leaped forward convulsively, and plunged down, knee-deep, in the soft earth of the grave. The dead had a mount.

It was black night by this time, and we filed back to the Agency, where I felt better for having the electric lights. There had been something gruesome in the whole proceeding. But it was a custom of the people, as the trader had said, and in other ways I learned from him that it is not wise for a strange Chief at once to take his people by the throat.

Now the first complaints were filed with me, and soon increased to scores. The Hopi has suffered for many years because of the willful depredations of his too close neighbor, the Navajo; and the Navajo in turn has community troubles of his own. There were complaints of damage to fences, and of ruined crops, and of peeled orchards; of the stealing of ponies, and the re-branding and butchering of cattle, the pillage of houses, and the unwarranted seizure and holding of precious water-holes; complaints of domestic wrangles and social scandals, of blighted love and too ardent affections; of marriage portions and the current price of brides, of mothers-in-law — ye Gods! even of witchcraft! Descent and distribution included not only real and personal property such as we know, for came a Medicine Man claiming to have inherited the paraphernalia of a deceased tribal doctor, and requested that I decide ownership, according to the rules, in the dried head of a dead crane.

The Indian welcomes opportunity to speak his piece in court, and if permitted will promptly set up as prosecutor and spring to the rapid cross-examination of witnesses. He will even incriminate himself if there is chance of making things unpleasant for someone else; and those of the accused found guilty and sentenced invariably request a chance to peach on some other poor devil who has evaded punishment. Witchcraft seldom appears in the open, but I recall one case that was unusual.

The favorite son of a Tewa died, and the father looked about him for someone on whom to blame this calamity. Indian grief, seldom long-lived, may be the more quickly assuaged if one can fix the blame. Suddenly the bereaved father discovered that a certain neighbor was a witch. He did not like the man anyway. So, finding him prowling around the house, — urged by a sympathetic curiosity, no doubt, — the parent seized him and dragged him into the room with the dead.

"Now," he cried, amid tears, "You see him plainer. Look at him. You are the one who killed him. You are a witch, and you sickened him with sorceries and bad medicine. Listen! When we kill anything, we always eat it. Now you eat him!"

This the alleged doctor shrank from doing, and forthwith the enraged father administered a terrific beating. The nose of this unfortunate neighbor was hammered out of all resemblance to a human organ, and other features of him were sadly damaged. They both appeared before me the next day. The father then expressed penitence and disavowed a belief in witches; but I could see that his conversion had been too rapid. In his troubled heart the witches prevailed. He seemed not to mind his sentence of a week at hard labor, having had action for his sorrow.

Having once opened a docket, the word seemed to go forth to the mesas and the cañons to bring in their complaints. The cases became legion. One would begin to examine witnesses in so simple a matter as horse-stealing and record quite a bit of evidence, to discover suddenly that the animal in question had disappeared eleven years gone, the complaint having been duly entered by seven different Indian Agents sitting at this and other Agencies. It became necessary to impose a statute of limitations.

The first real trial concerned a medicine man and his collar-bone. One Horace Greeley, of Sitchumnovi, in the First Mesa District, at that time reputed to be seventy-four years old, and by profession a bone-setter, had not pleased a member of his tribe. Or perhaps he had conjured only too well with the misplaced anatomy of the patient, and charged according to his skill. At any rate, a relative of the patient took umbrage, and proceeded to handle Horace in a rough and unseemly manner. Among other things damaged was Horace's own collar-bone. He could not very well set this himself, and naturally distrusted his confreres; so he was forced to send for the Agency physician; otherwise I should not have heard of the case. But Horace being found with a fractured collar-bone and numerous contusions, the matter was reported, and his complaint entered for the next session of court.

The Regulations of the Indian Service direct that the Court of Indian Offenses shall consist of two or more intelligent and trustworthy Indians, acting as Judges, whose verdicts shall be reviewed by the Indian Agent, should an appeal be taken to him. As many Indians do not understand their right of appeal, the Agent is compelled to be present either to sustain or to overrule the verdicts.

And did I not have two such Judges, all properly commissioned? Did not Hostin Nez have a treasured "pretty paper," and was not Hooker Hongave an equal Judge? Did not the Government, looking for justice, generously crowd on each of them the princely salary of seven dollars, each and every month, "fresh and fresh"? Now was the time to avail myself of native wisdom.

Judge Hooker was a figure in the First Mesa community. At one time he had been a Hopi of the Hopi, and had fought the new system of schools and school regulation with all his crude ability. To prevent his children from being enrolled, he had walled them up at home; that is, he placed them in a small room of his house, gave them food and water, and then walled up the entrance door, hoping that his fresh mortar would not arouse suspicion. To-day he is hated by pagans because he has tried to assimilate the doctrines of Christianity, and is looked on by some Christians as an arch-hypocrite. Such are the trials of the savage.

Actually he is a childish old fellow who has tried to merit the confidence of the mission folk, with little concept of where paganism ends and Christianity begins. His great-

Photo. by Emri Kopte

JUDGE HOOKER HONGAVE
Indian Court of First Mesa District

est sacrifice in life has been the abandonment of tribal ceremonies. From his house below the mesa can be seen the famous Walpi dance-ledge, like a miniature stage high in the thin air, thronged on pagan festal days with multi-colored costumes, where faintly sound the chanting and the drums. But he never attends these feasts of rhythm and song, save at the biennial Walpi Snake Dance, when he joyfully receives a dispensation from the Agent to go as an official of the Government, he being a Judge and the authorized Crier. Many times did he cry down the aim-less chatter of tourists during my administration, that solemn announcements might be made to the brethren and the visitors cautioned against the making of vile photographs and unseemly levity. Garbed in a magni-ficently beaded waistcoat that had decked some long-vanquished Sioux warrior, and bearing his staff of office, a knotted club out of Africa, he presents a strange and not undignified figure on these occasions.

Therefore the two who shared the woolsack were con-trasts. Hostin Nez, a Navajo pagan of the pagans, a Medicine Man, a leader of chants and a priest of the sand-paintings; Hooker Hongave, a simple-minded savage who had turned halfway toward the Church, with the low-toned booming of hide drums in his ears, and in his heart perhaps a longing for the mysticism of his ancient people.

The day of hearing having been reached, and all assem-bled, the Judges listened to the story of old broken Greeley, who had by no means recovered and was still swathed in bandages. The accused was a burly fellow under forty, powerful enough to have challenged a middleweight, who did not deny or extenuate the assault.

"It is a very bad thing this man has done," said Judge Hooker, clucking his tongue and shaking his head sadly.

"Yes, my brother," agreed the Navajo jurist. "It is a serious thing and it must not happen again. We must make an example of this man so all the people may know of it."

"We will," said Hooker; and they withdrew to frame up a sentence.

From their determined expressions I feared that friend prisoner would get at least a year in the hoosegow — an embarrassing piece of business, for the Regulations do not recognize any charge as deserving more than ninety days, and the Territorial Court had thought three years sufficient for cold-blooded murder in a recent Indian case. The judges reappeared.

"He is a bad man," said Hooker.

"Yes, he is a dangerous fellow," said Hostin Nez.

"And so we will send him to jail for — ten days."

"Ten days!" I cried out. "Why, he nearly killed Greeley! That old man will suffer for weeks. You mean ten weeks, don't you?"

"No," they said. "Ten days is a long time in jail."

The appellate power came into action.

"Your decision, gentlemen, is overruled."

Hooker brightened, expecting a remission of at least five days, which would save his face at the mesa and perhaps prevent the prisoner from hating him for many years.

"The prisoner will be confined for the period of sixty days, and during that time he will be employed at hard labor."

Hooker gasped, trembled, and was speechless.

"You are a man without mercy," declared old Hostin Nez.

That was my last session of the Indian Court in the

Hopi-Navajo country with native judges sitting. One might as well expect justice from a goose.

For an Agent who wishes to evade responsibility, the "judges" are an excellent smoke-screen. He can always say — "It was done by the prisoner's own people": Pilate's method. Aside from its having all the elements of farce, it breeds dissatisfaction and ill will among the people, while teaching them nothing. I know of nothing more unjust, unless it be the trial of an unlettered Indian according to the strict letter of white man's law and the unwavering standard of the white man's boasted morality.

Thereafter I paid the salaries, and pleasantly chatted with the old gentlemen when they visited the Agency; but of their legal wisdom I wanted nothing. The Court proceeded to business without them.

So large an area of country, nearly four thousand square miles, occupied by two dissimilar tribes and these ancient enemies, should have some measure of control. The police force I found consisted of three individuals, two Navajo and one lonesome Hopi. The Agent had found things so peaceful that he did not need police; which is one way of saying that he did not bother himself about policing the Empire. And when the first serious bit of police work became necessary, after five years of peaceful neglect, the War Department, at the request of the Secretary of the Interior, detailed one hundred and twenty-five men of the Twelfth Cavalry as an "escort" to Colonel Hugh L. Scott. This officer of long experience at Indian diplomacy was sent to review the situation and conditions. The work completed, he recommended to the Secretary of the Interior that the Indian Agent should have a force of not less than twenty men, in charge of a white officer. The

Department, therefore, being unable totally to ignore the opinion of the famous Colonel Scott, increased my police to eight men, all natives, and left me to whatever success I could contrive. In 1921 Major-General Hugh L. Scott told me that he had not changed his opinion.

The Hopi do not make good policemen, and certainly not in a cohort of one. Their very name implies "the peaceful ones." Their towns are ruled largely by pueblo opinion. If a resident acquires the reputation of being unreasonable and unfeeling, as a policeman often must, his standing in the outraged community may affect all other phases of his life. Therefore the Hopi is not likely to become a very zealous officer when operating alone. And too, the Hopi fear the Navajo, as it is said the Navajo fear the Ute, and are useless when removed from the neighborhood of their homes.

But many years ago, when the Hopi were sorely pressed by nomad enemies and had not even the consolation of telling their woes to an Indian Agent, they sent emissaries to their cousins, the Pueblo Indians of what is now New Mexico, and begged for a colony of warriors to reside with them. In response to this plea, and looking for something to their advantage, in 1700 came a band of the Tewa from Abiquiu on the Chama River, from that section where Onate found San Juan de los Caballeros. To these people the Hopi granted a wide valley west of the First Mesa, known as the Wepo Wash, providing they would stay and lend their prowess in future campaigns. They built a village atop the First Mesa, now called Tewa or Hano, where their descendants live to-day. Some intermarried with the Hopi, and a few with the near-by Navajo; but they have not been absorbed, and it is a curious fact that while all the Tewa speak Hopi and Navajo with more or less fluency, after two centuries of living side by side few of the Hopi can speak the Tewa dialect.

The Hopi invited warriors, and the warriors have graduated into policemen, for one learns to police the Hopi districts, and even to discipline some of the Navajo, with Tewa officers. They are dependable and courageous, even belligerent; that is to say, they will fight when it is necessary and, strange thing among desert Indians, with their fists, taking a delight in blacking the opponent's eye. But one has to learn that the Hopi as policemen are fine ceremonial dancers.

The Navajo cohort had been selected following a frontier fallacy. Many of the old Agents believed that a good police force could be built from the "bad men" of the community.

"The cattle-thief will know all other cattle-thieves," was their reasoning. "The gambler will not be deceived as to those who waste their herds and silver playing monte. And the meaner an Indian among his own, the more respect and fear he will stimulate when garbed in a uniform and authorized to pack a gun."

As reasonable as if New York officials should make a special deputy of Gyp the Blood.

Hoske Yega, commonly known as Old Mike, a tall and unscrupulous Navajo, carried the Chief's badge. It was said that he had killed more than one man; and while I am not so sure of this, certainly he was no example of righteousness. The second officer was not so mean a specimen, but one of the same system. They had been policemen of the jurisdiction for many years, believed themselves entitled to the positions, and knew the game. A Navajo policeman has nothing to learn from the bulls of the whites as to methods of graft and the blackmailing use of his badge. The Indian Service has used native police since 1878, and I will admit that occasionally one finds a jewel of an officer, of good judgment, trustworthy, brave, and loyal; but for the most part the Indian policemen of the Desert are go-betweens and grafters.

Providing that the Indian accused of wrongdoing is not of the policeman's clan, providing that the policeman is not afraid of him or of his clan, providing that there is no witchcraft involved, the Navajo policeman can serve a warrant and get his man as quickly and as unerringly as any Sherlock Holmes. A skilled tracker, he can read the trail as an open book; and often he does not need to follow it. Indians leave their visiting cards behind them. My first knowledge of this came when the corral of Clezzi Thlani was relieved of several good ponies, and Old Mike was sent forth to investigate. He recovered most of the stock from the open range, and reported:

"They were taken by Sageny Litsoi."

Sageny's idea had been the common one among Navajo, dating from wagon-train days: to run the ponies a little further each night until distance had convinced him that he actually owned the animals. Then a little tinkering with a hot wire would so confuse brands as to bring even the records to his support.

"Why did n't you bring him in?" I asked.

"Did n't see him — just got the horses."

"Then how do you know that Sageny is the thief?"

"Went to corral; saw his tracks. Yisconga dahtsi" (to-morrow perhaps) "I bring in Sageny."

"You mean the trail will lead to his hogan?"

"No, No! Went to corral; see his tracks — Sageny's feet. No two Navajo have feet alike."

And when Sageny was brought in, although he had many

excuses and claimed that he had raised the animals, he
did admit taking animals having another's brand; and
he occupied the guardhouse for a period as a guest of the
Empire. Several of my Navajo police graduated later into
the same rest-room, which seemed a humorous proceeding
to many, and was not altogether different from the experiences of some white lieutenants.

It was when I discovered that Tewa could be depended
on that better police-work followed. The point of view
was different. One day I summoned the tall and spare
Tewa chief of police, and said to him: —

"Nelson, I want Hostin Chien Bega. You know him?"

"Yes; me know him — call him 'Bull-Neck.'"

"'Bull-Neck' it is. Can you bring him in?"

"Dahtsi."

"Well, here are handcuffs. Suppose you try it."

He took the cuffs and walked away. A short time after
he returned, and I saw that he had buckled on his guns.

"You want 'Bull-Neck,'" he commented. "He mean
Navajo — carry two guns all the time. Sometimes bring
in whiskey. Now, how bad you want him? You want him
dead?"

Well, to be plain about it, I did not want Hostin Chien
Bega, alias Bull-Neck, as a morgue exhibit. He was mean
enough in the flesh. And I foresaw the later experience of
a brother superintendent who ruled the reservation on
my west line. His domain was if anything a trifle wilder
than mine, reaching to the Grand Cañon and the most
remote places of the Utah border. Its area was a trifle
more than five thousand square miles, inhabited by at
least six thousand Navajo, many of whom had never
touched civilization. One Taddytin had graduated from
the police force into a bully of the countryside, and it

became necessary to impose on him a bit of his own medicine. Taddytin was a giant in physique and quite the meanest man of that territory. Messages summoning him to the Agency were of no avail. He pleaded illness, that cover to which retreat all those who do not wish to testify. Taddytin not only resisted the persons sent to arrest him, but did his level Navajo best with a .45 gun to get them before they subdued him. The Navajo is quite handy with a gun at close range. Most of them go armed from the time they make money enough to purchase a heavy weapon at the nearest trading-post — a trade permitted by the Indian Office, although in utter defiance of both Federal and Arizona State law.

The affair came off in a hogan, which is entirely too restricted a place for serious shooting. Taddytin's gun twice missed fire, and the persons sent to arrest him, having been in line with the gun, became nervous and, strange to relate, lost their judgment. They should have reprimanded Taddytin for carrying a defective weapon. Instead, they felt it necessary to shoot Taddytin several times, and although not using one of those fancy .22's that O. Henry was wont to ridicule, the first two bullets failed to knock him down. Unfortunately the last shot killed Taddytin, which was entirely opposed to all policies of moral suasion.

My brother superintendent, who acts as Indian Agent no longer, defended himself in the Federal Court, first against a murder charge, and then one of perjury, from the Spring term of 1916 to and including the Spring term of 1918. He stood quite alone, save for the testimony of all those who knew anything about Indians and Taddytin in particular. It cost him quite four thousand dollars in cash, to say nothing of time and mental disturbance.

The full history of this case may be found in a Congressional Report (*House Doc.* 1244) to accompany *H.R. Bill No.* 5639, dated September 19, 1922 — a bill to reimburse the man after his persecution had ended; a report that is probably forgotten. According to that report, the superintendent, acting as Indian Agent —

did not receive the support from the Indian Bureau in connection with this matter to which he was entitled, but instead he was vigorously, and your committee believes unjustly, prosecuted by the Federal authorities.

You see, the superintendent became the official goat, and suffered that a glowing policy of big wind and puffery might not be embarrassed.

As this affair occurred to my next-door neighbor, it had a serious effect on law-and-order conditions within my by no means peaceful jurisdiction, to the end that I was once reported as murdered and often threatened with having the report confirmed.

No; I did not urge my Tewa policeman to give a too realistic picture of loyalty to my commands.

XIII

A DESERT VENDÉE

One noticeable thing about all the Calhoun letters is the complaint of inadequate support from Washington. — ABEL: *Correspondence of James S. Calhoun*

It was a hot sweltering desert day in July when I proceeded westward from Oraibi to survey for the first time the contentious pueblo of Hotevilla, Chief Youkeoma's retreat. I did not expect to meet this strange personality, but his very name caused me to have an interest in so rare a character: You-*ke*-o-ma, or "something quite nearly complete" — as one might say, "almost perfection." An American Dalai Lama.

Several miles beyond the little grotto of the Oraibi war-gods, a concealed shrine of quaint images, passing that place where Youkeoma's adherents lost the contest to decide their traditional rights in the town of Oraibi, one came to a wall of shattered rock. These Hotevilla cliffs have little of dignity; they picture chaos, as it was left by the rending and scarring of some violent earthquake in the ages gone. To-day the ubiquitous Ford may ascend that wall on a wide and evenly graded roadway, because I grew tired of risking my neck there; but it was not so in 1911. My team had a tug of it up a dipping and winding trail that the Indians, under guard, no doubt, had crudely torn from the masses of tumbled sandstone.

The second steppe was dotted with thicket from which, on the winds of springtime, stirs the fragrance of heliotrope. There were patches of deep sand, and more of rock outcroppings, and then appeared the fields of the natives, irregular gardens of corn and beans and melons, growing profusely. These people can make a rock-quarry bloom and produce food. The Hotevilla are always one year ahead of famine. At some time in the past they must have suffered desperately from crop-failure, and that bitter lesson taught them never again to trust a single harvest.

The pueblo itself was on the westernmost edge of the mesa. There, where the rocks dropped away again in huge broken steps, overlooking the vast Dinnebito Wash country, they had built their curious little houses of stone and mud. If not balanced on the edge of a precipice, apparently the Hopi are not happy. Fatalists — when the aged or blind plunge over it is regretted, but not grieved about sufficiently to disparage the site. Alcoves of the mesa benches were fenced with cottonwood boughs, and served as hanging balconies for their burro stock. They had no cattle, few sheep, and fewer horses; in fact they were and are the poorest of the Hopi people, having rejected all tenders of acquisition and progress; but in those things that do not run counter to the traditions, such as cornmeal and burros, they have great wealth.

There was one man with me, and he advised against going down into the village. Indeed, I was not inclined to insist on it, for coincident with our topping the last rise the roofs of the highest houses had been posted with guards, watching, watching us in an ominous manner: a custom that prevailed for many years, and one that causes the stranger to feel a trifle less than comfortable.

"Very likely they feel that we slipped up on them," I said to my companion.

"Not at all," he replied. "They have been expecting you for days. They knew when you arrived at Oraibi yesterday. Be sure of it, old Youkeoma has gone underground and will remain in hiding until the coast is clear. Those watching fellows simply want to know where you go and when you depart. If we sought to take off a kid or two to school, there'd be a fine row. They know we have no backing. I'll bet they knew when you left the Agency and started out this way."

All of which proved to be true, and I had later to learn to circumvent and deceive such mysterious methods of information.

We sat on a baking sand-hill and surveyed the place. It was simply a dirtier duplicate of the other pueblos I have described, without their picturesque setting. And if there is a place in America where aroma reaches its highest magnitude, then that distinction must be granted Hotevilla on a July afternoon. The sun broils down on the heated sand and rock ledges, on the fetid houses and the litter and the garbage, and all that accumulates from unclean people and their animals. Multitudes of burros and chickens and dogs. Hosts of dogs. Lank, slinking, half-starved, challenging dogs. Poisonous-looking dogs that would attack one.

Hotevilla's sloping streets end at the mesa-edge, and below are the sacred spring and their sunlit fields. Far away in the northwest, as a dim blue sail on the horizon, showed Navajo Mountain, that peak of Indian mystery where the last of their secrets have found refuge. The Hopi had migrated from that country centuries past, south to the Little Colorado River; and then, like the back-wash of a wave, had drifted and settled in his present place of stagnation. Perhaps Hotevilla had proved his Promised Land.

The smell of cooking arose from the houses, a muttony

odor, — although it may have been burro-haunch, — mingled with smoke and the thick incense of smouldering cedar. In and out of the doorways the women passed at their tasks, and one sat weaving a reed plaque. They were all indifferent, with a contemptuous sullen indifference, to the stranger. There was a perfect swarm of children, wary, watching children, ready to dart and hide, long-haired and dirty, and most of them as nude as Adam.

At one end of the village, and a little apart from it, stood a house with a peaked roof. This had been the station of the Mennonite Mission, but when last threatened, the good people departed. It required a brave spirit to live close to the hostile Hopi. One was likely to reflect on the fate of Fray Padre José de Espelata, of the Kingdom of Navarre, and the difference in theological teaching lent very little comfort.

Until 1915 the Hotevilla mesa was a very lonely place. The nearest white neighbors were seven miles away, with rough cañons between, and no telephone wires; and the nearest authority of the Government, the Indian Agent, quite fifty miles distant, with no road-condition assuring speed of rescue in case of trouble. One brave white woman lived alone on that hilltop until the building of a Government school brought neighbors. This was Miss Sarah E. Abbott, a field matron. For many years she had been stationed at the First Mesa, where she had acquired a knowledge of the Hopi language. She received orders to confront the Hotevilla, and she did it. But it was necessary for me to send police several times to arrest those who sought to intimidate her, and the longest term of imprisonment ever given old Youkeoma himself, perhaps the longest ever given an Indian at an Indian Agency, was because of his threatening this woman.

When it grew near to sunset the men began returning from the fields, plodding in with their sacks and staves and huge planters' hoes. Many of them were aged, their long hair matted and snaky-looking; but there were enough of the burly, thickset fellows to give any official pause if he contemplated dictating to that outfit. Even those who closely observe these people wonder at this evidence of physique. The Hopi lives largely on a vegetable diet. His teeth are blunted and worn down like a horse's from the eating of flint-like corn. Because of isolation and clan ceremonial exclusion they have become devitalized through centuries of inbreeding, and quickly succumb to disease. And yet these same Hopi are famed for two things requiring raw strength and sustained energy: they can lift and pack on their backs the heaviest burdens, and they are great long-distance runners. Many of their ceremonies include the foot race, notably the sunrise competition on the day of the Snake Dance. Given a long desert course, fifty to one hundred miles, and the Hopi runner will wear down a horse. Their ability to bear burdens comes from both sides of the house, since for ages the women have packed water from the springs to the heights, and the men the harvests, the firewood, and the rock for building. I have seen two moving piles of wood on a mesa-trail, to discover one a burro-load and the other covering a man, with small difference between them.

And they must have carried weight over distances that compared with their runs, for how else were the Spanish Missions roofed? The great timbers were brought on the backs of men. About 1629 the Hopi, obedient and enslaved, brought these timbers from the San Francisco Mountains to Oraibi and other points, a feat equaled only by the Acoma Indians, who built a huge mission atop their penal height, the beams coming from San Mateo or Mount Taylor. Each of these packs was more than fifty miles. One of the unused timbers may be seen to-day in the *convento* part of the Acoma Mission. It is a log measuring more than thirty feet in length and two feet in thickness. Without mechanical equipment, the raising of it to the mesa-top would tax any man's ingenuity.

Especially would an official pause in dictation at the time of which I speak, for the Hopi had defied two former superintendents and for several years had done exactly as they pleased, in utter disregard of all admonitions emanating by mail from Washington. Of course official Washington had not worried, and for the rest of the world the Hopi do not exist; but the example to about fifteen hundred other and disciplined Hopi and to several thousand unregulated and undisciplined Navajo, all in constant touch with these rebels, was not good. The Agents reaped the effect of this timid policy, and it had given them concern.

The Hopi had so acted at other times, and the methods adopted to correct them had not been of the happiest. Officials had threatened and, when the native did not stir, had offered bribes.

"Your bones will bleach in the sun!" one set had promised — to be followed by: "Won't you come in and be good, for a nice new contract stove?" Now the bleaching process had affected only those so unfortunate as to die naturally, and the Hotevilla people were content with their piki stones and adobe fireplaces. *The Indian does not respect those who seek to buy him. When a threat proves as empty as it is boastful, he is strengthened in no small degree.* Washington has been given to bluffing, and buying.

The Indian Service had not greatly concerned itself about these strange people until 1887. Between 1847, when the Hopi were acquired as one of the blessings of the Mexican War, and 1887, when the first school was planted in Keams Cañon — forty years — they had lived practically as undisturbed as since their coming from the cliff- and cavern-dwellings in the northern cañons of the Utah border. A few traders had visited them often enough to be known; and one of them, Mr. John Lorenzo Hubbell, has told me of his witnessing a Snake Dance in the seventies, a solitary white spectator where now several thousands congregate annually. The tourist was not in those days, and had he been, under the circumstances of the back-country, it is likely he would have been going away from a Snake Dance rather than attending one.

In 1890 the defiance of the Oraibi first caused notice. Old Lo-lo-lo-mi, their good chief, had been to Washington, and had agreed to place the children of his faction in the school. His counsels were disregarded by the opposition; in fact they imprisoned the old man and threatened him with death for this lapse from the traditions. Lo-lo-lo-mi was "too good," as his name implied. The sub-Agent, Mr. Ralph Collins, arrested several of the war-chiefs and sent them to their Agent at Fort Defiance. When they returned they busied themselves making more trouble; so troops were sent to pacify and coerce them, and the first great blunder was made by an army officer. This officer accompanied Collins to the Oraibi mesa. They were warned that the hostiles had armed and meant to fight. Believing this to be so much bluff, they ascended the mesa to the pueblo. A war-chief, who had refused to attend a council, stepped out on one of the terraced houses. He was painted for the occasion, carried a rifle, and looked the part of his office. He was joined by a medicine man, who wore a raw sheepskin that dripped blood and besmeared his body. These two, knowing of many sympathizers within the hovels, dared the whites to combat and greatly abused them. The two white men prudently retired after an abortive parley.

Then came five troops of cavalry. The commanding officer invited the hostile headmen to a council below the mesa, and gave his word that they should be respected. They came, but stubbornly refused to change their minds as to this white man's educational propaganda. They were then seized and bound as prisoners; and were afterward marched up the pueblo trail as a screen for the soldiers. This was rank betrayal, and the effects of it live in the Oraibi country to this day.

"Some white men do not keep their word." And at Oraibi, or at least among unreconstructed Oraibans, who are now at Hotevilla, it is wisdom to suspect all white men.

Collins, the civilian and sub-Agent, had no part in this. He advised against it and deplored it. It would have been better to risk a bit of bad marksmanship, for which the Hopi is noted; it would have been better to beat a few worthless war-chiefs and medicine men to death, if that were actually necessary. One can forgive a battle — but betrayal rankles in the heart.

The prisoners taken at this time were sent to Fort Wingate. In a few months they were released on promise to be good, but when they returned from captivity they too refused to keep the parole given. The goose of an officer had produced a flock of ganders, and his work was to live for nearly three decades. In 1894 troops were again in demand at Oraibi, and nineteen of the Indian leaders were sent as prisoners to Alcatraz Island. They were imprisoned about eight months, and returned impenitent.

In 1898 the Hopi suffered from smallpox. It was not so bad as that epidemic told of by the Spanish, but it was severe enough. Superstition and fright, combined with fatalism, are hard things to conquer among a people who know nothing of vaccination, who trust no stranger, but prefer to die unassisted by aliens. Troops were necessary, to affect quarantine and to cremate bodies. In 1899, say the records, troops came again, and once more prisoners were sent to Fort Defiance.

All this time internal dissension was at work among the Oraibans, and in 1905 differences as to the views of local oracles concerning the traditions reached a climax. This quarrel involved nearly everyone within reaching distance. The Commissioner of Indian Affairs, Francis E. Leupp, the best supporter of discipline the Service has had in three decades, was at odds with his Agent on this station and, to tell the truth, this Agent had met one Waterloo at the Chimopovi pueblo, where an outpost of the Oraibi dwelt. His effort to coerce the Hopi with an enlarged Navajo police force had nearly resulted in bloodshed and real war; and at the end of this fiasco the Navajo mercenaries threatened his life because the pay-chest was not promptly thrown open to them.

So the Commissioner came to exert a strong personal influence. And he found speedily that his personal influence in the great Desert amounted to very little. The Indians had a keen sense of the fitness of things, and they resented his appearing to negotiate with them without an official sponsor.

"Who are you?" asked the troubled Oraibi, when invited to a council with him.

"I am the Commissioner from Washington," he stated, a fact that was known to President Roosevelt, the Gridiron Club, and the *New York Evening Post,* and that should have been patent everywhere.

"Why do you come here without Moungwi, then?" they demanded. "He should introduce you to us. We do not know you. Moungwi is not here. Why do you come in the back way, from Winslow, and call a council without Moungwi?"

Indians are often peculiarly consistent. They did not regret that recent fracas with Moungwi, when they had seized him by the beard and threatened to toss him bodily from the gigantic Chimpovi cliffs, — action prevented only by his Navajo police threatening to open fire, — but they did know something of official courtesy between and among all Moungwis or Chiefs, and there is such a thing as having the proper entrée, even with an Indian tribe in the far-removed hills. Very likely the Commissioner said something about the respect due his office; when arose a big Indian, who declaimed to this astonishing effect: —

"This man comes here alone, and he has a crooked mouth. His words go two ways. He is no Commissioner of Indian Affairs, or the Moungwi would be here to tell us. I myself saw this man working with a shovel on the railroad section-gang not three weeks ago. Don't listen to him. He will lead you the wrong trail."

Now this was a terrible blow to dignity, and hurt all Washington. Matters did not improve, and by 1906 the trouble had increased to the point where troops were necessary once again. They came. They rehearsed their parts perfectly, and prisoners were taken. A special inspector was sent in to observe matters, and he found himself in a very embarrassing position. The one hundred captives had arranged a hunger strike. Receipts for their prison mess-equipment had been demanded of them, in strict accordance with the farcical methods of accounting then in vogue. The true Hopi hostile, loyal to high-priest Youkeoma, has never signed for anything. He is reared to be wary of the white man's papers. As he cannot read them for himself, he classes everything in the nature of a document along with the white man's word, as illustrated by the first army officer who betrayed him.

"If they won't sign, let them starve," said the soldier in this case, and he was not at all worried about it. But the special inspector was very much worried about it. He had to be more careful of his civil job; so he managed early one morning, with the seductive aroma of boiling coffee and the alluring scent of fried bacon, to develop a hungry Judas among the younger men, who signed for the whole lot; and lo! by such means all tribulation was avoided.

This time seventeen leaders were sent to Fort Huachuca, seventy-two were put to work on the roads of the reserve, and a lot of younger men, rebels in embryo, were dispatched to distant Indian schools, in the belief that enforced education would bring calm to their troubled spirits. Eight of these young men went to Carlisle. I had to deal with them when they returned, some seven years later. In fact, the Commissioner of that time advised me that they would prove a help in administering the affairs of the reservation. They returned arrayed in the clothing of the white man, but only three of them showed any signs of repentance. Those of the Hotevilla, with one exception, shucked the clothing promptly and went back to the blanket. They were sullen and suspicious, and they had not lost their memories.

I did not blame them in great measure, for at least four

had been married men when taken from the pueblo. Their wives now had other consorts, other children. The children of the rebel fathers would not forgive them, because they repudiated the faithless wives. The fathers blamed the Government for not protecting their households. And the women said to me: —

"You took our men. We were left alone. We had to keep the children alive, and this meant tending the fields and the sheep. Speak not to us of morals."

At least that was the English meaning of their argument and reproof, whatever the Hopi terms of it. Quite so many "'Lispeths": "You are all liars, you English"; and in the same manner their sons and daughters took to their "own unclean people savagely."

Now a tribal marriage is a legal marriage, or so the courts have decreed, of course far removed from the haunts of the alien and having no specific knowledge of him or of his conditions. So, in strict accordance with sacred property rights and the Great Book of Platitudes, it was my duty to say to the outfit assembled: "You, hussies, are guilty of adultery, and many of your children are illegitimate; while you, impenitent rebels, may not take other wives, since by so doing you would commit bigamy; and each of you, every one, all and several, to wit, should have long terms in the guardhouse."

That is what I should have said; but being of sound mind, and having very little use for platitudes, especially those courageously hurled by mail across two thousand miles, I did nothing of the sort. I had a convenient place in which I kept the sacred book hidden, and had trained myself into a complete forgetfulness of it.

But notwithstanding my sympathies, I could never soften the hatred of one of the sons. He hated his father because of his mother's treatment, and above all this he hated white men, including me. The stupid sins of one Moungwi are inherited by another in the line of succession.

"You took my father," he said to me, "and left my mother to work hard in the fields; and when I grew big enough to work you took me to school, so she was left again without help. Then, when my father returned from Carlisle, he would have nothing to do with my mother. And you would not let me go home to her. I have no use for these ways of the white men. I will not cut my hair, and I do not agree to continue at school. You are strong enough to make me, but I will not do these things for you."

He could tell me this in straight English, as at my desert school he had received a good grammar foundation; and he was not interrupted or punished, because I encouraged the pupils to come to me and speak their minds. But, being stronger, I elected to do these things for him, having in mind his individual interests as separate and apart from the feuds of the past; but I could not severely blame him for his stubborn opposition. He was a very bright lad, and became an exceptional student; but just as surely he returned finally to his "own unclean people, savagely." Three weeks on the roads, breaking stone and wheeling sand, would have done more to cure that father's rebellious attitude than those years at Carlisle, exiled from his household and all of life that he understood and cared for. To be sure, — and to be fair to his instructors, — the man learned a great deal at Carlisle, which was a very fine school; and more than this, he saw the wonders of the white man. He was one of the first to witness an air flight. And when he told his ancients at the pueblo of these strange and unbelievable things he had seen in Philadelphia, they arose in wrath, knocked out their ceremonial pipes, and denounced him as the greatest liar unhung. So even by the elders, whose lost cause he had espoused and suffered for, he was repudiated and damned. Few patriots get such treatment as this. He was completely ostracized at home. To keep him in food, I employed him as a local policeman, hoping he would revenge himself; but this commission brought him only additional scorn and reprobation. For long he lived at Hotevilla as a pelican in the desert; where else could he live? Was it not home?

But we had reached 1911, with the same old situation burning on the Oraibi mesa, save that the hostiles were now in a pueblo of their own, and could be dealt with, however justly or unjustly, without affecting those who had never actively resisted the Government. It was sheer nonsense to begin again the farce of supplication and argument, of cheap bribes and equally impotent threats. No bones had "bleached in the sun," and there were not enough native police and loyal employees to risk an attempt at coercing this sullen horde. I returned to the Agency and wrote a very impolitic report. Anything of truth that the Indian Bureau does not wish to know is impolitic.

I recited the facts, and recommended, as the Government had found it necessary to send in troops so many times before, and always after much backing and filling and abortive negotiation, — all to the amusement of the savage, — why not send troops now, and quickly. This recommendation was dated July 28, 1911.

Government moves with a truly fearsome swiftness. I realize now, after thirteen years of report-swapping and buck-passing, that some miracle happened in that my suggestion was considered at all. I have been told that a friend assured the Secretary of the Interior that I was not a maniac. But it required until September 27, 1911 to request the Secretary of War to detail cavalry from a distant point, when troops were idle at Fort Apache only one hundred and eighty miles away—quite in the neighborhood, as desert spaces are considered. Another month drifted by, and on October 28 the Secretary of War detailed Hugh L. Scott, then Colonel in rank, as an officer of Indian experience likely to have influence with these strange people. Under date of November 15 I was directed to coöperate with Colonel Scott, and as no allowance was made for the fact that it was winter and mails likely to be delayed along the one hundred and five miles of wagon-transport, the great Indian diplomatist and his officers and men reached the Moqui Agency before my orders. Four months had been devoted to the delicate untwisting of red tape that a telephone conversation between Departments and a telegram to the nearest post would have settled in twenty-four hours' time. How comfortable if those Hopi had been Ute, Apache, Navajo, or Sioux!

XIV

SOLDIERS, INDIANS, AND SCHOOLS

Now it is not good for the Christian's health to hustle
the Aryan brown,
For the Christian riles, and the Aryan smiles, and he
weareth the Christian down.

— KIPLING

IF you seek information on an Indian Reservation concerning things outside the line of routine, never ask the Agent in charge. He will have the important papers locked away from prying eyes, and will likely comment that it is none of your business. Why invite this rebuff? Go to the mess-cook, the farrier, or the seamstress. They will have had all the essential details from some other post, from a mess-cook, a farrier, or a seamstress, who will have zealously garnered it from some leaky official, or mayhap from the telegraph operator. Who told Sitting Bull that Custer had divided his command? By long odds, it was a camp cook.

And when the school disciplinarian asked me one morning, as he was checking his watch with my chronometer, "When do you expect the troops?" I knew that an unusual order had issued. He was correct in his assumption, for the laundress had been notified. Now I do not presume to assert that the Secretary of the Interior had notified the laundress — but she knew. Perhaps some other laundress had found the order in the Colonel's wash. Anyway, the column arrived just when she predicted.

It made a striking picture filing down the long Cañon

hill-road, black riders against the sky and yellow sand, the field flag and troop pennant fluttering; and there was about it a certain campaign note that caused as much consternation throughout the back country as if war had been declared, with Kit Carson back in the saddle.

Those of the wavering Hopi who lived apart from Youkeoma but leaned toward his policies when they dared, and who had been awaiting developments, began to rush their belated children to the schools. The smiling "friend-lies" industriously continued minding their home affairs. And the Navajo, after one excited survey from the oppo-site mesa-wall, completely disappeared from the land-scape. Not a Navajo was to be seen about the Agency for a very long period. Their old chiefs, such as Hostin Nez and Billa Chezzi, could recall the captivity at the Bosque Redondo, and the younger men had heard them tell of it. This was no time for argument with the Nah-tahni, and while they had lost nothing in the back country, still it invited a peaceful hegira far from the tents and bugles of that column.

The whole affair was against all tradition. Three former Agents had argued and threatened and waited in vain, and the third had lingered helplessly at his post until revolt blazed out to singe his beard. Now this new Nahtahni had said very little; in fact, he had seemed depressed and a trifle bewildered. But here came the soldiers, a very different sort of Se-lough from those three uniformed natives he was thought to depend on. The effect was immediate and lasting. And more than one official, hav-ing actual knowledge of conditions among the isolated Navajo, has agreed with me that such a column should file through that country every little while. There would be in both Indians and white men more of respect for the orders of the Government, and fewer murders in lonely places.

And then I found the famous Colonel Scott seated at one end of my desk. I apologized for being so ignorant, having received no Departmental orders, and supposed that he would be thoroughly informed. Aside from the request that he coöperate with the Agent in this little frontier squabble, it appeared that his mission was a survey, and action would await further instructions. Quarters were arranged for the officers and a camping-place for the men, and then the Colonel and I sat down to a discussion of conditions among the Indians of the reserve. Having read of his career among the warriors of the Plains, I felt that the less I said to this experienced soldier and tribal expert the better would be my chances for making no mistakes. I hoped to create an impression of wisdom by keeping my mouth shut.

But Colonel Scott would have none of that. He had then and has to this day a most disconcerting method of propounding a question, and then boring one completely through and through with a pair of gimlet-like blue-gray eyes that pierce as if made of steel. He could see that I was very green and young at the business of being an Indian Agent, but he would not permit me to retreat before his age and superior rank.

"I propose first to go among these Indians, and learn something of their reasons for this refusal to obey the wishes of the Department," he said.

I remained silent.

"I will go alone," he said.

I said nothing.

"You do not think they will receive me unpleasantly?"

"Oh, no!" I hastened to make up for lost time. "They

are peaceful enough, so long as they are permitted to have their own way. Very likely they will receive you with much of courtesy and even hospitality."

"That is as I thought," said the Colonel, who has always gone alone into hostile camps — a method of conciliation that would give most people pause. "I will reason with them," he continued, "and I believe I can bring them to a sensible view of the matter we have to adjust."

I said nothing.

"What do you think of my plan?"

"Why, Sir, I would not presume to suggest — "

"That is not the question. You should be somewhat familiar with these Indian people by now. Will my plan succeed?"

His eyes punched through mine, straight back into the brain, out through the skull of my rear elevation, and I knew they were drilling on through the stone wall immediately behind me.

"Considering the experiences of former agents, and even soldiers, Colonel Scott, and — "

"Do you think my plan will succeed?"

"It is a very good plan to try, Colonel. It has been your method with other tribes, and it may prove successful here."

"But what do you think?"

There was no way of avoiding the truth. He would have it.

"You will not succeed."

He studied a moment or two.

"I have dealt with unreasonable Indians," he said, slowly.

"So I am informed, sir. But you have not dealt with

the Hopi Indian, who is a religious fanatic; and since you pressed me for an opinion, I had to give it. I can ask only that these people be not promised anything that will not be fulfilled. That has provoked half the trouble of the past. The Department has threatened them, and then curled up. They are accustomed to being betrayed by soldiers. They will talk endlessly; but if you expect to bring a Hopi to reason without a show of force, it is too much. You will not accomplish it."

Whereupon the Colonel seemed satisfied that he had procured an answer from me, and next day he departed for the pueblo of Hotevilla, with an interpreter and a striker to attend him. His extraordinary knowledge and uncanny skill in the sign-language would avail him nothing among the Hopi, for few of the Southwest Indians use this method of conversing. The deserted mission house was placed at his disposal. The troop remained encamped in Keams Cañon at the Agency.

That night the mail brought those belated orders, in duplicate, from the Commissioner of Indian Affairs to me, and from the Secretary of the Interior to Colonel Scott. I read them with amazement and a complete mixture of feelings. They had been drawn without deference to the facts, and were as completely garbled a set of instructions as one could imagine. By merely accepting the conditions imposed, the Indians could win, and the whole expedition be reduced to farce. Washington had been so careful to preserve a shield between it and the sentimental critics of the country that, no matter what I proposed doing and no matter what the officer agreed to assist in doing, the fat was in the fire if those orders were recognized.

And here were more than one hundred men, with mounts and extra mounts, and a pack train, and a wagon train en route with additional supplies. Hay for the horses was being purchased locally at sixty dollars the ton, and oats in proportion; and these were but two items of the expense. A very costly piece of humor, indeed.

But the Colonel was at Hotevilla; and there he remained for ten days, talking, talking, talking, when he was not listening to Youkeoma. I had one report from a messenger, who found the old chief seated in the centre of the floor, facing the Colonel on his camp-bed, the interpreter to one side. It was the seventh day, and Youkeoma, in the recital of his traditions, had reached a date only four hundred years removed. To give the old chap credit, he never weakened. The Colonel, sitting bolt upright, would go into a doze, finish a nap, and pick up the thread of the discourse immediately on waking, to continue as long as daylight lasted.

Of course there were breaks in this programme. They invited the officer to a rabbit-hunt, and gave exhibitions of their fleetness in running and their skill with the rabbit-club or Hopi boomerang; and he witnessed some of their ceremonies. But the end of it all was talk — so many words arranged one after the other, one string in slow, even-toned English, studied, level, monotonously imperative; the other in imperturbable Hopi, rising and falling as Chinese, started with a long intake of the breath and finished in whispers when Indian lungs were exhausted.

Youkeoma began at a point in his traditions before the period of the Dawn Men, when they came up from the Underworld. Wells' *Outline of History* is not half so elaborate. And without a break or hesitation, supporting his statements with pieces of pictured rock offered as indisputable evidence, much as Moses woud have brought forth the Tables of the Law, he progressed down through

YOUKEOMA, ANTELOPE PRIEST AND PROPHET
Who told the tale of the Dawn Men

the ages. The troop surgeon, who had joined the Colonel, furnished me a rough transcript of this legend, which, boiled to a bare consistency, follows: —

Hopi Genesis according to Youkeoma, Chief Priest of the Hotevilla

The Hopi came from the Underworld, down in the earth. They had their chiefs and medicine men, and their villages, in the Underworld, the same as now and here. But the people drifted away from the traditions. They had too much love of a good time, and refused to hear their wise men. They held social dances, and forgot the old religious ceremonies. First the girls, then the women, and finally nearly all the Hopi people came under this influence. They forgot everything else. And even the wives of the priests became evil.

Then the good chiefs and medicine men held a council. They were against these evils, and decided to look for another world. They discussed many methods of leaving the Underworld. And they made experiments. First they planted pine trees, and by ceremonies grew these trees very tall. The pine trees grew up to touch the roof of the sky, but they did not pierce it. Their tops bent over and spread along the sky. And the good Hopi knew that pine trees could not help them.

Next they planted sharp-pointed reeds, and these grew tall and pierced the sky.

Now to find what sort of place was above them. They sent up birds as messengers, to go out through the holes in the sky and find a land for the good people. They told the birds to return and tell what they saw. So they sent humming birds first. These flew up and up, circling the tall reeds, and resting on them when tired. But the humming birds became exhausted, and fell back into the Underworld.

Then they sent up a chicken hawk. It could fly much swifter, but it too became exhausted. The swallow was sent, but he did not reach the top of the reeds. Each bird was dispatched by a clan. And finally the catbird was sent. He flew with such a strange jerky motion that they never expected him to reach the top — but he did, and went through the hole in the sky, and came to Oraibi. There he found the Red-headed Spirit.

The bird asked the Ghost if it would permit the good people of the Hopi in the Underworld to come and live at Oraibi. And the Spirit was willing, so the bird returned with this message.

Most of the people were still busy with their social dances; but the chiefs and medicine men and the good people, when they had the news, began to climb the reeds. In this they were helped by the two Gods of Hard Substances, who made the reeds firm. These people managed to crawl through the hole in the sky. But those who had given their time to frivolous things were shaken from the reeds by the chiefs, and they dropped back into the Underworld, and the hole in the sky was stopped up.

Search for the new home was then begun. But the head chief's daughter died. This delayed things. He believed that some powerful witch had come out of the Underworld with them, so he called the people together and made some medicine of cornmeal, saying that the meal would fall on the witch's head. It did fall on a girl's head. The chief then decided to throw this witch back into the Underworld; but when he looked down through the hole in the sky he saw his daughter playing there, in the old place, as a little child; and he knew then that everyone went back to the Underworld after death.

Now the witch told the chief that if she might live with him he would be kept from many hardships and difficulties, and that some day his daughter would return to him. So the witch was spared.

It was utter darkness when the Hopi arrived on the earth. They counseled, and sought a means to create light. They cut out a round piece of buckskin, and on it put bits of the hearts of birds and beasts, and of all the people, and then told the buckskin to give forth light.

But this was not powerful enough. So they took white cotton cloth, and put the bits of their hearts on it, and set it in the East for the Sun. Thus the Sun gave light for every living thing, and to-day we all welcome its coming up in the East.

The head chief then called the mocking bird, and told him to give to each group a language. The older brother's people received the first language, which is that of the white men.

The clans now went in different directions. The older brother of the chief, with his people, was directed to go where the Sun rises, and to stay there. In time of trouble he would be sent for. The chief told him not to be baptized into any strange fraternity.

Then the clans went their several ways, each to find a country. They would travel for a distance, and stop to raise a crop of corn, and then go on. Sometimes they stayed at places two or three years. And the older brother, with those who made up his company, traveled fast to the East, and has not yet returned.

The Ghost clan finally arrived at Moencopi, and there too came the Smoke and the Spider clans. The Bear clan reached Chimopovi. Two brothers were chiefs of this division, and one of them settled Oraibi, where the Ghost and other clans later joined them.

Within the Ghost clan were two groups — the Ghost clan proper, and the Ghost-and-Bird clan. Youkeoma is of the Ghost-and-Bird clan. They were known as the bravery clan, and acted as guards. When came a war with the Ute, Navajo, and Apache, the Bear clan and the Ghost clan tried to win without the aid of these brave men of the Ghost-and-Bird clan. But they did not succeed, and had to ask their aid. So the bravest of the warriors then put explosives in pottery, and threw these bombs among the enemy, and scattered them. Then the Ghost-and-Bird clan lived at Oraibi, and were taken into the sacred fraternities, and were known as warriors.

Now the traditions say that a stronger people will come upon the Hopi, and try to get them to adopt new ways of living. And it is in the traditions that the Bear clan will yield to these stronger ones.

Many years ago, when the Spaniards came from the South, they sought to make the Hopi accept their ways. They were here four years. And the Bear clan yielded; and the Spider clan yielded; but the Ghost-and-Bird clan did not yield.

Then the Spanish black-robes came to live at Oraibi; and after four years these priests of the strangers wanted to baptize the Hopi. That caused much trouble. It was against the traditions. And the warriors of the Ghost-and-Bird clan were unwilling to assist the larger clans, like the Bear and Spider, because they had yielded to the Spanish. The Ghost-and-Bird clan knew that the sea would swallow up the land if they accepted these new teachings. Finally, the Badger clan killed the Spanish black-robes.

Then came a great battle, between the Oraibi people on the one side and the Spanish helped by the First and Second Mesa Hopi and also the Navajo on the other. The Oraibans drove the enemy into Skull Flat, named because of the heads that were piled there. And the people of Oraibi recognized the Ghost-and-Bird clan as their bravest men; and they lived in peace for many years.

Next came the white men—at first but a few, looking through the country; then more; and then they brought a school. This was to teach the Hopi children new ways — to lead them away from the ceremonies and the traditions.

Again some of the Oraibi people yielded, and took on the new ways taught by these white men of the Government. But the Ghost-and-Bird clan would not yield.

And then came the soldiers of the white men. They have come many times. Youkeoma has been a prisoner eight times, and has been taken away to forts where there were many soldiers; but he has not yielded. Five years ago, because of these troubles among the people, the Ghost-and-Bird clan left Oraibi and settled here at Hotevilla. Youkeoma looks on the Oraibans as traitors, for they have more than once received strangers and yielded to strange teachings.

In the end, all the enemies will combine against the Ghost-and-Bird clan. So say the traditions. These things will come to pass. Youkeoma cannot change it, nor can he go contrary to the traditions. The talk of the white men is incited by witches. And Youkeoma knows that these white men are not the true Bohanna, who will come some day and who will know the Hopi language. These white men are simply forerunners; they are not the Bohanna. They have treated him kindly when a prisoner among them, but they have never encouraged him in his way of living.

Now the way for the white men to conquer the Hopi is to cut off Youkeoma's head. The traditions say that the head of one of the Oraibi chiefs will be cut off, and then the trouble will cease. But Youkeoma cannot yield; for then the Sea would swallow up the land, and all would perish.

Ten days of it. Priestcraft and sorcery, superstition and cruelty, differ very little among primitive peoples. The Hopi beginnings were very like our own. And in the ages past they had out-talked many enemies. The old man flattered himself that so long as the Colonel listened, he was gaining credence; and that when the officer became completely hypnotized by weariness, he would capitulate, and cry, "You win, old man! For God's sake, give me a rest!"

Whereas Colonel Scott was awaiting a reply to a telegram forwarded through me four days after his arrival at the pueblo. He had recommended to the Secretary of the Interior that the children of the village be removed to schools, without further regard to this old fanatic and his sacred traditions. Youkeoma had confirmed my view of the situation. At the same time, Colonel Scott had written to me: "There is no use in arguing with a lunatic. If the Secretary says 'Take the children,' come on with your transportation and police and the troops."

These messages were carried by riders to the nearest telegraph point. To send them by the archaic mail-route would court long delays. Hotevilla was forty-five miles from the Agency and the railroad eighty miles south of that, so a round trip required two hundred and fifty miles of riding.

On the eighth day answers were received in duplicate, repeating the original conditions. Realizing that the buck was being passed in strict accordance with our traditions, I forwarded the Colonel's copy to him by messenger, and ordered all necessary wagons to Oraibi. The Lieutenant commanding the cavalry put his men in motion a little before midnight, to reach and surround the pueblo before dawn of the next day. Guided by Indian police, and following the shortest trails, they went directly to Hotevilla and had about it a picket-guard before the wondrous piece of White Cotton Cloth, holding the hearts of all the people, swung up out of the East.

I found Colonel Scott at an early breakfast in the little mission house, and reported to him that everything was right and ready save one.

"I am directed to read this telegram to Chief Youkeoma and, should he have brains enough to seize on its provisions, this whole affair will spell failure."

"Well, can't you do these things?" he asked in surprise.

"No one of them can be carried out. The placing of the children in the boarding-school at the Agency is made contingent on certain equipment being at hand for their comfort, and the Office knows perfectly that such equipment is not at hand. I informed the Office to that effect some time ago, and the Office has not corrected the situation. Then parents are to be given the privilege of selecting the school in which their children shall be placed — either at the Cañon or one of the local day-schools. The day schools are not close enough to permit attendance. The Indians know it. Should they accept the day-school proposition, it would require a troop of cavalry to get the pupils in each morning. Moreover, this whole attitude is equivalent to indulging a group of contentious savages in the belief that they are to be consulted, and that they shall have the privilege of decision."

"What do you propose to do about it?" he asked.

"Why, sir, since it would appear that Washington has none, I would supply a bit of intelligence and read it into these orders. And there would be a result."

"Are my orders the same as yours?"

"Exactly the same — they are in duplicate."

"Well, I am a soldier, and I do not break orders."

This came in a tone of utter finality, and I could see that it would be useless to advance argument.

"Very good, sir. Then I suppose you will withdraw your men. This thing will go by default."

But the Colonel had studied old Youkeoma for ten days, and actually he disliked as much as I did the accepting of stupid instructions issued by a Department that has a long record in buck-passing. And he felt that our dilemma might be solved by permitting the obdurate Indian to hang himself on the horns of it.

"Let us have in Youkeoma," he said; "and you propose to read the telegram to him, stating plainly that these are orders from Washington. If he does not at once accept the conditions, will you be prepared to collect the children promptly, with a squad of soldiers and your police?"

"I do not think I shall need the police, and I do not want the soldiers in the village. If you will keep the picket-guard as it is, and have a squad ready in case of trouble, I will go into the houses with two employees who know the people. I will bring out the children for medical examination. But I certainly do not propose to enter into debate with each savage as to schools, bedding, and commissary matters."

"Will you wish to make prisoners?'

"Not unless there is positive resistance. That has been done before, and I cannot see that any good resulted. It simply indulged the ringleaders in their idea of persecution."

"Very good. Have the old chap in."

Youkeoma came wrathfully into the council-room. His anger was like that of a trapped animal; his eyes gleamed with hatred, and he fairly quivered with rage. All morning he had fumed, realizing that he had wasted ten days of perfectly good oratory and traditions. He squatted on the floor.

"This is your Agent," said Colonel Scott. "He wants to shake hands with you."

I held out my hand to him.

Youkeoma looked me over carefully, and drew his blanket around his shoulders as if he had been insulted.

"I am done with white men," he said. "I will not shake hands with you or any other white man."

"Here is a telegram from Washington. It must be read to you."

The interpreter explained.

"I do not care to hear anything from Washington."

A MESA ROAD — OLD STYLE
The trail to Hotevilla

A PRETENTIOUS HOME AT HOTEVILLA

"But I must read it to you." And I straightway began. The interpreter translated the first sentence, the second — when the old fellow stood up. He waved his arm toward the soldiers outside, and cried angrily: —

"You have your men here; why not go ahead and do what you want? You can cut off my head. Why don't you do it? I will have nothing more to say to you. I am through with white people."

He stalked from the council-room, the maddest man in Arizona; and that was the last of him for many months.

"Now, Colonel, if you please, I will search the pueblo. Will you lend me your flashlight?"

"What do you want with that? It's broad day."

"I shall have to crawl into every corn-crib and cellar in the place, and none of them have windows."

He directed that soldiers accompany me through the village, but at the first house I asked them not to come inside. They remained in the street. This was followed throughout the search. The two employees who had some knowledge of this population entered with me.

"There should be three children in this house," one would say.

There were never any children in sight. The long, narrow, principal room would seem to have no doors leading from it. Racks of corn, carefully piled, and blankets and folded skins lined the walls. The employees, having assisted in such matters before, began lifting down these blankets and piled furnishings, to reveal usually a small door, and beyond this door would loom the blackness of a corn-cellar. The flashlight showed more corn racked up, melons in piles, and filled sacks; but no children. I would scramble through the little trap to make a closer investigation, recalling how Judge Hooker had walled up his brood, years before, when the Hopi of the First Mesa protested against education.

In the first of these places there was no room for hiding between the sacks, and when I moved against them I could feel the corn they held. I prepared to leave the place, and was at the opening, when I heard a sigh, as if someone had long held his breath and could hold it no longer. Back I went. No one among the melons, nor behind the racked corn. I began moving the sacks. Three were filled with corn on the cob; the fourth — my hand grasped the top of a Hopi head. It was like the jars of wine and the hidden thieves.

From the sacks we delivered the three children of that household.

When they appeared in the main room, laughing, the father caught them in his arms; and when they were taken from him, the mother proceeded to play the same trick. It was easy to break his hold on them, but not so easy to handle a woman without giving grounds for complaint as to rough usage — a charge the Hopi like to make. But those three children went into the street, notwithstanding all this hokum, and other employees took them before the physicians. There were three doctors present, the Army surgeon and two physicians of the Indian Service. Each child received a thorough examination, and only those fit and above the age of ten years were taken from the village.

I do not know how many houses there are in Hotevilla, but I crawled into every filthy nook and hole of the place, most of them blind traps, half-underground. And I discovered Hopi children in all sorts of hiding-places, and through their fright found them in various conditions of cleanliness. It was not an agreeable job; not the sort of work that a sentimentalist would care for.

In but one instance was real trouble threatened. On coming from one cellar, I found the head of the house sitting in the centre of his castle with an axe at his feet. He protested against the removal of the children, and grasped the axe as if to use it. The men with me promptly removed the implement, and threw him into a corner.

By midday the wagons had trundled away from Hotevilla with fifty-one girls and eighteen boys. Our survey of the place in July had warranted an estimate of one hundred and fifty pupils, but in the five months that had elapsed an epidemic of measles and its terrible aftermath of bronchial pneumonia had swept the town.

"Where are the others?" the interpreter asked of a villager.

"Dead," he replied, solemnly.

So much for expediency and Departmental delay.

Of those taken, nearly all had trachoma. It was winter, and not one of those children had clothing above rags; some were nude. During the journey of forty-five miles to the Agency many ragged garments went to pieces; the blankets provided became very necessary as wrappings before the children reached their destination. It was too late to attempt the whole distance that afternoon, so the outfit went into camp at the Oraibi day-school, where a generous meal was provided, and the next day their travel was completed.

Across the great Oraibi Valley was the pueblo of Chimopovi, perched on the highest of the mesa cliffs. And this place had a suburb, dominated by one Sackaletztewa, a direct descendant of the gentleman who had founded the original Hopi settlement after their emerging from the

Underworld. Sackaletztewa was as orthodox as old You-keoma, and it was his following that had given battle to a former Agent and his Navajo police. I proposed to Colonel Scott that Chimopovi should be visited.

"Take the troop to-morrow morning, and finish it up yourself."

So next day the same scene was enacted. It was a short job, only three children being found; but here occurred something like resistance. All the protestants congregated in the house of Sackaletztewa. When I entered, a man opened a little cupboard of the wall and produced a packet of papers. They were offered to me as documents of great value. And they were strange documents — letters from people of the country who had read in newspapers of Youkeoma's visit to Washington, and his defiance of the Government. I suppose such persons have nothing better to do, and write letters of sympathy to the members of every Indian delegation that parades itself eastward in feathers and war-paint to present a fancied grievance. I recall the words of one of these papers, from some weak-minded woman: —

Chief Youkeoma: you are a noble man. Do not let the Government have your children. Their schools are not the place for your Indian lads who know only the hunt and the open spaces. Resist to the last gasp. Die rather than submit.

Very like, she is now writing scenarios. Of course this correspondent had read Fenimore Cooper, and was filled to the neck with the storybook idea of Indians — lithe, clean, untouched by disease, and painted by romance. The Southwest has no such Indians; and Indians, whether lithe or not, are seldom clean and never romantic. She knew nothing of filth and trachoma and child-prostitution, while the Hopi had brought such things to a fine degree of perfection. And she lived in Indiana.

Now there is a wide difference between demanding the rights of Indians, rights that should be sacred under agreements, — and perhaps foreign treaties, such as those of the Pueblo Indians of New Mexico, — and inciting them to warfare and rebellion when teachers and physicians are striving to recover them from ignorance and disease. There is a vast difference between the argument that a title confirmed by three sovereign Governments be not attacked for the sake of political loot — as in the case of the Pueblo Indians of New Mexico — and denouncing the educational system of the United States and advising a group of benighted savages to kill in a distant and lonely desert. That writer from Indiana should have been a field matron for a little!

I have no sympathy with this type of sentimentalist. I deported some of them from the Hopi desert country when they appeared with their box of theoretical tricks.

I handed back the documents, and asked where the children were. Accompanied by my Tewa policeman, I entered a small room off the main house and found these three mentioned surrounded by relatives. The room filled up to its capacity and a harangue began. At Hotevilla we had not listened to argument, but here I thought it best to placate them, to explain things, rather more in line with the moral-suasion programme outlined from Washington. All talk led to one definite answer, growing sullenly louder and louder: "You cannot take the children."

We had to make an end. When I proceeded to lift one from the floor, in a twinkle two lusty Indians were at my throat. The Tewa (Indian police) came to my assistance, his face expanding in a cheerful grin as he recognized the opportunity of battle, and three or four others draped themselves around his form. The sound of the struggle did not at once get outside. The Tewa began to thresh out with his arms and let his voice be heard. An employee peered inside and set up a shout. Then in plunged several very earnest fellows in uniform, and out went the protestants, scrambling, dragging, and hitting the door jambs. The Tewa followed to see that these things were properly managed, he being the local and ranking officer in such affairs. I remained behind to counsel against this attitude, but did not remain long enough, for on going outside the house I spoiled a little comedy.

Sackaletztewa, the head man, a sinewy fellow of about fifty years, when unceremoniously booted forth, had challenged the Tewa policeman to mortal combat. He declaimed that no Indian policeman could whip him. The soldiers had greeted this as the first worthy incident of a very dull campaign.

"You have on a Washington uniform and wear guns," said Sackaletztewa, "But without them you are not a match for me. If you did not have those things, I would show you how a real Hopi fights."

Now this Tewa always rejoiced in a chance for battle. The fact that no one at Hotevilla had been arrested had filled him with gloom. Unbuckling his belt and guns, he handed them to the nearest trooper; then he promptly shucked himself out of his uniform. Twenty or thirty of the soldiers made a ring, their rifles extended from hand to hand, and into this arena Nelson was conducting Sackaletztewa for the beating of his life. It was a pity to issue an injunction. If I had remained only five minutes longer in the house, those patient soldiers would have had something for their pains, and the grudge of the Indian police, who had suffered in esteem at Chimopovi five years earlier, would have been wiped from the slate.

Sackaletztewa was a good man physically; he had courage; but he was a Hopi, and knew nothing of striking blows with his fists. He would have relied on the ancient grapple method of combat, and the proficient art of scalptearing. Perhaps he would have tried to jerk Nelson's ears off by dragging at his turquoise earrings. He would have scratched and gouged, and, if fortunate enough to get a twist in the neckerchief, would have choked his man to a finish. All this is permitted by the desert Indian rules of the game. But unless Nelson had been tied to a post, he would have accomplished none of these things; for the first rush would have carried him against a terrific right smash, accompanied by a wicked left hook. Behind these two taps would have lunged one hundred and sixty pounds of pure muscle. And a very bewildered Hopi would have spent the remainder of the day holding a damaged head, and wondering how he would manage a flint-corn diet without his teeth.

That night, blaming myself for the necessary interference, I joined Colonel Scott at the Agency.

Now you will please not strive to conjure up a harrowing scene of terrified children, removed from their parents, lonely and unconsoled. They were not babies. They were nude, and hungry, and covered with vermin, and most of them afflicted with trachoma, a very unpleasant and messy disease. Some of them had attended this Cañon school in the past, that time before their parents' last defiance, and they knew what was in store for them — baths, good food, warm clothing, clean beds and blankets, entertainment and music, the care of kindly people. There would be no more packing of firewood and water up steep mesa-trails, and living for weeks at a time on flint corn, beans, and decaying melons. There would be meat, — not cut from hapless burros, — and excellent bread of wheat flour, gingerbread even; and toys and candy at that wonderful time the Bohannas call Christmas. There would be games for both boys and girls, and no one at this school would interfere with their innocent Indian pleasures. Their parents would visit them, and bring piki bread — and the parents very promptly availed themselves of the privilege.

So there was nothing of exile or punishment involved in this matter; and if you have any true regard for childhood and defenceless children, there will be seen a great deal of protection and happiness in it. I fancy that many of the girls — especially those who had reached that age when the maternal uncles, the ogres of the family, assign them in marriage and as the old men pleased — had been counting the days since the first news of the troop's coming.

It was a busy time for the corps of school employees when the wagons arrived. Seventy-two children had to be recovered from the dirt and vermin that had accumulated during their long holiday. The less said about this the better; but I would have been amused to see the critics at the job of hair-cutting!

Those children spent four years at the Cañon school, and without vacations. When the school departments were closed in 1915, because certain buildings showed weaknesses and I feared their collapse, the Hotevilla children, having reached eighteen years, might decide for themselves whether or not they wished further education. With few exceptions, they elected to attend the Phœnix

A HOPI YOUTH WHO IS PREPARING
FOR COLLEGE
His ambition is to be a physician

A HOPI SCHOOLGIRL
This same girl is shown in native dress
opposite page 358

Indian school. They had no wish to visit Hotevilla, and very frankly told me so. To illustrate their standpoint, Youkeoma's granddaughter, an orphan, was not of age so to elect. She feared that I would consult the old man about the matter, and she knew that he would insist upon her return to the pueblo life. So she secreted herself in one of the wagons that would carry the older pupils to the railroad, and went away without my knowledge.

I had advised against the immediate recall of the troop of soldiers, and had expected that a sergeant's squad would remain for some months to return runaways and to preserve discipline among those who might risk the power of my army of three policemen. It was not improbable that a band of Hotevillans would come to the Cañon to demand their children, once the soldiers were withdrawn. They had staged this play before, and in 1913 certain Navajo did not hesitate to make off with pupils. But trouble on the Border called. It was then I sought the Colonel's counsel. For a time he evaded a direct statement of his views, but I was insistent, and he said: —

"I would never permit an Indian to remove his child from the school against my orders to the contrary. They would find me sitting on the dormitory steps. Other methods of prevention you must devise for yourself."

He concluded with the words I have quoted before: "Young man! you have an empire to control. Either rule it, or pack your trunk."

Very early the next morning the troop departed. There was a light fall of snow, to be followed by more and more, until the stark Cañon cliffs were frozen and white in the drifts. The little campaign in the hills had closed just in time.

Twice thereafter Colonel Scott, accompanied by the

cavalry, came to the Desert; once to pacify the truculent Navajo at Beautiful Mountain, after they had threatened the San Juan Agency at Shiprock, New Mexico, and once to quiet the Ute on our northern borders. But the Moqui Reservation was left entirely to my ruling. The Department read the Colonel's report through a reducing glass, and gave me eight policemen instead of the twenty he advised. With these and a few determined employees I contrived to have peace and order within the Hopi-Navajo country — not always easily or pleasantly, but without actual war. And I did not pack the proverbial trunk until the latter part of 1919, eight years later, when ordered to take charge of the Pueblo Indians of New Mexico.

XV

AN ECHO OF THE DAWN-MEN

"According to the law of the Medes and Persians." — *Daniel*, vi, 12

THE sending of a small army to one's home, and the imposing of rigid Governmental regulations, would seem to be sufficient to give any rebel pause. But not so You-keoma. He stood faithfully by the traditions; and unfortunately for him, the traditions obstructed or became entangled with everything that a white official proposed for the best interests of his community. No doubt the old man had been amazed, and I think somewhat disappointed, when he was not sent away as a prisoner. He could have made capital of another entry in an already lengthy record as a political martyr. But he did not propose to soften in consideration of this amnesty. He very likely thought it an exhibition of the white man's weakness, and gave his ancient oracles the credit.

Nothing was heard of him until the next early summer, when came time for the dipping of sheep on the range. The Hotevilla flocks were the poorest of all the Hopi stock, which is saying a good deal, since the Hopi is a disgraceful shepherd at any pueblo. But whatever their condition, the head man of Hotevilla did not intend to recognize the sanitary live-stock regulations issued by the peculiar Bohannas. They paid no attention to the Indian crier who announced the order, and they did not move their sheep toward the vats. It was necessary to send police, hire herders, drive the animals to the dip about twenty-five miles from their village, and return them to the sullen owners. Naturally, in such a movement, there are losses. Youkeoma came to the Agency, at the head of a delegation, to file protest against this action and to present claims for damages. He came modestly clad in one garment, a union suit, and without other indication of his rank.

During the hearing a few of the Hotevilla children came in to greet their relatives. It was a satisfied little group of clean and well-fed youngsters, having no resemblance to the filthy, trachomatous urchins we had gathered at the pueblo.

"Your people's children are happy here," said a clerk.

Youkeoma looked at the girls in their fresh frocks, and noticed their well-dressed hair, which had not been weeded with a Hopi broom.

"They should be dirty like the sheep," he answered, "as dirty as I am. That is the old Hopi way."

His claims for damage were disallowed, and for much angry disputing he spent a few days in the jail; then, very much to my surprise, he promised that he would not counsel resistance to future Governmental orders.

"I will attend to my affairs hereafter," he agreed. "For myself, I do not promise to obey Washington; but the people may choose for themselves which way to go — with me, or with Washington."

This was all that was asked of him, and he departed.

A year passed without incident. When the pupils were not returned in vacation time, the parents filed regular complaints. They very truthfully admitted that, were their requests granted, they had no intention of permitting the children to return, so it seemed best to deny them.

And now the other children of the village were growing up. At the time of the first gathering, only those above ten years of age were taken; and given a few years among the Hopi, without epidemic, children spring up and expand like weeds. A census was taken, not without acrid dispute and a few blows, which showed that the pueblo held about one hundred children of age to attend primary grades. So I proposed to build a complete school-plant close to their homes. This was another terrible blow to the traditions.

When selecting a site, great care was taken not to appropriate tillable land or to invade fields. The school stands on a rock-ledge. For a water-supply it was necessary to develop an old spring, one that the Hopi had long since abandoned and lost. It is the only Hopi school on the top of a mesa, and the children do not have to use dangerous trails.

The villagers watched us very suspiciously as we surveyed the lines for seven buildings, and they respected the flags marking the site-limits. But when materials and workmen arrived, and the buildings began to go up, they uttered a violent protest.

"We do not wish to see a white man's roof from our pueblo!"

They declared that all such buildings would be burned. Guards were necessary whenever the workmen left the camp. The school was built, however, and the smaller children rounded up and into it. Two dozen men managed what had required a troop of cavalry; but do not think that we approached it in a spirit of indifference. The town held about one hundred husky men, and one never knew what might happen. Once again I had to crawl through the corn-cellars of the place.

The old Chief was not to the front, and his body-guard of elders was conspicuous by its absence. Great credit was given them for keeping their word. I flattered myself that the contentious Hopi spirit and the backbone of rebellion had cracked together. But he was simply waiting for a more propitious date, in strict accord with prophecy, perhaps. The fire in the kiva had not burned with a flame of promise; the cornmeal had not fallen in a certain sign; the auguries were not auspicious. A little later and these things must have strengthened him, for one night he appeared at the door of the field matron's quarters, accompanied by his cohort, the whole band evidencing an angry mood.

"It is time," he said, wrathfully. "You have been here long enough. We will not drive you away to-night, but in the morning do not let us find you here. There will be trouble, and we may have to cut off your head."

The field matron was alarmed, but she did not leave as directed. She waited until they had gone away, and then slipped across the half-cleared desert space to the school principal's home. He promptly saddled a horse and came into the Agency that night. There were no telephones across the Desert then. Next day he returned with definite instructions.

It is not wise to permit Indians of an isolated place to indulge themselves in temper of this kind. One bluff succeeds another, until finally a mistake in handling causes a flare-up that is not easy to control, and one is not thanked in Washington for fiascos. I have pointed out how quickly Washington moves itself to aid when there is revolt.

A capable field-matron or field-nurse is a good angel among such people. She supplements daily the work of the visiting physician, dispensing simple remedies according to his direction; she is foster-mother to the little children of the camps and to the girls who return from the

schools. All social ills have her attention. She maintains
a bathhouse and laundry for the village people, and a
sewing-room for the women. In times of epidemic, these
field matrons perform extraordinary labors, and have been
like soldiers when facing contagious disease. With one
other, Miss Mary Y. Rodger at the First Mesa, Miss
Abbott of Hotevilla ranked as the best in the Service; and
having ordered her to remain on that station, I determined
that she should live at the pueblo of Hotevilla in peace,
if every one of the ten-thousand sacred traditions reaching
straight back to the Underworld went by the board.

It is necessary first to catch your rabbit.

Whenever wanted and diligently sought for, Youkeoma
was somewhere else, and an unknown somewhere. While
it was said that he and the other old men spent their time
in the kivas, I had failed to find them there. Like the coyote that scents gun-oil, he smelt business from afar; and
this time it was business, and I wanted him.

Summoning the Indian police, I dispatched them under
two white officers to attend a Navajo dance in a distant
cañon, forty miles east of the Agency. Hotevilla was
directly west from the Agency and about the same distance removed. Having placed eighty miles between my
police and the scene of action, I informed my office force
that I intended visiting the railroad town on business.
This would take me eighty miles to the south. Others of
the white men were sent to work at different range
points. No one suspected a Hotevilla mission. We went
our several ways.

But I did not go to the railroad town. A messenger,
sent from the Desert, recalled the two officers and the
Indian police from the Navajo encampment and, going
roundabout the trails, they joined me at the Indian Wells

trading-post on the south line of the Reserve. After dark on the second night we hiked across the southern Desert, avoiding all Indian camps and settlements, to reach the Second Mesa about midnight. There we halted for a pot of coffee, and rested an hour or two. Then on again, crossing the Second Mesa in the wee sma' hours, we avoided alarming Oraibi, that always suspicious pueblo. The rangemen were collected from their different stations. In the black, before the stars had begun to pale, we arrived at Hotevilla and, without disturbing a soul, strung out around the town.

With the first streak of red in the east, the Hopi became aware that strangers were present. A perfect bedlam of noise arose. It seemed that thousands of dogs came into vociferous action, and made the morning ring with their challenges. But no man got out of the place.

We found our slippery friend Youkeoma and his supporters. They were taken to the school and identified as those who had threatened the matron. And once again the wagons started for the Agency guardhouse. This time friend Youkeoma joined our Cañon community permanently, for I had no idea of releasing him while in charge of the post. This occurred in the summer of 1916 and he remained at the Agency until the autumn of 1919.

He did not complain. In fact he seemed quite contented in his quarters. He was not imprisoned in the sense of being locked-up, but was given the work of mess-cook for the other prisoners. This in no way offended his dignity. The more able of the men were required to work at odd jobs — the cutting of weeds, the herding of sheep, the tilling of small fields, and an occasional bit of road-mending.

Life as prisoners was not very irksome for these old

men. The guardhouse was very like their home kiva. Instead of cold stone benches, they slept on good beds; for rabbit-skin quilts and sheepskins, they had good blankets; and in place of a central smoky fire there was an excellent egg-shaped stove. Aside from being clean, with walls freshly painted and floors scrubbed, it was very like their kiva indeed. No one disturbed them in it. I fancy their discussions were the same, and the ceremonies conducted according to the calendar. Certainly they occupied themselves in weaving belts and other talismanic articles.

And as prisoners they developed fully some very peculiar tastes. Required to bathe regularly, they came to like soap and water very much. I recall the first time Youkeoma found himself under a shower. He had soap and towels, things considered entirely unessential at home, and he looked for a tub and water. Suddenly the ceiling opened and the water came down from Lodore. He was scared speechless at first, and then began chattering as if this were some rare form of white man's magic. And he liked it!

They received new clothing, sufficient for the different seasons, but they would refuse to don these garments until ordered to do so by Moungwi. A clerk would make the issue from commissary, and would succeed in getting them to pack the articles to the guardhouse. Next morning they would appear in their old rags. When a solemn Governmental pronunciamento was hurled at them, something smacking of excommunication, the traditions were satisfied, and forthwith they would array themselves.

They very diligently prepared and sowed certain fields — small patches of corn, beans, and melons, such as they used at home. They weeded and cultivated and watched the plants, until told that the harvest would be theirs to supplement the guardhouse ration of staples. They refused to work at once. It was against the traditions. They would not willingly raise a crop, to accept it as a reward from Washington. Their work must be wholly in the nature of punishment.

"So be it," I said, washing my hands of them; and they continued working those fields faithfully, once they knew that others would possess the fruits thereof.

One by one, the men were released for good conduct, until only Youkeoma remained. I told him plainly that he would not return to foment trouble until I was relieved of authority. Often in the long, drowsy, summer afternoons I would talk with him. He would sit on my porch-floor, hugging his knees in his skinny arms, and amaze me by his observations.

"You see," he would say, "I am doing this as much for you as for my own people. Suppose I should not protest your orders — suppose I should willingly accept the ways of the Bohannas. Immediately the Great Snake would turn over, and the Sea would rush in, and we would all be drowned. You too. I am therefore protecting *you*."

He stated such things as an infallible prophet. There was no malice in the old chap, and I did not bear him any grudge for his pertinent reflections.

"Yes; I shall go home sometime. I am not unhappy here, for I am an old man, little use, and my chief work is ceremonies. But I shall go back sometime. Washington may send another Agent to replace you, or you may return to your own people, as all men do. Or you may be dismissed by the Government. Those things have happened before. White men come to the Desert, and white men leave the Desert; but the Hopi, who came up from the Underworld, remain. You have been here a long time now

— seven winters — much longer than the others. And, too — you may die."

He had many probable strings to his bow of the future. I had to admit the soundness of his remarks, but I did not relish his last sentence. There was a little too much of hope in it.

And it came to pass that I was sent to another post. My last official act as a Moungwi was the dismissing of Youkeoma. Our differences would not affect the success of a newcomer. We shook hands this time, pleasantly, and he smiled. I asked him for no promises, and preached him no sermon. He departed down the Cañon afoot, for his hike of forty-odd miles. Quite likely he would stop that night with his married daughter at the settlement of the Five Houses, a Christian family, and the next night with Sackaletztewa on the Chimopovi cliffs. He was too old to make the journey in true Hopi fashion, jogging tirelessly. I venture that he did not visit his hereditary rival, Tewaquaptewa, at the original stronghold of his people — Oraibi had slipped too far from the traditions. But I would like to have witnessed his entry into Hote-villa in the sunset, a tired old man, but steadfast in spirit and unconquered, and to have heard the talk at that first all-night conference of the ancients in the kiva.

In 1921 I visited the Agency; and lo! he was in the guardhouse again. He was squatted on the floor, sifting a pan of flour for the prison-mess, his old trade. He looked up, to recognize me with a whimsical, not unwelcoming smile.

"Hello!" he said, "You back?"

When I saw him last, he was talking to Major-General Hugh L. Scott, who had spent ten days listening to him ten years before. Youkeoma was again reciting the legend of the Hopi people. Many things had happened in those wild and unreasonable ten years. The world had suffered discord and upheaval; merciless war had lived abroad and bitter pestilence at home. Nations had quite lost identity, and individuals had become as chaff blown to bits in the terrible winds. Scott had heard the great guns roar out across Flanders. Nearly everything had changed except the Desert — and Youkeoma.

He was the same unwavering fanatic, "something nearly complete," a gnome-like creature that would have better fitted dim times in the cavern cities of the Utah border, where his cliff-dwelling forbears built and defended Beta-takin, and Scaffold House, and the Swallow's Nest. In those wild days of the Dawn he would have been an evil power; but now he was simply a belated prophet without honor in his own country, one who had set his face against progress, and whose medicine had failed. Quite lonely too, for most of his followers had drifted from him.

But miserable and impotent as he seemed, and perverted as he proved, we somehow admire steadfastness of purpose and the driving will that does not flinch under adversity. This Youkeoma of Hotevilla was not malicious. He was simply a deluded old savage, possessed by the witches and katchinas of his clan, living in a lost world of fable. A Ghost-and-Bird chief. The last of the Hopi caciques. A faint echo of the Desert Dawn-Men.

XVI

FIDDLES AND DRUMS

For you and I are past our dancing days. — Romeo and Juliet.

HAVING had charge of the Hopi for a longer period than any other official of the United States Government, — eight years and two months, to be exact, — I venture to picture them and their empire. To have visited and counseled with them, to have wrangled with them, to have traveled long distances in all sorts of weather because of their childish factional quarrels; to have arrested and judged and disciplined them; even married them, — if that may be separately classed, — to have cared for them in severe illnesses and advised in times of stress; to have ransomed them from enemies; to have espoused their uninteresting cause in the face of Departmental opposition; and when their meagre business of living was over to have buried them — well, this ought to embrace an angle of vision.

Yet, I hesitate. Reflection cautions me that this may be presumption; for, after all, what do I know of the Hopi Indians?

During those eight long years I met on the reservation thousands of visitors — students and their mentors; painters and etchers and sculptors of distinction, and those who thought they were; photographers and lens-artists; ethnologists, philologists, and sociologists; ballyhoo men from Eastern department-stores and half-wits taking an outing; journalists and authors and publishers; geologists and common "water-witches"; motion-picture men and others wearing puttees; actors and lecturers; composers, musicians, and vocalists; museum scouts and "scratchers"; clergymen and soldiers; Oxford men, Harvard men, men from Bonn; retired statesmen and unretiring politicians; representatives of foreign governments; persons from the far-famed city of New York; tourists, and caparisoned dudes, and simple guides; plain gentlemen and plainer roughnecks.

Some of them sought me out courteously to explain their missions, some of them just happened to see me *en passant*, and a few earnestly avoided me. The permit system was very irksome to those who did not have a good excuse. And I listened to many theories concerning the Hopi and their curious customs, and I made a brave effort to answer in some pleasant manner ten thousand questions. Finally, I prepared a plea in avoidance: —

"Don't ask me. I have lived here only six years. Ask the chap camped now at the trader's post — he came last week."

I plagiarized this method from a brother superintendent who knew much of the Navajo and their rare designs in weaving.

"Now, my dear Mr. Shelton," the tourist would ask hopefully, "Does n't that sign indicate the rabbit-foot following the lightning?"

"Make up your own story," he would gravely reply, "and then you won't forget it."

So with Hopi secrets. The little of their history that is known I have already related. The rest is speculation. The believed facts of their ethnology may be had in Smithsonian Reports, moisture proof, dessicated. The bones of their ceremonies have been diagrammed and painted,

their chants recorded in scaled notebooks, their odd ceremonial objects looted and catalogued. Sentimental word-
pictures one can procure from those journalists who flitted
rapidly in and out seeking impressions, and who never
failed to get them.

But I am not one whit more ignorant than any other
white man. Despite reams of theories, no one has learned
anything of Hopi lore that the Hopi did not want him to
know. "Make up your own story, and you won't forget
it." When certain Christianized worthies of the tribe
have pretended to expose their knowledge, I have paid
little attention, since I knew the mental calibre of such
fellows before conversion, and the depth of their gray matter was never impressive. The last who gave evidence
proceeded well in his story until, with a foreign fervor, he
began to lie about the Oraibi happenings within my own
time, and as I had taken his testimony under oath in
Hopi trials, I knew just how many Bibles to trust him on.

Moreover, being the recognized Moungwi or Chief of
the Hopi, and having some instinctive conception of the
manner in which an alien and suspicious people should be
governed, I respected their privacy and reticence, to gain
and hold their own respect. One cannot play with an
Indian in the morning, and expect to summon him to
judgment after noon. The poorest stick of an Indian Agent
I have seen is he whom Indians address by his first name,
or familiarly without a title. When one lowers himself
to an alien's social level, he seldom achieves more than the
privilege of dipping his food out of the same dish. It was
my job to manage all things for their best interests, against
their strenuous efforts otherwise if that were necessary —
as it often was; and I hoped to restore to them a confidence
in white men, whereas they had come to believe that all

white men were a mixture of abnormal curiosity and treachery, coupled with an astounding rudeness.

As for their psychology, no itinerant will ever grasp the subtlety of these people. It is something elemental and therefore indescribable. Those who have lived among Asiatics will know what I mean. Fatalists, they are as patient and immutable as the Pleiades. Much of this is vanishing with the elders as they wend their ways from the mesa stages to the Great Place of Ceremonies that Youkeoma has told me of. The pastoral peace and solemnity of the desert shrines is passing before the roar of motors and the harangues of "dude wranglers."

Now I remember a curious red-haired visitor who came into the Agency one drowsy afternoon, herding a squad of burros. He looked a figure from a Conrad novel, and would have graced any one of them. His animals were packed with matting hampers having an Oriental touch. His flaming head was bare to the summer sun, his worn and rusty boots of cordovan preceded war-time styles and spoke of long journeys. The seat was absent from his trousers. An astonishing man.

His first question of me was: "Who is the new French Premier?"

It just happened that I could tell him. He handed me his credentials, and I found that this dilapidated tramp represented the French Government in his wanderings after strange cacti and other plant life. He strewed the contents of his hampers over my quarters and forgot to sort the wreckage for a week. Meantime — in my bath — he was analyzing Hopi corn and rare Indian dyes.

And he related to me strange things. He had been to Lhasa with the Younghusband expedition. He said that the Hopi were duplicates of the Tibetans, and that he

believed the languages contained similarities. That fellow
knew how to reach the heart of a secretive people. He
had procured seventeen distinct varieties of Hopi corn,
and other seed, as well as old dye-formulæ and samples
of ceremonial cotton.

"Zey call me, ze man wi' ze burros," he said, naïvely.

You see, he had walked in on their level, prodding his
patient beasts, covered with the desert dust, a wondrous
simplicity on his face. He had touched the Hopi heart.
He could have told one things of the Hopi people — but
the opening guns of the Great War summoned him away
to die at Verdun.

> Know ye the trail that the Salt bands go?
> Close by the Rock where they carved their names?
> Know ye the hills of the Navajo
> And the barren sands that the Hopi claims?
> Dim in the cañons of the dead,
> Where the towns are dust and the last scalp dried,
> Their swords are rust, and the desert crow
> Scarce can tell where the Spaniard died.
> Slain at Zuni and Cañon de Chelly,[1]
> By the Mesa Black and at Santa Fe;
> One of them killed by a Pecos clown,
> One of them dropped by Walpi town.
> — *Song of the Spanish Bell*

The Hopi live in northern Arizona, surrounded by the
reservations of the Navajo. They speak a Shoshonian
dialect, and are often miscalled Moqui. The Department
for forty years libeled them under this misnomer. Moqui
is a Hopi term, and has been used against them by Navajo
to signify anything inert, unpleasant, cowardly, dead.
The dignified Navajo has another distinct title for the

[1] Pronounced *Shay*

Hopi, and uses it when filled with courtesy. Moqui is probably a Keresan word originally, since it is found as "motsi" in Cochiti and San Felipe pueblos of the Rio Grande, whose warriors and rebels fled to the Hopi country for sanctuary after the rebellion of 1680.

Near the centre of that huge space on the Arizona map marked "Moqui Reserve" are the Hopi towns. These were known to the Spanish conquistadores as the Seven Cities of Tusayan. There are now nine pueblos.

In that early hour of geologic time when the receding waters carved the great gorges in the face of northern Arizona, the more resistant sandstones and clays and coals were left as shattered cliffs, and from these reach out many bony headlands — long fingers, at the crumbling tips of which, like villages clinging to a rocky coast, are the eyries of the Hopi. Below them, as sea-floors, are the sandy valleys and drifting dunes of the Painted Desert.

These nine little towns are set oddly in groups of three, and so are the Hopi divided, quite as into three distinct provinces. Three are balanced on the narrow backbone of the First Mesa, a knife-like projection that rises hundreds of feet above the valley, and is at one place not more than twenty feet in width. These are old Walpi, beloved of etchers, and Tewa of the warriors, and Sitchumnovi. Three are built on the broad mounds of the Second Mesa, known as Machongnovi, Chepaulovi, and Chimopovi. And perhaps the oldest and certainly the youngest of the villages are at Third Mesa — Oraibi, the aged; and tiny Bacabi; and redolent, sullen Hotevilla.

Their first contact with white men was made in the dark of an autumn night in 1540, but it was in the next dawn that they realized invasion by a new and strange enemy. Most of Hopi history has the dawn atmosphere. Their

THE WALPI HEADLAND, SEEN FROM THE
DESERT ORCHARDS

footprints lead back to the caves of the Dawn Men. Their homes face the rising sun from the highest point of the landscape; their ceremonies and hunts begin at sunrise. They are a dawn-loving people.

Contact with the Spaniards was broken by the revolt of 1680, and completely ceased with 1700; but the gifts of the enemy remained in fruits, and wool, and beasts of burden, and perhaps some loot of swords and Church vessels hidden to this day. The obstinate Hopi were not worth the effort at reconquest, and later the Mexican Government did not bother them. For more than one hundred and fifty years the Hopi knew only the Navajo and Apache and Ute as his enemies. With the close of the Mexican War and the treaty of 1848, this nearly forgotten tribe came under the nominal guardianship of the United States. I say nominal, for their first Agent was located in far-distant Santa Fe, and unlike the Spanish, he had no missioners to risk martyrdom for the spreading of his doctrine. In 1849 he accompanied an expedition against the Navajo, and reached Cañon de Chelly, about sixty miles from the First Mesa. One year later a delegation of Hopi visited this chief to petition for protection against the Navajo. I fancy them plodding afoot, behind their burros, timidly crossing the Navajo country to pass through the provinces of their kinsmen, the Pueblos, and on to the City of the Holy Faith. In that same year, 1850, their Agent was prevented from visiting them, as he wished, *because he lacked an escort of troops.*

Many estimates of the Hopi population were made in the early years. The Spaniard was an expert at overestimating for the benefit of distant kings. His thousands were always given as tens of thousands, and when he wanted money and help toward new colonies he stressed the saving of souls and could easily imagine millions of baptisms. But it is recorded in 1780 that smallpox had reduced the Hopi to less than 800. In 1899 their first resident Agent stopped guessing and made a count. He found and listed 1832 Hopi. In one hundred and nineteen years the population had little more than doubled. In 1912 there were 2068 on the Reserve, and in the next seven years they gained 217, or 31 per year — 15 per thousand annually. They lost nearly sixty per cent of this seven-years' gain in 1918, the year of Spanish influenza. In 1919 there were 2158 Hopi on the Reserve, and adding the absent, who had increased and multiplied in the west, at Moencopi, there were less than 2500 of these Indians alive. But this handful has interested more distinguished men and women than have many greater nations.

While there is much of Hebraic resemblance in the Navajo Indians, — their pastoral life and their religious customs, — a matter that strikes every thinking visitor and student, there is more of this in Hopi history. Their retreat southward from the cavern villages, from Betatakin Cave, from the Swallows' Nest and Scaffold House — stopping to build a hamlet here and to reap a harvest there, leaving always testimony in potsherds and corn refuse — to their present cliffs, was much the same as the migrations of the Jews. Perhaps, having lost one citadel, they moved on to the next best position for defense; or perhaps a remnant of a once-powerful tribe fled; for we do not clearly know whether these cliff-dwellers migrated from choice, or to escape pestilence, or to avoid captivity. Across the relatively narrow territory of their hegira the Navajo and Apache — the once-combined "Apaches du Navaju" — and perhaps the Ute fought and harried, the Hopi quite as helpless as Judæa between Egypt and

Babylonia. When they retired finally to such a place as old Walpi, to barricade the narrow causeway at the mesa-end and to defend the Walpi stairway, just wide enough for one enemy at a time, surely this was a desperate people making a last desperate stand. I have no doubt that the Hopi, peaceful as they have been and are named, fought some worthy fights before the white man was known on this continent. The determination that wore down the Spaniard must have had its martial quality when facing enemies armed no better than themselves. It required a brave war-party to attempt to storm those mesa strong-holds. And their foes must have stood somewhat in awe too of Hopi incantations, made so impressive by their Snake legends and solemn mummery. The Snake gods protected them more than once, according to their priests, and are remembered in the ceremonies.

And the resemblance is not only in fanciful surmises. The daily life of the people duplicates in many ways the customs of the Judæans. A people of legends and portents. In the quiet nights they have watched those burning signals of the heavens that mark wars and the birth of kings. Perhaps their shepherds too have been summoned by such signs, inspiring them to missions and pilgrimages, bearing gifts, relating to that mythical Bohanna who will one day come to redeem and revivify the people. From the great chart of the heavens they take their calendar. And certainly, in the sunsets of that quiet and ever-tinted land their pueblos reflect the Old East, with its donkeys and goat-bells, and simple gardens by the springs, and the blurring dust of sheep in the half-tones of desert twilights.

Government reports of to-day give the unqualified fact (?) that the Hopi have a reservation of 3863 square miles, large enough, in all sense, for twenty-five hundred people! But the Hopi exist on and use less than one fifth of this semi-arid land, the remainder being held and dominated by their old plague, the Navajo. The Hopi Indian Agent has absolute jurisdiction — on paper — over all those Navajo living within the boundaries of the Hopi Reserve; but this does not mean that he is or ever has been able to control that undisciplined element of Navajo who pillage the peaceful Hopi whenever in the mood. Many bitter and scathing reports have been sent to Washington concerning this. Agents have not minced words, and have not always spared themselves in an effort to get justice — well, let us say, "consideration" for the Hopi. When reports failed to procure attention, one or two started crusades against the Navajo, not always successful, that ended in blows and bruises, to say nothing of the chance of sterner wounds. A difficult task to find the offender; if found, he was invariably supported by a gang — his gang. I recall one investigator who stated blandly that it was similar to conditions often found in cities: that of a corner gang. Quite so. But the investigator did not ask to see the corner, nor did he evidence any anxiety to encounter the gang.

The nomadic Navajo have a vast country to make themselves scarce in, quite 30,000 square miles of wilderness, much of it untracked; there is no quick communication between the six Agencies established to govern these people. It has been possible to coördinate business methods, so as to have uniform stock-regulations, for instance; but nothing has been arranged to guarantee the peace. There have been numerous murders in Navajo country. Representatives of the Board of Indian Commissioners, particularly Major-General Hugh L. Scott, and inspectors of the Indian Department have fired verbal volleys in support of Hopi Agents. Navajo have been dragged to the Agency guardhouse, and other Navajo have been haled before the Federal Courts when the Agent could arrange locally all the details of the haling. A one-time United States Marshal, charged with the duty of assisting, remained conspicuous by his absence from the scene. The matter finally attracted the attention of a sub-Committee of Congress, and brought about a field investigation of Hopi conditions, pictured in a printed report. I know that the report was complete, for I wrote it; in fact, I had prepared that report in 1918, and placed it before Congress two years prior to the appearance of the sub-Committee. The gentlemen graciously inserted it as a tailpiece to their otherwise innocuous comments.

But the wall of political indifference to anything that does not furnish a vote has not been dented. It is a mere matter between obscure tribes, a squabble in the hills, which occasionally embarrasses an Indian Agent and constantly annoys a helpless people who have no other court of appeal. Neither tribe nor Agent can threaten a politician. Both tribe and Agent are kept mute by an uncaring Bureau.

Announce, however, that these same Hopi Indians are wont to dance with live rattlesnakes! Ah! that is a different story, and received with different emotions. The politician rushes in to view the spectacle. The Bureau sheds crocodile tears about it. Reams of reports are called for and written. During the past twelve years the Hopi Snake Dance has troubled the Solons of the Interior Department far more than any signal of Hopi distress. The Christian ire of three administrations has been aroused by this primitive pagan ceremony. Result: the Hopi Snake Dance is as well advertised as the Grand Cañon of the Colorado!

Most picturesque of the Hopi towns is Walpi. You can procure a fine appreciation of this, the effect of standing on the roof of the last Walpi house and viewing the entire First Mesa therefrom, the narrow rugged top and the deep valleys on either side, the trail down to Polacca, the whole vast sweep of that distant and beautiful landscape — simply by visiting the New York Museum of Natural History. The artists have constructed a wonderful reproduction of that Enchanted Empire citadel. My friend of various wild spots in Indian country, Mr. Howard McCormick, magically brought the charm of the Hopi eyrie to the edge of Central Park.

I recall a particularly drab day in New York, one of those having a wintry edge that comes only off great waters, when I wandered into the Museum, seeking this exhibit. I had anticipated something of the usual order — papier-maché, plaster, dust, and a ticket; but behold! I found myself at home, on the mesa-top, below me the First Mesa and the Wepo Valleys; and to my right would be Huh-kwat-we, the Terrace of the Winds, and in the dim distance Moits-o-ve, or Yucca Point. I felt that in a moment I should surely see Harry Shupula, the chief Snake priest, emerging from his kiva; and half aloud I addressed one of the group as "Quat-che" (friend). And at the foot of the winding trail, a little beyond the spring, would be the camp of the water-witch and a desert welcome — such a welcome as "Mac" and wandering Indian Agents receive. A great feeling of *Heimweh* came over me. I wished for a magic carpet, that I might step instantly from the lonely desert of New York into crowded, speaking Hopi-land.

I remember a conversation with a clergyman from Canada, as we stood at the inner edge of the crowd on the

THE WALPI STAIRWAY, A ROCK-LADDER TO
THE SKY

Walpi Snake Dance ledge, passing that bit of ominous wait just before the entrance of the Antelope priests for the annual ceremony. That is the time when the Hopi Indian Agent meets most celebrities and makes most of his enemies. Some words passed concerning the picturesqueness of old Walpi, and the magnificent view from our position. The plain below was bathed in a lemon light.

"Yes," I said, casually, "the people would be better off in the valley, if we could get them to remove."

"What!" he cried out in pain and direst astonishment. "Would you have them leave this beautiful place — this beautiful life!"

I had uttered sacrilege. No Hopi of the old school could have bettered the clergyman's utter horror at the thought. But the gentleman, I am sure, gave little attention to many things an Agent sees that are not beautiful, things of distinct menace, hideous things. Walpi is a scenic place, a ruined castle in outline, and always steeped in color effects; but there is the dangerous ledge-road up which all supplies and wood and water must be packed, a road that has accounted for more than one Hopi when the brake would not hold. And did he not forget that women did much of the packing on their backs? And the old and blind, who had plunged over the sheer face of the cliff? And above all, the constant danger of the filth-infested houses, where trachoma and tuberculosis abide? These are things that a tourist does not notice, and when he is away from the color effects and the sound of drumming chants, they do not impinge on his vacant — his vacation mind.

Destroy Walpi as a picture? No. But as a human habitation, Yes!

I recall a visit to the Indian Office at Washington shortly after one of my characteristic reports on this very subject.

"What!" said a Bureau chief who, because he signed a great many letters daily without reading them, believed himself intelligent. "You recommended dynamiting the First Mesa — the destruction of that oasis of beauty, and peace, and — and — "

"And trachoma, and tuberculosis, and child prostitution," I finished for him, as he gasped and his words failed, as I knew they would. Words always fail a Bureau chief. Like the long-range gun of the Germans, he is accustomed to firing things across the continent, secure in that the other fellow cannot immediately crash his words back into his teeth.

I had not recommended that. I had simply advocated the destruction of the road leading to Walpi, since the Government and its Bureau Chief would not advance sufficient moneys to make the road safe for travel.

That is the viewpoint of tourist and bureaucrat, — the artist has one of pure sentimentality, — of all those who have viewed the Hopi, who have been charmed by the color of his life, but who have been utterly blind to his miseries, and who have contributed nothing to his well-being.

No one has a keener appreciation than I of the artistic value of the Hopi pueblos — those old streets of worn rock where the bearded Spanish walked; the curious archways and the irregular little balconies from which children peer over at one; the thought of phantom Mission bells from the peach orchards. But I was not stupid enough to over-look that these same streets contained offal, that the houses were not ventilated, and that there were various unseemly stenches in the air. A tourist must leave his olfactory organs at home. And I knew, being in charge, that all the labor of industrious and conscientious field-matrons was not enough to keep those quaint streets and courtyards clean.

I remember another visitor at another Snake Dance, a man sitting on the parapet of a Hopi kiva, looking down through the ladder entrance. I saw that a number of dancers were below there, preparing costumes. They had an array of skins and masks and feathers, with many cans of bright paints.

"I suppose you know a good bit about that too?" I asked.

"Well, I recognize some of the signs, common to Indian people."

"Shall we go down? You can give them a hand," I suggested.

"I should like to, very much; but — won't they object?"

"Perhaps I can arrange that," and I started down the ladder. Several of the Indians glanced up, but, observing it was only Moungwi, said nothing.

"Here!" I called to them. "Here is a real friend of yours. You may not know him, but he understands many tribes, and their ways, and their signs. Put him to work. He can help with those costumes."

One looked up from a robe he was painting, and thrust forward a brush and paints, as if to say: "Welcome, brother; fall to!"

The white visitor showed a rare facility. The Indians noticed it.

"You know him?" asked one, pointing to a design.

"Yes," he said, naming it.

They laughed delightedly, and soon he was friend to them all. I left him in the kiva, busily working with them and chatting as much as possible with a limited vocabulary and many descriptive gestures. This was Ernest Thompson Seton. I have not seen him since, but afterward he forwarded a letter, thanking me for his entrée to the wardrobe-room of the First Mesa, and giving some excellent advice concerning the things we had discussed before he signed on as costume-painter for the Hopi tribe. Among all the visitors I met in Hopiland, he was one of very few who sensed the things that should be done and those not done for their welfare. Briefly, his idea was that the community life should not be violently disrupted, for fear of the effect our own isolated rural populations had suffered; and that efforts should be made to keep alive all that is best in the social and mesa-plan of living, without permitting the Indian people narrowly to confine themselves to it. This of course would include the harmless dances or shows, the social features that many confuse with ceremonies. I could recall the earnest efforts made by former Agents to induce the people to leave the mesa heights — notably that one beginning in 1891, when houses were built for them in the flats, and later completely furnished. By 1900 at least one hundred such houses had been placed at Hopi disposal. And I knew that in 1911 not more than half of those houses were used even temporarily. The people would return for the society of their kind, drawn, too, by intense religious feeling for the ancient mesa home.

I could recall two abortive efforts made toward the allotment of these people in severalty: the scheme to have them accept parcels of land, many of which were miles from water, and on which it would have been impossible for families to subsist themselves, to say nothing of maintaining their sheep and other stock. The first of these allotment plans blew up in 1894; but the Bureau, wedded to the allotment theory, was not deterred. A second and most expensive effort died in 1911, after friends of the Indian plainly showed the farce of the proceedings, if they said nothing as to the inhuman side of it. This did not please the allotting agent, eager for his pay and job, nor his son, nor his assistants, nor the camp cook and the other hangers-on of an allotting crew. But thank God! it died, nevertheless.

The average bureaucrat, admiring the Allotment Acts, thinks that an Indian's head may be jammed into a regulation lathe, and with a few twists and spins turned out a full-fledged Mid-west agriculturist — just such a man as Thompson Seton said needed community centres made for him, to keep him from becoming an inmate of an insane asylum. Just so. But it cannot be done, my masters, with the speed of the mimeograph that grinds out your tirades and exhortations. Your Allotment Acts have been good friends to South Dakotans and others who wished to speculate in lands; but they have produced untold misery among the Indian peoples, and have utterly destroyed an innocent and simple phase of American life.

Now I never agreed with the ecclesiastical gentleman who thought that the Hopi mesa system was wholly one of beauty and idealism. But the writing man did force on me a realization of the utility and sanity to be found in the life that the Hopi had unconsciously adopted. Begun as a defense against enemies, the result in peace times was for good, if accompanied by sanitation and the protection of the younger generation. And I accepted a new view of the Indian ceremony and dance.

Until we furnish something as good in place of the Indian social dance, why rave about it? We might easily have a large number of low-spirited, sullen, and even dangerous Indians on our hands if it were not for these joyous occasions. So long as the dances are clean, can any one quarrel with a Ya-be-chai of the Navajo, a Corn Dance of the Hopi, or one of the Pueblo spectacles, half pagan, half Catholic? I have seen scores of such dances, not as a tourist, but as the man on the ground in charge, and I have not been able to figure out that they are one bit worse than a country picnic among our own bucolic population of Texas or South Dakota, for instance. I have seen a South Dakota Rotary Club cut as many fool antics as a Southwest Indian clan.

I recall an illustration from my very short stay among the Sioux in 1922. It was the Fourth of July, and I had permitted the old Indians to hold their dance on the hills. It had long been the custom to stop their merrymaking at sunset, and a very good ruling too. But this Fourth was unusually quiet, the booze-runners not having appeared as per schedule. The Indians petitioned me to permit just a little dancing after nightfall. It had been very quiet, and my special police force was large enough, and seemed loyal enough, to assure good order.

"All right," I said. "But please remember that I shall have a squad of police there, and I shall be there myself; so don't start any shines."

They had a very creditable evening party, and the peace was not broken. Later I visited the Agency amusement hall where a number of whites, visitors from the countryside and more than one mixed-blood couple of education, were enjoying themselves to the latest jazz. Now I am no authority on dancing and, having lived among Indians,

I am not easily shocked; but the postures and attitudes of those South Dakota whites were — well, a trifle extreme, to say the least of it.

"We have looked at them both," said an old Sioux to me, anxiously. "Au-tay-ah-pe (Father), there may be something wrong with the Indian's drum dance, but — *I do not like the white man's fiddle dance.*"

I told him very frankly which I thought the worse. There is no use in trying to bluff an old Indian. He can see through a hypocrite quicker than any man I know.

This is not a sentimentalist defence of the old Indian dance. I have bitterly excoriated the "secret" dances of the Pueblo Indians of New Mexico, but could never get sufficient backing from the Department to end them. Such indecencies may be found among all primitive peoples, and those of the Pueblos who indulge in them are most primitive — the barbarians of San Felipe, Santo Domingo, and other decadent backward pueblos. But I have tried to envision the social side of an alien people who have no other form of diversion than the spectacle of the dance. Were the Government to put them on a moving-picture circuit — but we were discussing the decencies.

And, to repeat: When we have established among them an amusement as appealing, simple, and inoffensive, it will be time for the condemnation of those features that are innocuous and foreign. And it will be long before I shall forget the comparison, by an Indian, between the dance of the Sioux with drums and sleighbells, a noisy soul-stirring hullabaloo, and — the seductive, suggestive "white man's fiddle dance."

XVII

SERVICE TRADITION

When first, as an employee of the Government, I answered the grave salutation of the red man, the buffalo roamed at will over the great plains of the Sioux country; the iron horse had not crossed the Minnesota boundary; the dull, plodding ox was the courier and herald of the culture that was stowed in embryo in the prairie schooner; Chicago was just beginning to throw off its swaddling-clothes under a blanket of smoke; St. Paul was the frontier to the Northwest ... and that was only a generation ago. — McLAUGHLIN: *My Friend, the Indian*

THE work of this reservation was that of a frontier. Until the late nineties, army officers, acting as agents, had administered affairs from Fort Defiance, distant about eighty-five miles from the First Mesa of the Hopi. The country between these points is rough, and in winter often impassable. The commanding officer did not make the two days' journey frequently, and when he did, entertainment at trading-posts would occupy most of his time. There were no other local stations. Until 1887 no official of this Government resided permanently within the Hopi territory; so that, from Spanish times until that date, these Indians had received little attention.

In 1886 a petition, signed by twenty Hopi head-men, requested Washington to give them a school, that their children might "grow up good of heart and pure of breath." But one of these men, Honani of Chimopovi, always a friendly chief, is now alive. Shupula, who signed as Second Chief of the Moki, died, a benign old man, in 1917.

So in 1887 a school was started in Keams Cañon, at the site of one of Carson's old camps, a picturesque alcove of the walls having a group of springs, and where Tom Keams, a trading Englishman, had long kept a post. Twelve years later a resident Agent, having authority to act as one in complete charge, was appointed.

Between the years 1890 and 1916, sub-Agents and the later Agents accomplished much permanent work for the people. The first school was succeeded by a modern training school in the lower Cañon. An Agency radiated orders and the tools of civilization. In the field at the pueblos were six day-schools to care for the younger children. Five hundred pupils attended regularly. The Indian youngsters advanced from the kindergarten and primary day-schools to the training school, where they received some knowledge of trades, and from thence to the larger non-reservation schools, patterned after Carlisle, such as are at Albuquerque, New Mexico; Phœnix, Arizona; Riverside, California.

But not only in point of education had there been progress. Tracks of the reserve had become roads, as the Indians were supplied wagons and implements; and ascending the rocky mesas, linking the different villages, were highways that had been cut from the solid rock, and that, considering the means and cost, were fair pieces of engineering. The Agents had built and enlarged the schools, and had opened mines to supply the winter fuel. The live stock of both tribes — for the Navajo came to this Agency — showed improvement. A most important advance had been made in medication. Three physicians attended the several districts. Trachoma had been greatly reduced. There was no longer the dread of uncontrolled epidemics, such as that one of smallpox that nearly wiped out the Hopi in 1780. And after 1913 a well-appointed hospital received the serious cases, especially those requiring surgical treatment. Between 1911 and 1919 vaccines were freely used to combat smallpox, typhoid, tetanus, pneumonia, and influenza. The Pasteur treatment was given. Surgery, minor and major, was a matter of routine, and with low mortality.

Whereas in 1900 the first Agent had but twenty-one employees, in 1915 there were above one hundred serving the various activities of the Empire. A force of water-development men, locally known as "witches," had greatly augmented the water-supply to the pueblos and their stock, through enlarging mesa-springs and the drilling of shallow wells in the washes. The supreme water-witch of the Empire, Mr. A. H. Womack, in later years discovered artesian flows. And by far the most of this work was accomplished after 1910.

But of troubles there had been no end. It not only was necessary to conquer frontier handicaps, — the distance from supplies, the bitter winters that blighted transportation, and the frequent changes of a restless and dissatisfied employee-force, — but was also necessary to fight the superstition and not always negative resistance of a fanatical and unreasoning people. Five times between 1899 and 1911 troops were sent to this reserve to quell disturbances or to enforce Governmental regulations.

One of the great reasons for Indian unrest had been that few Agents remained in charge long enough to influence the people. It requires at least four years of patient work to know the Hopi, to gain his confidence, if indeed one ever gets it. And in the thirty-two years after 1887 there were eleven different officers in charge. Prior to 1911, the longest period of service had been a little more than four years. Men quit or were transferred before they had made a beginning. Twenty years of the time were divided among nine officials, little more than two years for each, scarcely long enough to learn the country and its divisions. I recall some lonely years in the Desert, when the Cañon walls seemed a prison, but I am now glad to write that I directed its Hopi-Navajo population for more than eight years, twice the time of any other Governmental officer.

Of those who had the early work, there were two who exerted a strong personal influence: Mr. Ralph Collins, who was twice appointed a sub-Agent, and Mr. Charles E. Burton, who was the first Indian Agent. Collins had not complete authority, and his efforts were not always supported, but much of suspicion among the Hopi could have been avoided if he had been listened to. Burton, having carried out certain fool orders, was hounded by sentimentalists during most of his service. But both these men accomplished things for the Hopi people, and are kindly remembered among the elders. Their improvements have not entirely disappeared, and wherever one finds an English-speaking Hopi of middle age, the credit may be given to one of these men.

But in 1911 two things had not been finished, and one important thing was only vaguely planned. There was no fixed policy for the development of the reserve, and no one had succeeded in breaking the power of Youkeoma, that hostile witch-doctor who had made trouble since 1887. One could not hope to succeed without the first, and the success of the first depended largely on the second. The health work had been sporadic, and was ineffective without a hospital. My predecessor had procured an allotment of eight thousand dollars with which to construct one, whereas thirty thousand — considering Service methods — would not have been too large a sum.

I felt that a consistent policy of control was vitally necessary; that the country and the people in it, both whites and Indians, must be brought under strict regulation; that Youkeoma's influence must be broken; and I proposed to use the eight thousand dollars, plus whatever additional sum I could talk out of Washington, plus the resources of the reserve in cheap labor, stone, sand, and equipment, mixed with something approximating brains, to have a hospital that would be a benefit to the Indians and a credit to the Service, which too often has constructed buildings that were neither.

Regulation and control required only horse-sense and a little vision. Resolution and earnestness, accompanied by justice and fair-dealing, make a combination that few Indians can resist. The man who fails in the Southwest Indian country is the one who ignores his people's conception of fair play, and who forgets to keep his word. There have been white men among the Hopi-Navajo who, unmindful of their own two thousand years of background, proposed to correct everything in an afternoon. Discovered in 1540, brought under supervision in the recent eighties, it was and is too big a job for an afternoon.

And why not view with sympathetic consideration the problems of the Indian who, having little education and no vote, being practically as inarticulate as a deaf-mute, childish and incompetent, must trust someone, and is inclined to trust the only official he knows?

Why not be a decent Indian Agent, out of respect for one's self?

There are relatively few people who know that the United States Indian Service has a history, a tradition as it were, to be honored and lived up to. Few men in the service have the lively curiosity and interest in their charges that is necessary for success among primitive peoples, few who rise above personal prejudice, who can resist feeble enmity. There have been the early-day McLaughlins, Sheltons, and Carrolls, each of whom built himself a Service name by one efficient means or another; but those men have been in the minority.

Now the Army officer has a tradition, and the Naval officer has one. Why ought not other Government officials to view their commissions on as high a plane? Should a reader interpose to mention "scandals" — why, to be sure; there have been many; but they have not destroyed the Indian, and they have not ruined the Service. All Departments of the Government have had scandals of greater or less degree. There was a certain Arnold, an army officer of very high rank; but we need not go back so far. There was enough doing in the year of grace, nineteen hundred and twenty-four, and enough is sometimes too much. There have been timber scandals, and land scandals, and oil scandals, as the wealth of the Indian country has been exploited. And there is the scandal — or should be — of manipulation of individual Indian moneys. And the scandal of keeping inefficients in office. And some Indian Agents have gone to jail, and some should be there, accompanied by those who have protected them. All true, and granted. Nevertheless, the body of them have an honorable tradition as old as the United States itself.

In 1786, in the Articles of Confederation, consideration was given to Indian affairs. Two superintendents were provided for, who had the "comprehension" of all nations of Indians south of the Ohio River and all west of the Hudson. Their exact "comprehension" was no doubt much smaller than their outlined territories.

The Federal Constitution of 1788 deemed it important that the Central Government should have exclusive power over intercourse with Indian tribes. The Supreme Court of the United States later amplified this to include everything that may arise out of our relations with the Indians.

Congress in 1789 appropriated the first moneys to defray expenses of negotiating and treating with the Indians. While the Commissioners were referred to as "agents," their authorities did not extend beyond treating with the native.

George Washington, in a letter dated August 29, 1789, instructed Messrs. Benjamin Lincoln, Cyrus Griffin, and David Humphrey as "commissioners plenipotentiary for negotiating and concluding treaties of peace with the independent tribes or nations of Indians within the limits of the United States south of the Ohio River." This commission made a report to the Secretary of War, and from its suggestions grew the licensed-trader system, although the first traders acted as factors, and to some extent as agents, for the tribes with which they were affiliated.

Congress in 1790 provided a method for trading with the Indian tribes under license, but no Indian Agents would appear to have been authorized, as such, by law prior to 1796, when were established the trading-houses on the western and southern frontiers, or in the Indian country, and the appointment of men to manage them under the direction of the President.

The factors were the first real Agents for routine Indian business. This was the first experiment. The law limited it to two years, but its life was extended from time to time until 1822, when the system of Government trading-houses was abolished.

Acts of 1800, 1802, and 1806 provided for other experiments; and after 1806 there were actually four types of Indian officials:

1. Governors of the various Territories, who were ex-officio superintendents of Indian Affairs within their jurisdictions.

2. Certain Agents who were primarily under the direction of these Governors.

3. A Superintendent of Indian Trade.

4. The Factors under his direction.

When in 1819 and 1820 Congress provided for the employment of persons to educate the Indians, the appointment of Agents to specific tribes began.

When the trading-house system expired in 1822, the factors disappeared. Indian trade is conducted to-day by licensed traders, who are under bond, and expected to live within Indian country.

In 1824 the Secretary of War, without authority, organized a Bureau of Indian Affairs, probably to ease his main office of details; and eight years later the President was authorized by Congress to appoint a Commissioner of Indian Affairs.

The Act of 1834 conferred upon the officers of Indian country the authorities they invoke to-day with respect to control of the native and those who may seek to oppress him. This Act did not apply to the Territories of Oregon, Utah, and New Mexico. The Agents for the Pueblo Indians of New Mexico were handicapped in their work until 1913, when the Supreme Court of the United States clarified that situation by the Sandoval decision.

In the early days, army officers were designated to

perform the duties of Indian Agents, and the Indians were brought under strict military rule; and this, taken in connection with the imperative language of the laws enacted, tended further to increase the powers of the Agent.

By an Act of 1847, directing distribution of annuities and treaty goods, most Indians were brought to a condition of complete dependence on the central Government. If prior thereto they had enjoyed any civil liberty, the fragment was taken from them. Many looked to the guardian even for food, and when the guardian was aware of him — most Southwest groups were outside this soup-kitchen zone — it was provided. And then came opportunity to those who made a scandal of the "ration" days, and presented Robert Louis Stevenson and other brilliant sentimentalists with a slur from which the honest Indian Agent has suffered. Wherever the Government had cognizance of an Indian, he was a child without rights other than those his Agent permitted him to enjoy. As late as 1922, acting as a Sioux Agent, and being overwhelmed a thousand times daily by the emasculated title of Major, I signed many permits allowing old warriors to leave the so-called Reservation — it was really a sanctuary for whites — for trading- and visiting-trips, a long-obsolete bit of red tape that the vanquished one still recognized. I could not very well have prevented his going without a permit, but as he saw fit to believe in the old system, I signed the papers cheerfully. At least those older majors of the army had instilled into the elder Sioux a respect and obedience, without destroying their pride or confidence.

In 1849 the Department of the Interior was organized, and it was authorized to have supervisory and appellate powers in Indian Affairs theretofore exercised by the Secretary of War. The Secretary of the Interior became head of the Indian Department, the Commissioner of Indian Affairs acting under him.

The local control of reservations remained quite the same. Native police were authorized in 1878, but the Agent continued to be sole judge of the guilt or innocence of Indians charged with offenses. In 1883 the Courts of Indian Offenses were devised, an idealistic experiment, no doubt originating in the far East. It was hoped to encourage the Indian somehow to discipline himself. But it has proved farcical, and when used at all is a mere instrument in the hands of the Agent. During the past fourteen years I have had charge of four Indian reserves: the "Moqui," — now correctly named Hopi, — where are many Navajo; the Pueblo; the Crow Creek Sioux; and the Colorado River Mohave; these extended into five states, comprising a total population of 14,000 Indians of six different tribes and many local divisions; and among all these natives I have found but one Indian having the requisite intelligence and unprejudiced standpoint to warrant his presiding as a Judge of the Indian Court. It would be unfair not to name this man. He is Pablo Abeita, of the Isleta tribe of Tihua — Pueblo — Indians in New Mexico. And after years of loyalty to his honored Agents (not all of them were honored) he has reaped as his reward tribal enemies, and political and civil ones. The one man who proved the value of the experiment was made the goat. Such are the fruits of idealism, preserved by new leaders who come staggering under many inventions for the benefit of Poor Lo.

These historical facts have been briefed from an article entitled "The Evolution of the Indian Agent," written by the late Kenneth F. Murchison, one-time Chief Law

Clerk for the Office of Indian Affairs, and printed in the Commissioner's Annual Report for 1892. The writer closed with this significant statement:

The Indian Agent now has almost absolute power in the Indian country, and so far as the people over whom he rules are concerned, he has none to contest his power. Appointed at first in the capacity of a commercial agent or consul of the United States in the country of an alien people, the Indian Agent, under laws enacted and regulations promulgated, has developed into an officer with power to direct the affairs of the Indians and to transact their business in all details and in all relations.

This is a very curious chapter in our history. There is a striking contrast between "ministers plenipotentiary" appointed by the United States to treat with powerful Indian nations, and an army officer, with troops at his command, installed over a tribe of Indians to maintain among them an absolute military despotism. Yet our policy of dealing with Indians has swung from one of these extremes to the other in a strangely vacillating way. Indeed at present (1892) the Agent among the Five Civilized Tribes performs rather the functions of a consul in a foreign nation than those of an agent . . . On the other hand, the absolute military rule finds its illustration in the present condition of things at San Carlos (Arizona) and in a modified way at Pine Ridge (South Dakota).

Now the superficially informed person will arise to declaim that this is ancient history. It is true this was written concerning conditions of and prior to 1892. But only recently were the troops removed from Fort Apache in the country adjacent to San Carlos; and very recently we have had cause to regret that the authorities of the Agent for the Five Civilized Tribes were ever revoked. The Indian Agent for the Pueblo Indians of New Mexico, considering their recognized forms of tribal government that the United States Courts have sustained, should perform the functions of a consul, plus all the duties of an Agent. It is difficult for the average appointee to perceive this subtle distinction.

And should the superficially informed person visit the Southwest and a closed Indian reservation, to witness the Snake Dance of the Hopi, for instance; to view one of the pageants of the Pueblo Indians of New Mexico; or to hunt on Apache grounds, — and always providing that such Indians have an Agent not afraid of his political shadow, he will find that the supervision and control of the Indians, and of the superficially informed person, is based on the authorities related, which have not been revoked, and which any Indian Agent may invoke at any time he thinks necessary. In Arizona the State Legislature has granted additional powers to Indian Agents, as the residents of this colossal State have no false ideas with respect to its Indian inhabitants, and wish them managed in the most efficacious way consistent with justice.

As instances, Arizona has these laws:

CIVIL CODE.

SECTION 3837: "All marriages of persons of Caucasian blood, or their descendants, with negroes, Mongolians or Indians, *and their descendants*, shall be null and void."

SECTION 3839: "All marriages valid by the laws of the place where contracted, shall be valid in this state; PROVIDED, that all marriages solemnized in any other state or country *by parties intending at the time* to reside in this state shall have the same legal consequences and effect as if solemnized in this state; parties residing in this state cannot evade any of the provisions of its laws as to marriage by going into another state or country for the solemnization of the marriage ceremony."

Arizona and its people have no desire for a population of half-breeds; and it is a pity that not all the sovereign States of the Union have been filled with an equal pride. There is one State where it has been found to be necessary to proscribe by law the usage of the term "squaw man." While the Agents of to-day have not the military with which to coerce obedience, they have, as Stevenson once wrote of dogs, a strong sense of their rightness and superior position in action. The moral authority is theirs, and the legal means has not been emasculated.

The Regulations for the Indian Service, dated 1904, and unamended in so far as control of closed reservations is concerned, were based very largely on the Act of 1834. Since these regulations were issued, the Indian Agents have been engulfed by 2000 additional rules, advices, warnings, sermons, and remonstrances; but no modification of law-and-order guides has been encountered; and these original regulations have been consistently sustained by the United States District Courts.

An Indian of the Enchanted Empire may be dealt with by his Agent as surely as were the Sioux of the '80's. I had occasion to revive the permit system for both whites and Indians, to supervise the conduct of whites within Indian country, to protect native ceremonies, ruins, and graves, to deport those visitors and Bolsheviks considered of no immediate benefit to the quiet Indian population, to arrest and arraign both Indians and whites for offenses, to sentence them, and to see that the sentence was respected.

Now mark you! This does not mean that every Indian

Agent is a functioning Agent. It may as well be said, frankly, so long as this is getting out of the family circle, that few Indian Agents perform their fully authorized duty when it is possible to intimidate them: a process often recognized by quavering superiors at Washington who hope to outlast a dying Administration.

But before coming to the field in 1910, I saw three Secretaries of the Interior steadfastly uphold these Regulations; and as an Indian Agent in the field I have been strongly supported by three other Secretaries of the Interior, to the end that my Indian charges, *until 1922*, were the best-protected people on earth.

XVIII

BUTTONS AND BONDS

And he sat down over against the treasury, and beheld how the multitude cast money into the treasury; and many that were rich cast in much. And there came a poor widow, and she cast in two mites, which make a farthing. — *Mark,* xii. 41, 42

I HAVE heard it said by old-timers, and they could very nearly prove their suspicions through comparison of customs and the dragging in of the Bible, that the Navajo are the Jews of the Desert, a lost tribe of Israel. And suffice it to say that the true son of David has never been able to prosper in their country. The closest approach of these wanderers to the Navajo has been an invasion by marriage of a certain part of the Pueblo Indian country in New Mexico. Those who once made the effort to penetrate the Hopi-Navajo area of the Enchanted Empire have withdrawn, defeated and outwitted.

But if this is the advantage that the Navajo as a trader has over his white brother, in what relation does the Hopi stand to the Navajo? I cast about me for a simile, and find none.

The desert post-trader welcomes the Navajo when he comes on a purchasing expedition, because the Navajo is a spender and makes for quick sales and large profits. It is when the Navajo is trading wool and blankets and silver junk for hard dollars that the post-trader peels his eye to the nerve, and then hopes he will not get skinned. But the Hopi is maddening as a buyer. It will take a Hopi longer to spend two bits than for a Navajo to squander a month's freight-earnings. An astute trader once described the Hopi method to me.

"You know," he said, as if in pain, "an Oraibi will come into my place, hungry. You can tell he is hungry by the look of him. Has n't had his breakfast. And he will have come to buy something to eat. And then he will stand before the canned-goods shelves, if I am not watching, and get a full meal by just looking at the labels. Yes sir! Seen it many a time — look at a can of pears and lick his lips until satisfied, then go out without changing a dime. Give me a Navajo every time."

This same trader at Oraibi — Charlie was murdered by the Navajo, for all his love of them as customers, — would praise the Hopi as bankers. He was located ninety miles from his headquarters and several hundred of miles from his bank. A trader must pay in cash or negotiable checks to Indians, according to the regulations, and on that reservation they had to do it. There was no "tin money," no trade tokens were used. Charlie would run short of cash.

"I can go to the door, and whistle," he declared, "and get a thousand dollars silver from the mesa."

The Hopi liked him, and trusted him, and once tried to protect him.

The bank the Hopi patronizes is his sand bank, or its equivalent — a hole in the wall of his stone house, cleverly concealed, a place under the hearth, or a sack in his corn-cellar.

It is seldom that the Hopi make presents. Curios have a potential value with the trading public, and the Hopi believes that the laborer is worthy of his hire. When they think well of one, likely they will wait until he is leaving

the country and then bear what is comparatively a price-
less gift, something different in basketry or pottery from
those hackneyed forms duplicated so often for the touring
invaders. Where the Sioux will impoverish himself in
feasting and gifting his friends, the Hopi regards brother-
hood on a different basis. But I have in mind to show
when the flood of his generosity was loosened.

The Great War opened, and later "Washington" was
involved. War is a lost art in the Desert, but old warriors
like to think of battles. The far-removed Indians were
interested in more ways than one. The registration of
them, a silly proceeding, caused not a little panic among
the unknowing. While Agents who knew law advised
that the non-competent and non-English-speaking ward
would not and could not be drafted, this made no difference to those who drew up the schedule. It caused more
than annoyance; it caused some little apprehension in the
Desert. Said Navajo chiefs to me: —

"You want soldiers for this war of Washington's? Very
well, we will select them, and then married men will not
be taken from their families, nor young men from helpless
parents. How many do you want?"

Was not their thought a trifle wise?

But it was not to be done that way. Little blue cards
had been printed, and the Indian Agent was nominated
registrar for all persons of his jurisdiction, whites and
Indians, including himself. The Navajo simply evaded;
but the Hopi lists were prepared, and so much time and
paper and little blue cards were wasted.

Some of the Hopi took an equally fantastic view of the
crisis. At Oraibi were located the Mennonite missionaries,
an earnest people, but many of them of German extrac-
tion. A Hopi delegation waited on them, saying: "In a

few days there will be war. Washington will be at war with Germany. You are Germans. You will be our enemies then, for we are supporting Washington. What will you do when Washington sends the order to kill you?"

This was no doubt a very discouraging vision to have before one.

The Hopi interest in war-time methods and inventions could always be aroused through the illustrations in the great dailies. My pictorial sections of the *New York Times* were in great demand. They would pore over them, remarking the vast number of soldiers, and would ask for many explanations. Men were flying as birds through the air, and carrying the war beneath the waters. They had seen locomotives and automobiles; and they could believe in the aeroplane and the submarine, because of white man's magic. But at wireless they balked.

"No!" said one old Indian, emphatically. "That is too much. The telephone — yes, I understand, for there is a wire, and the man's words go through that wire, inside — I see that. But now you tell me of a man talking from here to the mesa, twenty miles, without a wire? No — excuse me, but that is too much."

Then came the food regulations; and food in the Desert is a limited fare at best. The Indian menu is slim enough, and much of it in flour. He had no use for substitutes that the trader was compelled to have him purchase, and when his horses disdained cornmeal as fodder, the Navajo began to be aggrieved. He had offered to help Washington with his prowess, no mean gift, and he could not see how an empty stomach helped campaigns.

But came the first call for Indian help that could be accepted. A bazaar was advertised, to be held in Washington, the proceeds to finance a hospital unit. The Indians

were invited to contribute curios. Knowing Hopi thrifti-
ness, I did not feel that they would respond in great
measure. I sent out the call and waited. When lo! for a
time the sale of pottery to trading-posts ceased. My warehouse began to overflow with the donations. Hopi pottery
is fragile; does not ship well; and I felt that so generous a
response should have good packing for the journey of
twenty-six hundred miles to Washington. I know how
much they gave in clay products, for I personally packed
the major part of it. There was not time to ship by freight,
express gave no insurance against breakage, so it was forwarded by parcel post. There was a trifle of silverware; a
rug or two of Hopi weave; there were reed plaques, and
small baskets, and pottery, — bowls and trays and plates
and odd forms, — hundreds of pieces. A tenderly whimsical thought: the vision of some wounded lad finding
relief through an old Hopi woman's moulding and baking
clay figures, far from the hysteria of the cities, far from
the guns and stench of war, but contributing the one
thing she knew, while humming some chant, perhaps of
ancient battles.

Next came the bond sales.

Now there was a deal of press-shouting anent the millions invested by Indians in Liberty Bonds; and the Indians did invest millions in these securities. But an explanation throws an illuminating light on the Bureau's puffery.
Indian Agents, having Indian moneys in their control,
bought most of those bonds. There is nothing much to
shout over, or for that matter to weep over, — as a certain
Commissioner was wont to do when his emotions slipped,
—if an Agent calls in old Jimmie Crowfeet, and says to
him: "Jimmie, you have twenty thousand dollars to your
account, from the sale of your dead children's lands, the

leasing of your own and your wife's allotments, and the careful manner in which I have marketed your cattle. Now you will need but two thousand dollars to cover the next several years. I propose that you place the remainder of your money in Government bonds at four per cent. Savvy? You help Washington. Washington help you sometime mebbeso."

If Jimmie did not understand all at once, it was done for him anyway. In any case, it was done. The Bureau directed it. And that's that. A trifle different from the story pushed into the Sunday supplement.

But with the Hopi — the Hopi had no moneys in the hands of his Agent. The Hopi has not had lands for sale — thank God who made the Desert! and the Hopi has not had lands to lease, thank God who was stingy with the water. He sells his cattle for himself, and places the results down in that pocket which is his own.

It would have to be a selling campaign; and I had first to convince the Hopi, rude, unlettered, and suspicious always of documents, especially those of Government, that this green paper would prove the same as fifty or one hundred dollars in hard silver.

He knew of the country's need and danger. It was easy to explain that soldiers, armies, must have guns, ammunition, clothes, blankets, medicines, and grub. The Hopi has to have all of these himself, even on a peace footing. For him to propose to give curios, manufactures, even corn, his staff of life, was simple; but the Agent was asking for money, in lots of fifty, hundreds, and other multiples, the security being a piece of green paper that the Hopi could not read, that would be hard to safeguard from fire or theft, and that might prove only as good as some other promises of our slow-moving Uncle in the

East, who had often forgotten him and at least once betrayed him.

"What shall we do if hard times come, and we must have cash?"

I knew that a Hopi would never be able to grasp market conditions. Indeed, being of "the sticks," I had little idea myself that Government bonds would so quickly slump in value. It was necessary to convince and sell; and I held the confidence of these people to some degree.

"I will see to it that every man's bond is redeemed at face value, should he come to me in need. You will not have to wait for maturity. These bonds will not go begging."

And in some cases, I had it to do, regardless of the quotation. But these instances were few, and to the credit of the Hopi be it said that, once invested, the major part stood firm, treasuring their green papers, the first bank-accounts that many of them had ever owned.

It was at the Second Mesa that I held my first meeting, and a whole group of hold-tights and skeptical were swept into buying through the example of the poorest and most despised man of that district. They gathered at the council and asked many questions.

"But we are poor, and we have no money for bonds," they protested.

"I am not asking you for fifty dollars to-day, or to-morrow. I am asking you for one dollar, and the promise to pay out the balance in installments. When you have paid the full fifty dollars, with interest, I will deliver the bond to you."

"How can Washington sell a fifty-dollar paper for one dollar?"

"Washington will not. But I will go to the banks at the railroad, and borrow forty-nine dollars at interest for

OLD GLORY AND THE BOND
FLAG AT THE AGENCY

THE AUTHOR IN THE HEART OF
HIS ENCHANTED EMPIRE

each man who agrees to buy a bond. The bank will hold the bond as security until all your payments are made, and then deliver it."

They were dubious of that. Said one young fellow: "How can you borrow so much money? If twenty of us sign for bonds, and pay you one dollar each, you will have to borrow twenty times forty-nine dollars. Will the banks lend you that much?"

"With the bonds held as security, yes. Try it out."

On that basis I hoped to carry my district's quota; and as a matter of recorded fact I sold to one hundred and thirty Hopi Indians $11,600 in bonds, and for the whole reservation, including a few Navajo and many whites, $36,200 during the five bond-selling campaigns. I three times held the honor-flag for that county, competing with white men's towns, and my last honor-flag had three stars sewn to it, showing that the Hopi Reserve had sold three times its quota. It snapped in the breeze very proudly at the Agency, under Old Glory.

But these first prospects of the Second Mesa were holding back. If I failed here, there would be no use in going to other mesas. Indians are like sheep. The individual takes his politics from the mob. There was some suspense.

And then arose an old Hopi. His coat was ragged, and his hat battered. He had been a captive in Mexico, and spoke Spanish better than his native tongue. Perhaps he had drifted away in the early days, perhaps he had been taken prisoner in a Border foray, perhaps he had been one of those parted with at Corn Rock, *quien sabe?* He was a butt in the village because of his grand manner acquired among the Spanish people, and twice he had appealed to me for justice when the home folks were treating him unfairly.

"*Superintendente!*" he spoke out, "I will buy a bond."

There was a shout of laughter from the Indians. They knew that this poor fellow had no fifty dollars, that he did not possess a cash dollar. It was a joke; and Indian ridicule is cruel.

"All right, Wupa — come forward."

"*Señor Superintendente!* You will sell me a bond?"

"Yes, I will sell you a bond, as quickly as any one else."

"Upon the payment of a dollar?" he deliberated, gravely.

"That is right. You pay a dollar down, and I will give you a receipt for it; then I will borrow the rest for you, holding the bond as security until you have paid it out."

He looked around at his tormentors, as if to say: "You see, this man knows a Spanish gentleman when he meets one." All his Indian pride, plus all he had garnered from the Dons, was aroused. He came to the desk, while they continued to cry him down.

"Where's your dollar?" they asked mockingly. "You have n't any dollar!"

And I was much afraid he had not. A fluke would not do. It would mean losing the lot, and I knew there were many present who could afford to buy on payments and who would make good.

The old man grinned wisely.

"I will sign the paper for a bond," he said.

The blank was shoved forward to him. He daubed his right thumb on an ink-pad to make his thumb-print, the signature the Government accepts from Indians who cannot write. He pressed it down on the dotted line.

"Now where's your dollar, old father?" jeered the crowd.

Slowly he reached into his pocket, and drew out a rusty

jackknife. He looked all around him gravely, knowing, as a Spanish-Indian knows, that he and he only held the centre of the stage. And then, beginning at the top, he began to cut buttons from his old coat — Navajo silver buttons, coin of the Empire when in need. He placed them, one by one, on the desk before me, counting: "*Una — dos — tres —* "

They were worth fifteen, perhaps twenty cents each, as the desert market fluctuated. As he laid each button down, he looked at me to see if the dollar was completed.

"That is n't money," said one of the crowd.

"*Cinco —* " he counted, looking up.

"*Buena!* Lo-lo-mi! Write a receipt for one dollar, and mark Wupa down as having bought a bond."

"Thank you, Quat-che [friend]; you are the first man to help Washington."

We shook hands on it, and he was proud of himself. Turning, "You see — " he motioned to the crowd, and strutted back to his place. The others were now silent. In a manner of speaking, their bluff had been called; and by Wupa!

"Now who buys the second bond to help Washington?"

Those who had laughed and mocked the loudest were now quiet. They began to sway about, hesitating, looking from one to another, and then to come forward. In the next few minutes, twelve hundred dollars in Liberty Bonds were sold, most of them for spot cash. The old man from the border had "helped me out," as the Indians say, and when the selling was over I read them a mild lecture on making game of their first patriot. To my astonishment, several of them then offered to help him with a fence he was building all alone.

As I drove away, around by the Corn Rock, I heard a

shouting behind me. I pulled up, wondering what I had forgotten. It was the old man, coming down from his house on the height, bearing a bucket of peaches, the delicious Hopi peaches that are as a blessing of the Spanish padres. He put them into the auto and made a bow in the Latin style, hat sweeping, hand upon his breast.

I shall never forget old Wupa of the Second Mesa, a wanderer in strange lands, an alien at home, who bought the first Liberty Bond with buttons from his ragged coat.

At the First Mesa I expected more of attention, because they are the progressives of the Hopi, albeit they have progressed through being pushed. The First Mesa and its several settlements are but thirteen miles from the Agency headquarters, on the direct road to anywhere in the field, and so their people have received more of regular attention. The missionaries have made most progress there, and the Indians are fortunate in having had two field matrons assigned to that station. The first, Miss Sarah E. Abbott, who later faced down the Hotevilla, had proceeded to educate and influence them; and the second, Miss Mary Y. Rodger, has for the past fourteen years not only influenced and assisted them, but in large measure helped to direct them. They have also had the benefit of the Desert's chief water-witch, Mr. A. H. Womack, who has his office at their mesa, and who has greatly influenced and improved all the Indians of the Desert.

But in matters of purchase the thrifty Hopi, of whatever location, is inclined to pursue the label-tasting method. I found myself up against the same detailed explanations, although knowing that hundreds, perhaps thousands of dollars should be garnered there. Once again a patriotic Hopi came to my rescue. This was Tom

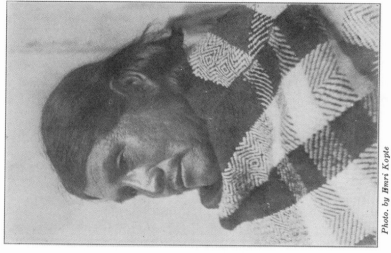

Photo. by Bmri Kopte

TOM PAVATEA: A HOPI MERCHANT
AND PATRIOT

ALBERT YAVA: INTERPRETER
FOR THE AGENCY

Pavatea, the full-blood Hopi merchant. Tom is one of those few Indians who have succeeded without the handicap of an education. Being a sensible man, he of course deplores the fact that he decamped as a child from the first school, and that a busy principal forgot him. Tom conducts an excellent store, carrying goods of standard quality, and his prices are not calculated on the altitude scale. Perhaps three-quarters of the Hopi trade in pottery is dispatched through his hands. He is fairly rich in livestock on the range, and has saved his money. Finance, however, troubles him at times, and I hope the last Western bank-crash has not caused him to suspect white men's accounting. Years ago he could not fathom the mystery of interest.

"Please explain," said Tom, quite perplexed, "Why should that bank pay me something for keeping my money? They have a strong steel box, and I get the service, and I should pay them for keeping my money safe."

Therefore I hope that he will never be deceived; because, on its being explained to him, he did not seem altogether easy in his mind. He had been rather of the opinion that his actual money always reposed in the vaults he had seen in the cities.

As to Liberty Bonds for the winning of the war, Tom had been solicited by an employee prior to my arrival.

"I'll match you buying bonds, when the boss comes."

"Match me?" inquired Tom, not grasping the idea.

"Yes — every dollar you spend, I'll match you."

"Dollar for dollar," said Tom, "one dollar, me; one dollar, you?"

"That's the game."

"Well," said Tommie, who always played as safely as he could, "I don't know these games; but you get your check-book ready."

He patiently waited through my talk to the curious but not over eager crowd, and then he came forward.

"This man, Leaming," he announced, indicating the employee, — a gentleman who has nominated himself in a number of campaigns for the mayoralty of Polacca, and invariably lost to the water-witch, — "this man wants to match me in buying bonds. I don't know about that. I have n't any cash to spare to-day, — but will you take him?" The "him" was a piece of paper. "If you take him, all right with me."

"Is Mr. Leaming to cover this purchase?" I asked.

"He tell me so. I buy — he matches me."

"That's my proposal," said Mr. Leaming, repressing a strong desire to view the figures on the slip.

"But, Tommie, this certificate of deposit will not mature for thirty days. Withdrawal at this time may cost you six months' interest, although I think I can arrange it that you will lose no interest. And another point — I am anxious to sell bonds, but this certificate bears interest at four and one-half per cent, and your bond will pay only four per cent. You may lose six months' interest, and you will surely lose one-half of one per cent interest each year."

"I know all that, lo-lo-mi," he answered; "Washington has a war, and needs the money. But you see that he covers it."

"Lo-lo-mi," I agreed heartily; "Mr. Leaming will please write his check for one thousand dollars, while Tommie endorses this certificate of deposit."

Two thousand in the first sale. It started them. The closest financial shark of all the Indians present hurried to his sand-bank and came back with four hundred dollars. And Leaming grinned a golden grin of relief when he produced his thousand to match the first sale.

"Tommie had me worried," the genial principal admitted. "I could meet him for several thousands, but Tom might have sold his herd of cattle, and I should have lost caste throughout the whole district."

Another evidence of Hopi thrift and credit is to be found in the "reimbursable" records. About 1914 the Government instituted a plan of loaning money to Indians, through their Agents, for the purchase of livestock, implements, seed, building-materials, and so on. I was not impressed with this plan, and to-day the Washington Office would like to have some one advise how to collect its outstanding reimbursables. The worthy charity provided many Indians with money without interest, and with practically no security assuring repayment. As an instance of this, the Mohave Indians found themselves embarrassed by these gifts, and in 1922 owed more than $34,000, they having had about forty thousand crowded on to them by a former superintendent. They had been crushed by debt for years. At least eighty-five per cent of the Mohave reimbursable was outstanding and delinquent, and with the best of fortune at least twenty per cent of it a total loss.

The always cautious Hopi approached this experiment gingerly. He is suspicious of Greeks bearing gifts. When he promises to pay, he expects to pay; and too, I did not rush forth, laden with money and generosity, to crowd them into debt. Between 1914 and 1915, my scruples having been argued away by a squad of non-visioning clerks who now wish that they had possessed a little less enthusiasm, I did advance $10,627 to the Hopi Indians. This money was placed in wagons, harness, and livestock. Within four years they had repaid seventy-five per cent

of the advance, and of the remainder it was estimated
that not more than $300 would be lost.

So the frontier work went on. We were building schools,
quarters, and a hospital; fighting dirt, disease, and superstition; improving livestock, and selling it, and washing
wool; experimenting with trees and plants; hawking bonds,
and lending money, and holding court; checking traders'
prices and guaranteeing Navajo blankets; policing Snake
Dances, trapping bootleggers, and offending tourists;
meantime struggling with the summer floods, and the
mud and quicksands afterward, and the winter drifts.
When the roads were destroyed, we somehow rebuilt
them — and then prepared to rebuild them again.

The Desert was a busy place. And when daylight failed,
I reported it all to an unappreciative, often snarling
Bureau, twenty-six hundred miles away, that understood
little and corrected less, while it asked senseless questions
that must be answered, made foolish decisions, and prepared for the field as many handicaps as distant ignorance
and lack of sympathy could contrive.

There were compensations, however. Drives along the
mesa ledges and across the wide vacant valleys gave time
for planning; and each excursion was an adventure. At
five miles the hour a sturdy team does not demand the
alertness that an auto compels at twenty. Traffic did not
bother one. Only an occasional flock of sheep, a straying
pony, or a somnolent freight-team blocked the road.
The drowsy hours of midday, filled with the humming
noises of the Desert, blessed by sunshine and the wondrous panorama of the Empire, could make up for many
frontier irritations.

Sometimes one caught vistas into forgotten ages. Far
away across the lower plain, as at the edge of a greenish

THE CORN ROCK: AN ANCIENT BARTERING-
PLACE OF THE INDIANS
A Second Mesa landmark, seen for miles across the Desert

sea, lifted those strange shapes, the Moqui Buttes. I had seen them frozen in a pallid sky; again half lost in the fog and swirls of dust-storms; and again as drifting mounds, with the one farthest west like a flat-headed Sphinx, touching the clouds; and always they had been somnolent headlands, half obscured. But one November day the sun burnt winter gold, and magic touched the Desert. It stretched a placid sea along their coast line of Parrish blue, that richest color of the fairies; and the many peaks were flat against a golden screen. Some lonely galley, heeling under old sails, was all it lacked; and I paused on the mesa-ledge to catch the sound of surf on enchanted beaches. The Coast of Romance! It would have ensnared that wanderer of the Greeks: —

> My purpose holds
> To sail beyond the sunset and the baths
> Of all the western stars, until I die;
> It may be that the gulfs will wash us down;
> It may be we shall touch the Happy Isles.

There they were, dreaming, awaiting a belated argosy of the years: the farthest Happy Isles, where — who knows? — in the days of the great waters, when the Desert floors were covered, some wily Ulysses may have landed and heard the songs of Circe.

XIX

OUR FRIENDS, THE TOURISTS

He expressed a particular enthusiasm with respect to visiting the wall of China. I catched it for the moment, and said I really believed I should go and see the wall of China had I not children, of whom it was my duty to take care.

"Sir, by so doing, you would do what would be of importance in raising your children to eminence. There would be a lustre reflected upon them from your spirit and curiosity. They would be at all times regarded as the children of a man who had gone to visit the wall of China." BOSWELL'S *Johnson*

THE Grand Cañon of the Colorado was once, in the minds of white men, an Indian fable. It exists to-day. It is now familiar ground. Getting there is an easy, quite luxurious journey, if one has the money. The Santa Fe Railway system has removed all the one-time misery and terror of the desert route to it. The hostile tribes, the sun and thirst that plagued Don Pedro de Tovar and Don Garcia Lopez de Cardenas in 1540, when given leave to discover what truth was in the Cibola stories, have been subdued by engineers and steam. Coronado's search for treasure cities and fabulous mines, for Quivira, ended in weariness, failure, disillusion; and his record in obscurity. Cardenas saw the Grand Cañon, while Tovar found something that should endear his name to the ubiquitous tourist. He located the Hopi Indians under their castellated cliffs. Now — had Tovar seen a Snake Dance! Although he arrived in August, that was denied him.

Thus a Wall of China was prepared in America nearly four centuries ago, and through "spirit and curiosity," male and female wearing pants, tourists seek it to-day. When the clans have all gone back to the Underworld, leaving their educated young to jazz and evangelists, the wall will retreat northward to the silent cavern-cities and the monuments of the Utah border, to Betatakin, and Kitsiel, and Inscription House. When a Service station desecrates the beautiful Laguna Cañon — the Tsegi — the wall will make a last stand at Rainbow Bridge — Nunashoshe — that great archway of the triumphant desert gods.

Tourists! Age does not wither them. I remember a very old lady, traveling alone. Alone she arrived on the mail-stage, obsessed by a mission, quite as Kim's lama. Having viewed one hundred miles of desert beauty from the mail car, she caught a little sleep, and then aroused me Sunday morning, quite early, with determined cries. Thinking that someone had been injured, I very nearly greeted her in pajamas, to learn that her search must be continued, and that it required an automobile or other conveyance. I referred her to the local trader, who also slept late of Sundays, and he sleepily turned her over to Ed. Ed told me of it later. He said that he "packed" her about sixty miles farther, hither and yon, around the Moqui cliffs and through the tinted valleys. She granted him not a croak of interest. And when he was thoroughly tired out, with the gas "about all," and the hour late enough to suggest a return to the post, she halted him with: —

"Now, my man, I've seen this, and it is very fine indeed; but — I came to see the Painted Desert."

"And we had been a-trompin' it all day!" said Ed.

Nor does their curiosity decay. I recall a party that

came upon us one evening, just at twilight. They erected tents, and stretched around them the fetish of a hair-rope, though no snake would have ventured near that camp for many gophers. Their cook banged his pan, and they came and "got it." The mail-stage pulled in late that season, and my miscellaneous collection of letters, newspapers, and books from everywhere would be dumped in the trader's private office, a combined place of business, art gallery, and Agent's rest. By the open fire I would dissect this mail, and reduce its bulk to ashes. But this night "dudes" filled the room and wrangled over a pile of Navajo blankets. An old man of the party pestered me with searching questions.

"Is this a good blanket — worth forty dollars?" he asked.

"Quite good. You may depend on Mr. Hubbell's prices."

"I would rather deal directly with the natives."

"May I advise you not to? The trader is regulated, the Indian is not. Many persons have lost their eyeteeth in a rug-deal with the Navajo. Besides, you have no guaranty from them. That blanket is guaranteed."

"And by whom?"

"By me, as Agent."

"But the Hopi, — or is it Moqui? — they are different. One of them offered to sell me a ceremonial altar at Oraibi."

"Sorry, sir; but you could not purchase it."

"Who would object?"

"I would, as Agent."

"And this prehistoric pottery I have seen — "

"It is recovered from graves, by Indians. It may not be sold or transported from the State."

"Who issued that order?"

"When the Office forgot it, I did, for this Reservation."

"Ah, yes — you are the Agent here. Now what are your authorities?"

"Well, one might say, the supervision of everything."

"Is that your mail — your official mail?"

"Yes, sir."

"You have many duties?"

"Quite a few."

"What is your salary?"

I dropped the letter of the Department that I had been trying to decipher between questions, arose calmly, and led the old gentleman aside.

"That," I said in a whisper, "is a State secret. There is an agreement between the War Department and the Interior Department, entered into just after the Navajo Treaty of 1868, and concurred in by every President since Andrew Johnson, that no Indian Agent of the Navajo country shall ever divulge the exact size of his reward. He may, with discretion, reduce the sum in speaking of it; but he may not under liability of extreme penalty, give out the true figures. It might encourage the native to revolt. You see my position?"

"Naturally," he said. He wiped his brow. He was simply overpowered. And he bothered me no more.

But Messrs. Weber and Fields' famous answer would have been more appropriate. "I'm ashamed to tell you."

And in early August come letters to the Agency. The queries are many and various.

"Please furnish the date of the Snake Dance."

"Will you send me a permit to Oskaloosa, Michigan?"

"Mail me a permit to the El Tovar, Grand Cañon, where I will meet my wife and see if she wants to come."
"Are moving pictures permitted, and if not, why not?"
"What are the rates at the Hopi hotels?"
"Is it good form to carry an umbrella in the Desert?"
"A Hopi woman sold me a loaf of bread in 1895. I want some of that bread this trip."
"Please reserve me a room and bath; I will arrive on the eighteenth."

All these should be answered, to the effect that the date of the dance will be given to the press as soon as known; that permits are issued when the permittee arrives; that there are no hotels; that the Agent can reserve nothing; that tourists should provide themselves with camping equipment and come prepared for rain. Does not the Snake Dance produce rain? The thunder mutters and the rain-clouds lower ominously, if no rain falls. There will be a drencher in the fortnight of the Snake Dance, one may be sure; and it often occurs so shortly thereafter as to cause one to wonder how the priests dope it out. In 1911 the storm broke just at the close of the ceremony. It broke immediately over me, as I perched on top of the Dance Plaza rock. That is an excellent place for an unobstructed view of the whole show, but it has an enormous — and unforeseen by me — disadvantage, in that one may wish to get down at a specific moment, as I did. And at that moment, the tribe's collection of snakes, scores of them, hissing, writhing, entangled, were thrown into the sacred-meal circle just below my dangling feet. I did not get down. I sat there in the rain, and soaked.

A slicker, or oiled-coat such as fishermen wear, is an important part of a desert outfit. It does not weigh much, it may prove useful in covering the hood of the engine

when bucking flooded washes, and it will certainly protect its owner after the Hopi prayer for rain. Pack one in
from the railroad towns; for while the desert traders carry
them, the demand is often heavy enough to exhaust stocks.
Like the Texan's gun, it may not be needed; but if needed,
it will be "wanted damn bad."

Comes also to the Agent a telegram from the Commissioner: HOPE YOU ARE DOING NOTHING TO ENCOURAGE
HOPI SNAKE DANCE — just that. Already advertising or
lurid press-stories have announced the date in Washington. The somnolent Bureau, that so often finds it inexpedient to administer justice, arouses itself and heaves
the telegram over three thousand miles. Never shall it
be said that the joys of the savage should receive sympathetic understanding. By no means permit them to be
happy in their way. Teach them to be happy in our way.
Encourage that broad spirit of charity we invite from
Kansas via the Civil Service examinations. But do these
things without hurting the native's feelings. Never act
so as to arouse or even risk antagonism. "Do nothing to
encourage the Snake Dance," but remember, if you have
an urge to discourage it, that we have not directed you to
do anything. We have simply expressed the hope that
you will successfully do nothing.

And the Agent, whoever he may be, has just finished
wrestling with the last of his fiscal-year accounts, closing
June thirtieth and requiring all of July to assemble. He
has signed 7863 papers of different colors and symbols,
all explaining his honesty. He has completed one thousand calculations forming the statistical section of his
Annual Report, long arrays of figures, giving the exact
value of each washtub, proving the altitude and longitude
of everything, from the number of sheep the Indians

devour in a year and why, to the number of tacks used in fixing the linoleum to his kitchen floor. He will have recently emerged from the impotent phrases of his narrative Report, a mandatory composition of past woes and future griefs, destined to fill an Eastern pigeonhole. These things are fetishes, thieves of time and destroyers of efficiency, worshiped by the Bureau as the documentary reason for its existence. Like prefaces, they are hopefully prepared, but seldom read, and certainly never acted on.

The Agent will pause long enough to sign a permit — a colored slip of paper printed over with regulations having a local significance. Read them; for he will not have time to read them to you. He has had them printed for a purpose — the purpose of relieving him of explanations.

Should the Agent appear a trifle acrid in manner, have patience. He may have just opened a batch of exceptions to his last year's accounts, rebuking him many times for intelligently carrying on the business of the Government, when absence of intelligence would have been much cheaper and approved. Or he may have received one of those Departmental questionnaires, calculated on the abacus of economy, and propounding solemnly something like this: —

It is noted that you mine coal, and request $3000 annually for the pay of miners. This seems beyond all reason. The Office has been informed on good authority that excellent bituminous coal may be purchased at five dollars the ton, f.o.b. Gallup, New Mexico. Would it not be advisable to purchase fuel in Gallup? You are directed to procure bids f.o.b. your station, and transmit them to the Office for consideration and comparison with your mining costs.

"Yes," you are startled to hear him comment aloud; "The advanced class in idiocy will now recite. Required: 2000 tons of coal, now mined within two miles of the bunkers, costing $1.50 per ton. Would it not be efficacious, not to say superb and miasmic, to purchase at Gallup, ship in cars one hundred miles to Holbrook, and thence haul eighty miles in wagons at one cent per pound cartage? Total cost, $27.00 per ton delivered, plus handling-losses and slackage. Ask me?"

But this inane query, signed by the Commissioner without reading, as he talked of the November elections with Congressman Grampus, must be answered. The record must be fixed in the mausoleum of files. The Agent will finally deny himself to Indians having real business requiring his attention, will neglect other duties, while he laboriously composes a fulsome answer, figuring the cost to five decimal places, and proving that $1.50 per ton in hand, supervised, is cheaper than $27.00 per ton on the road. He recommends — of course respectfully — that he be authorized to continue mining the coal God gave the Indians, until such time as the field may be leased to a syndicate; and then, with true official loyalty to those who arrange leases, to purchase from the syndicate, thus maintaining a perfect parity between whites who need money and Indians who do not need coal.

Before you harshly judge this desert pessimist, reflect a bit. He will be found sufficiently educated to issue you a permit. In the long nights of winter he has time for reading and reflection. The ignorance of the Desert is slowly disappearing before education; but no one has endowed a grammar school for the relief of those *you* place in Washington.

Classes in simple geography and numbers would help.

Each season more and more people come to view the Prayer for Rain. Not all are strangers. Many Navajo ride in from the ranges, tribal differences for the moment forgotten, just as they attend the fiestas of the Pueblo Indians in New Mexico; and the Hopi are equally hospitable with food and fruit at this their gala time. Many white guests repeat, year after year. Next to our trading friends, the Hubbells, father and son, who undoubtedly hold the record as to regular attendance, there is an engineer of the Indian Service who has viewed more Snake Dances than any other seriously engaged man. My own record is not insignificant. But this class is at home in the country, with business or duties or friendship to excuse it.

It is the sort of outing that true sons of Arizona enjoy. Carl Hayden, of Congress, has kept one eye on a Snake Dance and both ears open to Hopi conditions. Governors Hunt and Campbell have been found there repeatedly, and Governor Hunt has sought to preserve its record in pictures for the State Capitol at Phœnix and the museum of the University of Arizona at Tucson. In these men the Hopi have had good friends, and at least one Moungwi found them filled with understanding of the Desert and its peculiar conditions.

At Walpi one has a fit setting for a theatrical ceremony. Roosevelt wrote of it, "In all America there is no more strikingly picturesque sight."

The place of the dance is a narrow shelf at the very edge of the mesa. The houses of the people, tier on tier, terraced into little balconies, form a back-drop. Through these houses, and leading from the shelf, a tunnel gives on to another street. The ledge is simply a continuation of the rock roadway that skirts the brink of the village,

overhanging the wide First Mesa Valley. There is a sheer
drop from this edge, straight down at least sixty feet, to
the masses of shattered stone and drifted sand that but-
tress the mesa and shelve off hundreds of feet more into
the orchards. At each end of this shelf is an underground
kiva, marked by its projecting ladder-poles. A curiously
eroded rock seems to balance at one end of the little plaza,
between the houses and the precipice. Before Walpi was
evolved for purposes of defense, this rock existed. Probably it was because of this freak that the place was selected
for the rites of the tribe.

The ground-area available to spectators and dancers
measures about ninety feet in length and not more than
thirty in width. This approximate twenty-seven hundred
square feet must contain about forty Indian actors and a
large percentage of the mob, to say nothing of the snakes,
a most important and active feature of the meeting,
among which are many rattlers. It is like staging a nervous ballet on the cornice of the Woolworth Building,
knowing that fifty mice will be turned loose on signal.

The wisest of the visitors seek places on the balconies
and housetops; but not all of them can be accommodated
there. Many are forced, if they would see anything, to
stand on the ledge with the dancers. Dense groups mass
at each end of the plaza and along the house-walls, and
men and boys, white and red, stand four-deep on the outer
edge, facing the snakes, and with a death-drop behind
them. A tourist who would hesitate about hunting a
rattlesnake out of a bush will at this time develop courage
beyond all understanding.

When I first noted the possibility — the probability —
of accident at this unguarded mesa-brink, I proposed
stretching a stout rope along it as some small measure of

precaution; and I summoned the old Snake man to advise
him of its purpose. A rope there might easily have been
against the traditions, and I was new at the game of supervision. From the kiva came a nude figure and stood before
me in the sight of the multitude. The interpreter explained
my plan.

"I see," said the old man, nodding; "these people are
your friends, and you do not want them hurt."

Now I did not care to vouch for all those present, and so
corrected him.

"No, they are not my friends — not all of them; they
are people who travel about the country and come to see
your dance."

"Did n't you send them letters — write to them to
come?"

"No."

"Well," he concluded, "I did n't send for them. They
are no friends of mine. And you say they are not friends
of yours. Why should we care about it? Let them fall off."

But notwithstanding his unconcern, every year I had
a rope stretched there, and compelled the daring to stand
behind it. This too prevented them from crowding the
dancers, which the Indians appreciated; for when a man is
juggling an angry snake he does n't crave close company,
and I have seen an annoyed dancer thrash a tourist
across the face, using a live snake as his whip.

Some day the breaking of house rafters, or a flurry of
panic at the mesa edge may present tragedy as a closing
feature of this ceremony. "Let them fall off" may yet
have a grim sound.

The rites are conducted by the Indians with solemnity
and reverence. It is not a show in a juggler's booth, to
be guyed and ridiculed. But when one of the poisonous

DRAMATIC ENTRY OF THE SNAKE PRIESTS
AT WALPI

OPENING THE WALPI SNAKE DANCE
Antelope priests lined at the kisi

snakes has coiled, and is hissing and rattling and striking, just the time when one would think spectators would become more tense, that is when taunts are flung and a perfect bedlam of thoughtless merriment arises. Were there fewer visitors, as at minor ceremonies, they would be reproved; but the Hopi are a patient people, and they never insisted that these strangers behave themselves; they only expected that the visitor would keep his place, and not attempt to join the dance, a thing that some wild whites — including a few wild women — are only too ready to do. You now see all the standpoint of the old priest.

Each tourist packs one of those devices sold by Mr. Eastman. At many of the ceremonies, particularly the Flute Dance, cameras are barred by the Hopi, and I had their restriction respected. But when I proposed to increase the tribe's revenue by taxing each visitor a dollar for the camera privilege, the clan thought it good business, and asked me to arrange it. I had camera tags prepared, and the trails to the top policed. Each policeman was accompanied by a representative of the clan, who sold the tags, and who carried a sack of money to change anything up to a fifty-dollar bill. Usually twenties were thrust forward, and promptly nineteen hard, cumbersome cartwheels were dumped into the canny tourist's lap. It was disconcerting to those who sought that form of evasion. Occasionally came one who demanded a decision of the Supreme Court against this outrage, chanting invariably that he was a taxpayer, and often adding that he knew Wilson, or whoever happened to occupy the place of Chief Magistrate. But backing the collector was the imperturbable Indian policeman, who did not pay taxes and who did not know Wilson. The policeman knew Moungwi only, who had been found ready to "stand behind," as an officer put it. Either pay "una peso," "shu-kashe-vah," "thathli ibeso," or "one iron-man," in Spanish, Hopi, Navajo, or Americanese, whatever language you cared to have it in, or surrender that black devil-box in which a man's spirit may be imprisoned.

One dollar! Yet there were many who sought to evade, and forced unpleasantness; there were a few who flatly refused to pay and yielded their kodaks; there was even one who tried to steal a moving-picture film, who was hunted down at night in the black desert, caught in the early morning, handcuffed, lodged in the Agency hoose-gow, and had his precious record confiscated for Uncle Samuel, who preserves it in Washington to-day. This tricky envoy of a famous news-service has related in a magazine his harrowing experience, giving me full credit as his one-time host. I have not space in which to analyze his inaccuracies. Suffice it to say that he cost one very tired and harassed Moungwi and two hard-boiled range-men a night's rest. He should know that every trail to the railroad was watched, and he would just as surely have been apprehended and had his outfit confiscated had he escaped to the Mecca of Los Angeles, that windy city out of which he worked. The jurisdiction of the Indian Agent extended there, or for that matter anywhere, in connection with a plot affecting his wards.

There was a midnight conference with the visiting official then acting as Commissioner, who, surrounded by loneliness and an empty sterility, not having at his beck a Law Board, seemed bewildered. For once, delay could not be sought by mail. There was no one to receive the buck. A Departmental order was being laughed at. Despite the possibility of ridicule, the visiting mandarin feared that I might jar the gentle traditions and affect several votes in Southern California.

"I can handle him on the reservation," I said, anxious to be off. "What I want to know, and all I want to know, is, do you authorize me to follow him to the Coast?"

The Acting Commissioner shivered in his pajamas. It is cold at those altitudes, even on August nights; and when one is standing barefoot, you know, and being pressed for a warrant — he wavered into the wrong pew, for he said: "Ask Shelton about it."

Now Shelton was the most determined Indian Agent that ever wielded authority in the lonely desert. He and a dozen other Agents were among my guests. He was that one with a chipped-granite face I had met in the Office long ago, and whose language had failed when he tried to describe the subtle beauty of his domain. Roosevelt called him one of the best Agents in the Service, "who has done more for the Navajo than any other living man." He disciplined the criminal element among Indians, and protected all of them, good and bad, from exploitation. His Agency was a lovely garden wrested from a sterile immensity, where the Desert bloomed as a rose. Shelton is gone now. Only the Indians miss him. His place in the great Desert has not been filled. There are Nahtahnis and Nahtahnis. And I venture to say that the praise of Theodore Roosevelt, plus the few words I have written, are all the record shows for Shelton's many years in that empire of the San Juan River, where the Ship Rock trims its great stone sails against the desert winds.

Shelton rolled out and sat on the edge of his bed. He listened.

"How far to your line?" he asked.

"Nine miles by the road I think he has taken. He's

across the line long ago, unless the Jedito is running and has stopped him."

"Do you need me?" he said. He was not a man to waste words.

"No. But there is an early train west. He may be off the reservation. What would you do?"

"Get him," said Shelton, and went back to bed.

For it had been ordered that no moving-picture film of the Hopi Snake Dance should be made, unless by permit of the Secretary of the Interior; and it had been further decreed that such permission should be granted to representatives of State and National museums only. The Governor of Arizona had respected this order. The Commissioner had declined to request any modification of it. I was therefore anxious to find the fellow who had slipped in furtively, had procured a reservation permit by evasion, had been warned not to work, who had proposed a contract requiring the Secretary's approval, and who had broken his word.

For a week I had been on my toes, so to speak. Two thousand tourists, threescore official guests, including a dozen observing Indian Agents and the Colonel and everything, had caused me to become a trifle peevish. The Dance was over; the tumult and the shouting had died, the captains and the kings were departing. And so was an insolent crank-operator with a valuable film. Too much is enough.

We got him. He will never forget it.

Because of this untoward happening, and the wild cries of wounded vanity heard in Washington, the Commissioner became annoyed. He issued a crushing order that no photographs, still, animated, or out of focus, should be permitted thereafter. Thus all innocents are restricted to this day, and the official in charge reaps the criticism. He must locate and check the cameras on the day of the Snake Dance, a terrible procedure, bringing him into argument with almost everyone. This must be done because a few tourists may not be trusted to obey the order. A very foolish order. Nearly everyone was happy when he could bang away a roll of films for the family album and for a fee of one dollar. The tourist loses his chance to vie with Edward Curtis, and the Indians lose their feast money.

The reason for such an order against the movies? Well, it would never do to puff, through an entire administration, that all our Indians are domesticated, tamed, and engaged regularly in singing "Onward Christian Soldiers," and then to have a spine-thrilling vision flashed up in every movie-theatre each September. Some of the mildest of the Hopi are members of the Snake clan, and go their peaceful ways at Walpi; but they zealously enact their parts in the pageant every second year; and to see those fellows painted ferociously, garbed in savage dress, with snakes held in their mouths — yes, in their mouths; and two or three active snakes can weave a revolting mask for a painted face —

I can conceive of no more terrible close-up than that of a Snake Priest, coming toward one with eyes glaring, cheeks and chin painted black, his mouth a huge white daub, and snakes, some of them with rattles, feeling around his ears, through his hair, and about his face and neck. This would never do for general consumption. The public would accept such a pictorial news-item as proof that these continental United States contain savages very like those who beat the awesome drums in Conrad's *Heart of Darkness*.

Tourists! I remember the incidents of an Oraibi Snake Dance. At Oraibi the water-supply is limited. The assembled multitude drank the trader's well dry, and it was then a choice between the mesa-spring, an unsanitary flow, and the water-wagon of the day school. Trip after trip to a distant well this wagon made, the horses dragging through heavy sand; and as fast as it arrived the tourists emptied it. Precious water! But I had to appoint a guard to prevent their leaving the faucet running. Because my employee objected to several wasting the water, he was reported to Washington as a villain who had refused a drink to a suffering traveler in a burning and inhospitable Desert!

Then came an Indian who complained that they were taking his wood. The Indians at Oraibi have to haul their firewood a distance of ten to twelve miles. After one has brought in his winter's supply, he grows rather petulant to see another man, who rides about in an automobile, calmly burning it.

"Go back to them, my friend," I said, "and politely ask for payment."

"I did that first, but they told me to get out."

I directed a policeman to go with the Indian, and the policeman returned to report that he had been received — not to say insulted — with words. Whereupon the policeman departed a second time, evidently pleased with his mission, and efficiently led in a very angry gentleman. The complainant trailed along too.

"This Indian claims that you have burned his wood."

"Yes, we used some of it."

"He has to go a long way for that wood."

"Well, what of it?"

"I understand he has asked for payment. I pay six dollars a cord for firewood delivered by these Indians."

"Yes, he did ask for payment — "

"How much?" I inquired, thinking the Indian might have overreached.

"Early this morning he arrived, and demanded fifty cents."

"A very reasonable charge, don't you think?"

"Reasonable! We come seventy-five miles into this barren desert, and are denied firewood! Do you call that hospitality? Is that the way you educate Indians to view the public that supports them? A fine sense of courtesy!"

Having delivered himself of this rejoiner, the gentleman turned away to signify that the interview was finished; but the policeman happened to be standing at the door.

"Who asked you to come into this desert? This Indian did not invite you. You arrived without notice or summons. He is under no obligation to furnish your comfort. And you do not support these Indians. They are self-supporting. They pay the Government for everything they receive, other than the education of their children; and I'll bet your own children attend a public school. Suppose this Indian came to your town, camped without asking in your dooryard, and helped himself to your firewood. You would call him a vagabond, and he would get, very likely, a magistrate's sentence. Pay him a dollar."

"I will pay him nothing."

"One dollar, or I will show you the line."

The dollar was paid.

Tourists! Are all of them like this? I answer from a long experience in the Indian country that a very large percentage of them are just like this. Outside the reservations they form the bulk of unthinking sentimentalists, preaching a crusade for dissatisfied and malcontent Indians, stirring them against real friends and worthy tribesmen, making a pother and often a hell's brawl of half-baked accusations and charges. Recently a crew of them discovered "religious liberty" among the dangerous barbarians of certain backward pueblos in New Mexico. The knowledge of men of experience, the views of priests and ministers, the affidavits of eyewitnesses, the testimony of Indians who had emerged from the twilight zone and had accepted both education and Christianity, all availed nothing against those who would demonstrate that a Pueblo cacique, having a phallic doctrine to uphold, was being denied his "religious right" to enslave and debase the helpless of his community. A terrible banner for friends of the Pueblos to raise.

Whose fault? — Washington's. Washington has known of and winked at this disgrace for more than a decade.

Permit me to inform you that there are within the United States Indians as benighted and as evil as those who beat the drums in the *Heart of Darkness*. I have had them in charge. I have spent nights in their villages. I have faced the duty of restraining them. I have seen the results of their malicious performances. I have taken to hospital the unfortunates they viciously maltreated. I have arrested and prosecuted some of the guilty. I have protected a few of those they threatened — but not all; for I have exhumed their dead.

But do not think for a moment that I was *directed* to curb these evil clans of New Mexico. With my Indian police from other and freer pueblos, with determined employees both white and Mexican, and on one occasion backed by a United States Marshal's posse, I was fortunate enough to get away with it. The United States

Court, and the press, and the wholesome of the community, approved my actions and wished more power to me as Agent. A respect for law was being established. One New Mexican disgrace was being eliminated.

But lo! this became embarrassing to the East. Even as Nahtahnis, those in supreme command change and are different. Imagine being told that efforts toward control should cease, since the Government would find it inexpedient to lend support! What mattered it if a man were hanged until nearly dead, or a woman tortured, by caciques claiming "religious liberty"? As for violated children — who should presume to disturb the ancient Indian customs?

XX

THE GREAT SNAKE–CEREMONY

"On with the dance! Let joy be unrefined!"
                                H. L. MENCKEN

THE ceremony of the Snake Dance begins many days
before that public conclusion the tourist sees. The date
of the dance is announced by the pueblo crier from the
housetops. The priests of the Antelope and Snake clans
go to their respective kivas where, amid chants and exorcism, the wardrobe is looked over and all necessary tools
and sacred equipment are prepared. A certain number of
songs are sung each day, according to a strict ritual. It is
during this time that new members are initiated, whether
or not with revolting rites is for those to answer who know.

Then comes the snake-hunt, occupying four days, each
day to a different point of the compass, north, west,
south, and east. One would think that snakes have fixed
and respected neighborhoods, so readily do the hunters
procure them; and one monster bull-snake, fully seven
feet long and proportionately thick, must be trained by
the Second Mesa devotees, for it always occupies the
centre of the stage at Machongnovi. Very likely snakes
live to participate in many dances.

This facility in procuring snakes caused me to ask a
young Hopi how they were located.

"By tracking," he answered, pointing to the dusty
sand at our feet. "See! there is a snake's track. We can
follow him home and dig him out, if you want."

Well, we did n't do it, because I had something less dangerous on hand; and I must confess that I could not discern the delicate trail of the snake he referred to. But then, too, I have followed Indian trackers as they sought to run down a man. They would call off his movements as if reading from a book. As a desert tracker, I was a good Indian Agent.

Armed with a hoe, for excavating the more retiring, with a buckskin sack of sacred meal, — for this must be sprinkled on the votaries, — a larger bag in which to carry them, and a snake-whip of feathers, the hunters go forth. They wear moccasins and a loin-cloth only. An ordinary member of the snake family, such as a bull snake, no matter what his size, is picked up with slight ceremonial fuss. But the rattlesnake often objects. He is most likely to sound his displeasure, and to coil swiftly for defense. Perhaps he has never attended a Snake Dance. In this event, the hunter blesses him with meal and proceeds to attract his attention with caresses of the snake-whip. After several strokes of the long eagle feathers, the snake uncoils and seeks escape; but swifter than he is the unerring hand that nips him just back of the head. He is waved in the air, stroked with a quick pressure along his spine, and dropped into the sack with the others. And no more attention is paid to the sack's contents when carrying it back to the kiva than if it contained so much corn.

While the Hopi Desert contains large bull snakes and king snakes and long slender side-winders, the rattlesnake is a short specimen, seldom more than two feet in length. It is active enough for all purposes, however, and can produce extraordinary activity of movement on the part of those not initiated in the Snake clan. Once on a desert road I alighted from my car to arrange something. I heard a sibilant noise, a whirring dryish whistle or hiss that, peculiarly enough, is neither. There is no English word to describe accurately the rattlesnake's warning, but it is imperative, and procures immediate attention. In a thousandth part of a second I discovered the gentleman scuttling rapidly between my feet. He wished to avoid me, and I shared his emotions. It is of course impossible to assert exactly how many feet directly upward and sideward I impelled myself. There was a space of time in which I was oblivious to everything save the breaking of leaping records. I came to at a point entirely clear of the road, as my acquaintance disappeared into the sparse grass at the opposite side. Then, knowing where he was, and that he was safe and unharmed, I did not follow to put on any Snake Dance experiments. The swift grasp of the neck immediately behind the head, the triumphant wave in the air, the pressure along the spine, and the composure of the snake-gatherer, all may combine to render said snake harmless or indifferent; but — you try it!

The public part of the Snake ceremony consumes about twenty minutes of time. The kisi, a bower of cottonwood boughs, something like a miniature tepee, is erected midway of the plaza and to one side. The kisi screens a hole in the rock-floor, and just before the dance begins a mysterious bag is carried out and placed therein. It contains the snakes. The hole is covered or roofed by a thick piece of board.

Early in the day the crowd of sightseers has gathered on the mesa-top, and in late afternoon it begins massing at the Walpi plaza. There is the usual wrangle over prominent places, and the inevitable bickering as to who

engaged them first. Soon the roofs and terraces and balconies are hidden by the people. The odd stairways and
other points of vantage cause the crowd to group as if
arranged by a stage director. A dozen or more crown the
Snake Rock itself. They wait patiently, expectantly, as
small boys await the head of the circus parade. Old Judge
Hooker arrives, garbed for the occasion, and harangues
them with Hopi cries, announcing to all and several that
this great ceremony will positively be held on this date,
once, and once only this season, and imploring them to
grant it the respect it deserves. The Indians present pay
attention to his speech, for on this occasion at least the
Judge has the Agency police within call; but the whites
do not know what he has said, and so care very little about
it. This waiting in a too-crowded place is a monotonous
and tiring procedure. There is much stirring about,
leaving a good place and then wishing one had not.

And suddenly comes a distant sounding of rattle-gourds,
a faint but insistent noise, like dried peas blown against
glass.

"Here they come!" calls the ever-present small boy,
who perches perilously on a projecting house-pole.

Quietly, ceremoniously, the Antelope priests in single
file enter the plaza. Their gourds sound steadily, and
with slow measured steps they march about the stage
four times. When passing the kisi, each man stamps with
his right foot on the board that shelters the snakes. They
sprinkle meal. And they are followed by the guardian of
the bull-roarer, a tall man who carries a huge Indian bow
ornamented with feathers, and who stops in mid-stage to
sound his awesome instrument. With all the force of his
arm he whirls that wooden plumb-bob on a sinew string.
It moans with the wind voice of the Desert. Then the

Antelope men form a straight line with the kisi, their backs to the houses and their faces to the plaza.

Now sounds a hurried noise, much clatter and scuffling, as the Snake priests approach. They burst into the plaza as if determinedly answering a call to battle. They are headed by the most robust of the clan, large powerful men. With rigid faces, fixedly staring, their elbows set as runners, they stride down the plaza. The crowd massed at the far end is always in the way. The Snake priests must go to the farthest end of this shelf on their first round, after which they shorten each lap until four have been completed. The crowd must fall back. It has no license to be there at all, and there is nothing in Snake-clan etiquette signifying change because curiosity has come out of the East. Their rushing single-file of men is projected straight at the narrow end of the shelf. Finding that it was impossible to fix such a throng in place, I would station two guards at that point to warn and part the spectators. Just what would happen if the whites did not yield is problematical. I recall that once the head-man of the dancers took me in the side with his elbow. He did not stop to apologize. It was two hundred rapidly moving pounds meeting much less than that. I did not completely recover from the blow until the dance was over. A head-on crack like that might propel one over the cliff.

These Snake priests are nude to the waist, their upper bodies daubed in black, with the lightning sign traced in white. Their hair is disheveled and streaming, and crowned with red feathers. About their eyes are reddish smears, and a circle of white is thickly painted about each mouth. They wear ornamented kilts of knee-length, and moccasins; and with some show of uniformity each man packs all the trumpery the clan has adopted as part of its regalia. They have armlets and bracelets of silver, and necklaces of many strands — beads and bone and turquoise. From the rear of each belt dangle one or more handsome fox-skins. Fastened just below the right-leg knee are curious clappers made of tortoise shells. Thus, as they stride tumultuously about, there sounds above the dry rattling of the Antelope gourds all the hurried clatter of this moving harness.

Each time they pass the kisi they stamp fiercely on the board. It gives back a hollow sound. And perhaps the snakes of former spectacles know that they will soon be wanted on deck. "All hands aloft!"

Then the Snake priests quiet down a bit and align themselves in a long row, facing the Antelope men. A chant is begun. It is low in tone and quite ceremonial in spirit. Their bodies sway. A curious waving motion is made with the hands, one dancer's wrists engaging his partner's. The gourds whir their singing sounds. And an old Indian, a feeble, aged man, passes down the line with a bowl of water. This he sprinkles at the kisi. The age of this participant and his evident fervor always attract notice. He appears and disappears. And it is just at this point, when the action is most impressive, when all touring eyes are bulging to a degree, that the inevitable dog wanders into the sanctuary and begins to investigate. I have never known a Snake Dance that did not produce its uninvited mongrel at this time. He is never shooed or kicked away. He is always the most disreputable animal of a people noted for their impoverished canines. Lank and lean, with a cringing expression of dog humility on his face, he contrives to spoil the scene.

There is a noticeable pause. The line of Snake priests breaks into pairs and, with a curious, half-stamping dance, they pass to the kisi. The man on the right stoops, plunges his arm into the snake-hole, and brings forth a snake. The dancer is humped over now, his body bent forward, his head projecting. The one with him places an arm across his shoulders, and with a feather-whip attracts the weaving head of the reptile. The first dancer holds the snake by its middle for a moment, and then places it in his mouth, permitting the two ends to dangle freely.

Behind these two steps watchfully the "gatherer," and follows them about. With a humping irregular motion the pair dance around the plaza, and finally the snake is dropped to the ground. The gatherer quickly retrieves it, if it is a patient, well-behaved snake; but if it is a rattler and acts unreasonably, proceeding to coil and sound its warning, the gatherer swiftly acts with the deftness of a juggler. His eyes never leave the defiant snake. He pinches a bit of meal from his pouch and sprinkles it toward the unwilling symbol of the gods. Then he waves his whip over the snake. If it strikes, he will let it alone for a brief time. There in the little plaza is a fighting rattlesnake, a vicious coiled spring, fangs darting, restless, angry. The dancers avoid it. The crowd shrills its approval of the scene.

But the gatherer is watching. Soon the snake gives a quick wriggle and is off, darting for the mesa edge, and those forming the crowd there begin anxiously to shift their feet. Another second and the Indian has pounced down on it, swishing the snake from under the very toes of the spectators. He waves it through the air in the motion of his capture, strokes it into limpness as he watches his pair of dancers. Then it dangles from his left hand, and he proceeds to the next adventure.

Meantime, other couples have approached the kisi and

A PATRIARCH OF SNAKES
Priest with one of the squirming reptiles

THE GATHERER
handling a rattlesnake

have produced their snakes. The differences in reptiles now attract attention. There are long, thin, nervous snakes, and short, fat, sluggish ones. A shout of amazement goes up when a very large specimen of bull snake is seen, its tail almost trailing the earth. But varying snakes do not affect the priests. The Antelope men continue the whirring of their gourds, and with the Snake men the action becomes faster. Seven or eight couples are now stamping around, and the gatherers have a busy time of it.

And then comes the signal that the bag of the kisi is empty. All snakes have been produced in the open, and danced with, and dropped, and gathered up. Now two priests describe with meal a large circle on the ground before the Dance Rock. The dancers approach and throw all the snakes into this circle. They crowd around it as meal is sprinkled, and perhaps some exorcism is muttered. For a second they poise there, as if under a spell; and then certain appointed men thrust their hands into the squirming mass, catch up as many snakes as possible, and rush from the plaza to liberate the votaries in the far Desert.

Now one notes the reason for the tunnel leading through the houses to the west. At First Mesa they may go north, south, and west from the little plaza; but no dancer jumps off it to the east; the strict ritual suffers a change to accommodate this natural disadvantage. He seizes his allotted share of the snakes and proceeds along the edge to some convenient trail, turning eastward in the lower valley. The uninformed among the spectators have a happy faculty for packing themselves in that tunnel. The Indian runner means to go through it, without pausing or apologies, carrying an armful of active snakes. "Let them fall off" is his motto.

This distribution of the snake messengers ends what

one may term the intriguing features of the ceremony. Soon the panting runners return to engage in the so-called "purification" rites, the taking of the emetic; and a number of the curious follow them to be in at the death. It is not of importance that one should witness this part of the programme; it is simply a matter of taste. Physicians may wish to time the potency of desert brews. The priests are then washed from head to foot by the women of the clan. Water is poured over them from large bowls. Dripping, the priests disappear into their kiva. Soon the women are hurrying there too, bearing in trays all sorts of viands. The dancers, who have fasted, would absorb a bit of nourishment. God knows they have earned it!

Dr. Jesse Walter Fewkes, the celebrated ethnologist, writes that after the Snake Dance of 1883 two of the liberated snakes were caught and taken to the National Museum at Washington for examination. He states that their fangs and poison-sacs were found to be intact. He does not accept the belief that these Hopi Indians have an antidote for the poison of rattlesnakes. It is his view that the desert rattler can inflict a deadly bite only after coiling and lunging viciously on its victim. And there is little to the theory that the snakes have been drugged or dulled into lethargy, since I have many times seen the rattlesnakes coil and fight wickedly. Several persons, particularly Mr. Herbert F. Robinson, the Government Engineer for the Navajo and Hopi country, claim to have seen Snake priests bitten in the dance. I could not make such a statement. But it is possible that the paint with which the priests are liberally daubed has, for snakes, a repugnant odor; and having anointed their hands and arms, and especially their mouths, faces, and necks with this ointment, they secure a certain immunity. And the stroking of the snakes, when picked up, may explain the safety of the gatherer. This action no doubt produces a partial paralysis of the snake's muscular system. But this does not answer for those who thrust bare hands and arms into the snake-bag at the kisi.

If one must see a Snake Dance, the best show is at Walpi in years of odd numbers. The ceremony is held also at Machongnovi, Chimopovi, and Hotevilla. Since 1918 there has been no dance at Oraibi, perhaps because of factional disputes, although a disciple of Christianity has claimed part of the credit. There is a solemnity observed at Hotevilla, among the reactionaries, with prophet You-keoma, the second man in the line of Antelope priests; but the men of Walpi preserve more of Indian color and thrill of action in their performance. Perhaps they have realized the advantage of a good show, well staged and costumed and vigorously enacted. While they do not invite the tourists, they keep them coming, and business in Snake Dance week is brisk along all lines.

Not all of the Hopi people are members of the Snake clan. Those of the uninitiated are as diffident with rattlesnakes as the rest of us. This lodge has difficulty in keeping up its membership. Sometimes a Hopi is invited to join, or is ordered to report for duty in the Snake kiva, and he declines this honor. It is well for him to remain away from dances thereafter, or he may have to hold a punishment snake as a penalty.

It was through the courtesy of Mr. John Lorenzo Hubbell, that early pioneer and baronial trader of the Navajo Desert, that I chanced to view the most secret of the Snake Dance rites, the baptism or washing of the snakes in the kiva. This occurs in the morning of the day of the public ceremony. Perhaps one might call it the consecration of the messengers; for, as I have understood it, the snakes are the tribe's envoys to the gods, bearing its petition for rain and its thanks for harvests.

Perhaps, as Moungwi, I might have achieved this success earlier, but it was my method in dealing with the Hopi, an always suspicious people, not to display an interest in their secrecies. Of necessity — or perhaps I should say in good judgment — I had to police their dances, to prevent possible clashes between the non-understanding Indian and the nearly always unreasonable and over-curious tourist; but I have never asked an Indian, anywhere, to give me an "inside" concerning his primitive beliefs. Having to guide and often to judge that same Indian, it would have been an unfair advantage to take of my position, and would at once have classed me, the appointed mentor, as a piece of curiosity no different from the white men he so often wrangled with. Moreover, I had other means of acquiring information. The traders told me all they had garnered through the many years of trafficking with Indians, and each newcomer — tourist, artist, or itinerant official, — presented me with the varying chaff of his very swift and gullible gleaning.

The always helpful Mr. Hubbell bridged this dilemma by inviting me as his guest, and I could accept without losing caste. Hubbell had been admitted to the kiva many years before. Then Dr. Fewkes in 1899, as he relates, and since then the Indians have received Mr. Roosevelt, General Hugh L. Scott, and a few others. Perhaps not more than a score of white men have witnessed this ceremony.

In our little party were a visiting superintendent, an engineer of the Desert Service, and Mr. Ford Harvey, son of the immortal Fred who rescued so many hungry travelers along the Santa Fe in early times, and to whom should be erected a monument of bronze.

From the poles of the kiva ladder flew the feather-plumes that signify the progress of secret rites. An Indian met us at the top, and we filed after him down the ladder, into the cool, dim atmosphere of that underground rock-walled vault. It had a peculiar odor — perhaps an earthy, perhaps a snaky smell.

Kivas usually are empty places. Bare and cold, unless filled with eye-stinging smoke from firebrands, I had not found them inviting on my rounds of the mesas. I had held councils in them when making the first steps against factional religious persecution. Again I had sat in them, chatting with the makers of costumes and drums, smoking their bitter and powerful tobacco — afterward wishing sincerely I had not. Most often the kiva is the club for retired old men of the tribe, lonely, feeble fellows, where they curl up to drowse and sleep, or where they weave some ceremonial scarf. It is not good form to idle in the neighborhood of kivas when the feather-plumes are displayed, and one very distinguished gentleman, who has been referred to as "the great Caucasian marvel," was most thoroughly bawled out by the chief Snake Priest for seeking to introduce himself without first requesting leave.

The ladder ended on a stone platform, raised above the main kiva-floor. In the corners of this platform stood large clay jars, and greeting us, albeit silently, from the corners and about the jars, were snakes. Not just a few snakes that had wandered out of their pottery containers, but congested wads of snakes, piled carelessly in the corners of the kiva, and with nothing to prevent their leaving when the spirit moved them. However, they were now quiet, somnolent, save for beady eyes and an occasional slithery movement that caused one to watch his step.

At the upper end of the kiva was an elaborate sand-painting after the fashion of the Navajo, no doubt another adoption, of foreign origin. A sand-painting is a mosaic-like picture of Indian symbols and fetishes, worked out in colored sands. This was surrounded or fenced by peeled wands, placed close together on end. And at this ceremonial altar stood, practically nude, two of my school-boys, bronzed lads of about sixteen, who had taken part that morning in the sunrise race.

Under the ladder and on the main floor a number of older Indians were grouped, having close to them large bowls of clay holding water or other liquids. And these priests were arrayed for a ceremony. The sacred-meal pouches were in evidence. Soon a chant was intoned. The Hopi chants are primitive, but have in them an echo of Catholic litanies. I have seen a Hopi priest anoint with and toss the sacred meal just as his forbears saw the padres bless the people. The Hopi is an assiduous adapter. And while listening to the chanting, I have often expected to catch the response: "*Ora pro nobis.*" The padres were sacrificed to the desert gods in that red revolt of 1680, but their peaches dry each season on the pueblo housetops, and Hopi ceremonies carry an unconscious echo of the black-robes who taught the solemnity of ritual.

Around the walls of the kiva, at the height of one's head, were wooden pegs set in the stone, and draped over these were masks and costumes. As my position at the end of the platform brought me close to one of these bundles, I leaned against it and the wall, half turned, to give an eye to the nearest snakes of my corner, and another eye to the proceedings of the elders. A snake wriggled out

Photo. by Emri Kopte

THE CHIEF SNAKE-PRIEST.　LEADER IN THE
WALPI CEREMONIES

from the pile and came closer; but the Indian who had received us waved him back with a feather-whip. Some-one was watching that sector, and I grew more confident.

We stood there for a little time in silence. From above came the noises of the crowd, thronging through the village streets. One could look up through the square opening of the entrance and see the blue Arizona sky. The ladder was very comforting. Several of the guests sat down on the edge of the platform, but I did not. I leaned comfortably against my pile of regalia, and kept a wide-angled view of the whole interior.

Then one of the Indians crossed the platform, gathered a few snakes and passed them swiftly to the old men at the bowls. They uttered invocations, stretched the snakes out, and anointed them with meal, all the while chanting in a low tone. A number of the men had lined up against the wall, carrying rattles and insignia. They too began a chant. And then suddenly the old men plunged the snakes into the water of the bowls — a quick, unceremonious ducking; the choir raising its chant to a savage crescendo. It was no longer rhythmic and solemn. It was like a scream of death, a wild, unreasoning challenge that ended in a blood-curdling shriek; and at that final cry the snakes were hurled up the kiva, to fall on the sand-painting. The peeled wands were knocked over by their swirling bodies. Somnolent before, the snakes now waked up, and twisted about, seeking escape, their heads raised, their tongues darting in and out. A hissing and whirring sounded. Their movements in the sand caused the design to be obliterated.

Now came another handful of snakes, swiftly passed for the baptism, and again the low chanting, but faster now, faster, and always that wild ending of the chant, and the throwing of the reptiles. More and more snakes squirmed on the wrecked sand-painting. All the wands were down now. And in among the snakes, with a calmness that chilled the blood, walked my two schoolboys, nude as Adam, hustling back to the sand those that darted for the walls. Twice snakes reached the stone bench along the kiva's end and, climbing it, sought crevices of the upper wall. Each time a boy reached for the disappearing truant and nonchalantly dragged him back to his place in this wildest of pagan rites.

Finally all the snakes had been removed from our corners, and several inches of them made a moving carpet where had been the mosaic. There came a pause, a significant cessation of action, as if the priests had reached an unexpected, unforeseen part of the service. There was a quick consultation among the head-men. One of the boys, Edward, began looking around. He went to the nearest peg and removed some of the costumes, dropping a mask to the floor. He examined the mask. Then he went to another peg and performed this same search. And then he came straight toward me, at the end of the platform.

"What is it, Edward?" I asked him.

"We had sixty-five rattlesnakes, Mr. Crane," he replied stolidly, "and now we count but sixty-four. Let me look through those dresses you are leaning against. That other one may be — "

"Excuse me," I said hurriedly, as I went up the ladder.

XXI

DESERT BELASCOS

Of course all Indians should not be forced into the same mould. Let us try to give each his chance to develop what is best in him. Moreover, *let us be wary of interfering overmuch with either his work or his play.* It is mere tyranny, for instance, to stop all Indian dances. Some which are obscene or dangerous must be prohibited. Others should be permitted, and many of them encouraged. *Nothing that tells for the joy of life, in any community, should be lightly touched.* ROOSEVELT: *A Booklover's Holidays.*

WHEN I first read this, I thought of and began to compare the different types of Indian dances and ceremonies I had witnessed: the Butterfly, Basket, and Corn dances, the Snake and Flute Dances of the Hopi; the Medicine Sings, and squaw dances, and the Ye-be-chai of the Navajo; the colorful pageants of the Pueblos, after Catholic Mass is celebrated on the name-days of their patron saints, and the fiesta begins; the memorial ceremony of the Mohave, and their cremation of the dead. And those slam-bang, whirlwind dances of the Sioux.

Some of these were commemorative; some were fixed ceremonials; some were of little moment; some seemed nothing more serious than masquerades; some were filled with superstition and had just a touch of smoldering fanaticism under the veneer of paint and feathers. A few were social gatherings, a break in the monotony of existence, having in them "the joy of life." And while all of the native dances should have thrown around them a thin line of supervision and restraint, many of them should be by no means "lightly touched."

The Snake Dance may be dangerous, and it is certainly revolting at first sight. And perhaps it should be prohibited. That is a point of view. I am not thoroughly convinced of its danger to Indians, since I never heard of a Hopi dying from snake-bite. I saw so many Snake Dances that the edge has been dulled from my original thrill. If tourists were denied the pleasure of seeing it, I believe the ceremony would soon languish, and pass away entirely with the going of the elders from the mesa stage. Certainly I sought to prevent its perpetuation through the initiation of children, but without result, for I was unsupported in this, and alone I feared my inability to stifle a pagan war.

But of those things that should be dealt with gently, the tiny shows that the vacationist seldom sees and the Bureau has never heard of, I recall the Dance of the Dolls.

One afternoon, at First Mesa, I came along a trail toward the witch's camp, meaning to start for home once the team was harnessed. I met an Indian of the district walking with my interpreter, and was about to give direction concerning the horses when the latter said: —

"He wants you to stay and see the Dolls' Dance."

Now I had quite a collection of Hopi dolls, those quaint figurines carved with some skill from pieces of cottonwood, and dressed in the regalia of twig and feather and fur to represent the various katchinas of the clans. But I had never heard of a dance devoted to these little mannequins.

"What sort of dance is that?" I asked.

"It is called the Dolls-Grind-Corn dance," he replied.

"When — to-morrow?" thinking of those monotonous

open-air drills, having various names but scarcely to be distinguished one from the other.

"No. To-night, in the kiva."

This interested me. I could see that the interpreter longed to remain overnight among his people, and to take in this show.

"Well," I said, "is it worth climbing that mesa in the dark?"

"I think you would like it," he answered; "it is a funny little dance, and the children go to see it."

So I did not order up the team.

After supper, when the twilight had faded into that clouded blackness before the stars appear, I scrambled after my guide up the mesa trail. When we reached the end of that panting climb, the houses of the people were murkily lighted by their oil lamps, but most of the house-holders were abroad, going toward the various kivas. To the central one we went, and down the ladder.

The place was lighted by large swinging lamps, bor-rowed for the occasion from the trader, lamps that have wide tin shades and may be quickly turned to brilliancy or darkness by a little wheel at the side. I had expected to find it a gloomy place, whereas they had arranged something very like the lighting of a theatre. It was a trifle difficult to find a place in that crowded vault. The far end was kept clear, but the two long sides and the ladder-end were packed with Hopi women and their little ones. Just as I have seen in our theatres, the children could scarcely repress their nervous interest, now sitting, now standing on tiptoe, turning and watching, as if this would hasten matters.

I seated myself on the lower rung of the ladder, be-lieving this place would be most desirable from my point of view, because from it I had a view of the kiva's centre and could most easily make my way to the upper air when things became too thick. A crowded kiva is rather foreign in atmosphere when filled to its capacity and with lamps going. But I soon found that I would be disturbed. From above came the noise of rattles and the clank of equipment, calls and the shuffling of feet. A line of dancers descended upon me. I moved to let them pass into the lighted centre-space. They were garbed in all the color and design of Hopi imagination, and wore grotesque masks. They lined up, and I sensed that their mission was one of merrymaking. Two clowns headed the band, and soon had the audience convulsed. They hopped about, postured, and carried on a rapid dialogue. There was a great deal of laughter.

I had my usual experience in trying to gain a knowledge of the show through an interpreter, quite the same as that lady who accompanied an attaché to hear a speech by Bismarck in the Reichstag. You will remember that the visitor kept demanding interpretation, whereas the attaché remained silent, intently listening, as the Iron Chancellor droned on, monotonously voluble.

"What does he say?" asked the visitor for the fifth time.

"Madam," replied the attaché, "I am waiting for the verb!"

And that is about as far as I ever got toward exact knowledge of the clowns in any dance. I have tried it many times. The interpreter always enjoyed the show for himself, first, and left me in outer darkness. Occasionally he would attempt to explain some part of the horseplay in progress, probably such simple portions as he thought my feeble intellect would rise to.

"You see," he would begin, pointing, "he is one of the uncles!"

And apparently there are always two, paternal and maternal, I suppose. The uncle is the great man of the Hopi family. The father does not amount to much — he can be divorced in a jiffy and, while the mother is the household boss, she is always dominated by the grand-mother, if living, and dictated to by *the* uncle in matters concerning alliances with other families. Perhaps one should call him a social arbiter. He has a great deal to say about weddings, marriage portions, and the like. Whenever I have watched the clowns at these smaller dances, and have asked their rôles in the play, invariably they have been of the uncles. Perhaps the Hopi in this manner square themselves at the expense of the family martinet.

I could not see that there was anything to cause suspicion of evil in this little scene. In old Navajo dances the clowns would often engage in dialogue that interpreters feared to translate. This is the charge too against the clowns of certain Pueblo and Zuni dances; and the clowns of the Hopi have been known to indulge in antics that were not elevating. I cannot bring myself to believe, however, that the clowns of the Dolls' Dance were relating anything other than crude witticisms, for the little children laughed as loudly as the others, and it seemed sheer fooling. Had a slapstick been in evidence, I should have been sure of the nature of the proceedings; but the Indians have not developed exactly this form of humor.

Then the dancers filed out, up the ladder, and away.

"They go to another kiva," said my companion.

And almost immediately came another and different set of fun-makers. They took the centre of the kiva and soon had all laughing at similar jokes and grimaces. So, I thought, the old tiresome reel over again, to be continued throughout the night. For I had seen this dancing in relays last an entire day, only stopping for hasty meals and new costumes or make-up, and to one who does not understand the differences in scenes it becomes an intense boredom. As I once heard a man remark: "They are three days making ready for one day's dancing, and the rest of the week getting over it." This critic was not too severe, for there is much to be said about the time lost in Hopi spectacles, when one is seriously engaged in thrusting them along the pathway of progress. I arose and was about to depart; but my interpreter pulled me down.

"Wait!" he urged. "They will put out the lights."

This time the dancers did not leave the kiva. One of them came to the lamp just above me, and at a signal all the lights were dimmed. The kiva was in thick darkness. One could hear childish sighs of expectation. Perhaps the lights were off for thirty seconds, although it did not seem so long. Then they flared up, to reveal a curious little scene that had been constructed in the dark. I had not noticed that the dancers packed anything in with them. The setting may have been in that crowded kiva all the time; but where had it been concealed?

At any rate, it was a queer little show, quite like that of our old friend Punch. There was a painted screen of several panels, and in the centre ones were two dolls, fashioned to represent Hopi maidens. Before each was the corn-grinding metate. And farther extended on the floor before them and their stone tubs was a miniature cornfield — the sand, and the furrows, and the hills of tiny plants.

Hardly had the first sigh of pleased surprise from the children died away, when, even to my astonishment, the dolls became animated, and with odd life-like motions began to grind corn, just as the women grind daily in the houses of the villages, crushing the hard grain between the stone surfaces of the metate and the mano. These mannequins worked industriously, and with movements not at all mechanical. Then a little bird fluttered along the top of the screen, piping and whistling. Shrills of delight from the youngsters, to be followed by audible gasps, for from a side panel came twisting a long snake, to dart among the corn hills of the scenic field, and then to retreat backward through the hole from which it had appeared. These actions followed each other in quick succession. The fellow behind the screen was quite skillful in working his marionettes for the delight of those children of the tribe.

Perhaps in all this there was some deep-laid symbolism, checking rigidly with the North Star and the corn harvests of the past and future. Perhaps it was a primitive object-lesson, to encourage thrift and industry as a bulwark against famine. But if you ask me, I saw in it exactly a repetition of the district schoolhouse or the country chapel at holiday time, when Cousin Elmer obliges with a droll exhibition of whiskers and sleighbells and cotton snow-flakes. Sometimes the Hopi at these festivals for children give them presents too, and a handful of piki-bread bestowed by a clown, however bizarre his facial appearance, has all the gift-wonder of our childhood Santa Claus and his treasure-pack.

Touch gently! They — all children will be gone soon enough. A little while and you can rest from anæmic policies and sophist sermons. The Desert will be lonely without its simple shepherds and their simple customs. Those who strain to inherit it, through legislation, will pack with them no poetry and attract no culture. Great cattle- and sheep-camps, monopolies, grimy oil-rigs, and yawning coal-drifts will mar the Desert. A few old books, a few paintings, — their creators gone, too, — will picture what you once possessed, and experimented with, and auctioned off. For one Shelton, discredited perhaps by a clamor of sanctimonious mediocrity, you have entrusted these people and their empire to twenty Bumbles. Twice you have sought to partition their community life, to make swift the end, to hasten the advent of the speculator who follows estates and bids for the possessions of the dead. At length, — because at length you will succeed in selling the desert heritage, — there will be only the museum case, and dust, and a ticket.

The days of approach to a major celebration in the Desert, such as the Snake Dance, were passed in a ferment of preparation and a stew of unrest. All employees would be imposed on in one way or another. Some would be called on to act as stewards, others would surrender their quarters to house unappreciative idlers. And certainly the men would have to drag cars from muddy sloughs, ferry them across dangerous washes, repair them when broken, and perhaps by main strength push some into havens of rest. Certain camps would have to be arranged, and some supplied. No! we did not welcome these extra duties, so often repaid with meagre thanks.

But we did enjoy meeting cordial people, both neighbors and visitors, who, catching the holiday freedom of the moment, invigorated by the tonic of the fresh desert air, gave us entertainment of a kind that was relief from long monotonies.

The Snake Dance ends very close to sunset. The

Photo. by Emri Kopte

THE ENCHANTED DESERT AND THE MOQUI BUTTES, SEEN
FROM THE PUEBLO OF WALPI

crowds leave the mesa-top, down the trails afoot or mule-back, down the rocky roads in rough wagons, a scram-bling multitude. The sun is gilding the western walls of First Mesa, throwing the east-side roads and trails in shadow, and above, the ruined crest of the headland loom black in a gorgeous halo. The farther eastern valley is bathed in a strange lemon light The far-away northern capes gleam luminously in scarlet and gold, and then suddenly are gone. Huh-kwat-we, the Terrace of the Winds, pales in lavender and grayish green. Twilight, with its mysterious desert hush, steals over Hopi-land. Something has been fulfilled in accordance with an ancient prophecy. The desert gods have been appeased.

Soon it is dark, and stars appear as vesper candles. And then, all about the foot of the great fortress-like mesa, lighting the sand dunes, gleaming warmly through the peach trees, grow camp-fires. Where is usually a heavy silence at evening, broken only by sheep bells, now one hears laughter, many voices, the sound of the chef at work; and the smell of cooking rises. Coffee and bacon, desert fare, spread their aroma, and a ravenous hunger comes to one. Here is a tiny group about a tented auto, there amid horses and harness and camp dunnage are thirty around one board. "Come and get it!"

I recall incidents of my introduction to these scenes. Armijo, the trader's relative, had brought his treasured violin. I heard its tones from the trail, and when I came to Hubbell's camp, there a group of them, musicians of the posts, were making ready to match their skill against the melody that tourists bring. Supper put away, the concert began.

"How do you like this?" asked the master of the bow, and as he swept the strings, that saddest of memory songs

cried poignantly, a song fit for a desert night and a desert camp: La Golondrina! Such harmonies of double-
stopping I had seldom heard. It seemed to me — or was
it desert magic? — that Kreisler could do no more.
Silence. And then applause from fifty camps.

And Ed's guitar. Soon the lilting airs of old fandangos
would sing through the stunted trees, and one could imagine that the long-dead children of the padres made
fiesta.

"Now, Doctor," said someone.

"What do you play, Doctor?" I asked.

"I play the banjo," he replied — I thought with a shade
of mockery in his voice. Now I had just heard the
Spaniard's violin sob a song that had swept a nation, and
Ed's lightsome Mexican airs were no mean music for a
summer camp. Night, under the old trees and in the
shadow of the mesa of the gods, brings the romance of
serenades, especially soothing after a long tiresome, day.

But — a banjo! That thumpety, plankety, plunkety
thing! I was sorry I had spoken. He would oblige with
something to fit clogs and the levee, and the whole atmosphere of that evening would vanish, never to return! The
doctor opened a case.

"What would you like to hear?"

That is a terrible question from a banjoist, is n't it?

"Well — what do you play?"

"Oh! the — anything — popular classic stuff. Now
there's the Melody in F or Mendelssohn's Spring Song,
Schubert's Serenade, the Fifth Nocturne —"

"Great God!" I cried. "On a banjo!"

I think he pulled this little joke on all strangers, for,
after allowing it thoroughly to soak in, he brought that
wonder instrument closer to the fire and began strumming

the strings of it until its resonant cadences hushed all the noises of the camps. Then, softly through the grove, sounded the Melody in F, in organ tones.

Of course you will perceive that I am no musician and no critic. I have not the ear of the one, nor the language of the other. I am simply one of those who like to hear what I like — hopeless. The Andante from the Sonata Pathétique haunted and eluded me for years and, but for a wandering pianist disguised as an investigator, I might have classed it with a dream. Sordid duties dull one to accept coarser things on a phonograph.

"Yes," said the doctor, "I have played through the East and on Canadian circuits, but I don't care for the stage. I took up concert work, traveling with glee clubs and orchestras, but that wasn't much better. Hurried life. I like the quiet places."

And he was a doctor in the Indian Service!

Someone called: "Play it again!" And he played it again — on a banjo!

Down under the hill were camped a bunch of troubadours that once had trooped with a second company, passing as the Original New York Cast. By the light of a lantern they played accompaniments on an old melodeon, dragged from the schoolhouse. A rousing chorus, and then a tenor voice: the Irish Love Song. Followed a roar of applause that brought drowsy Indians to the mesa edge. Strange Americanos! Strange Bohannas, who mock at drums and chanting, and who then make such queer music and many cries.

And by midnight the fires would die down, one by one, to mere glows. The pueblo lights, high up along the mesa cornice, would be blotted out. Beyond the camps, only the sound of horses munching, the bray of a desert nightingale from the upper corrals, or the canter of a mounted policeman through the sand, as he gave a last look around before rolling in his blanket. Then silence under the dark star-strewn sky, a tranquil desert silence, to be broken, perhaps — who knows? — by ghostly sandals, as the padre walked to see that curious company, asleep in his one-time garden, guests of a pagan feast.

XXII

ON THE HEELS OF ADVENTURE

I have lived both at the Hawes and Burford in a perpetual
flutter, on the heels, as it seems, of some adventure that
should justify the place; but though the feeling had me to
bed at night and called me up again at morning in one unbroken round of pleasure and suspense, nothing befell me in
either worth remark. The man or the hour had not yet
come; but some day, I think, a boat shall put off from the
Queen's Ferry, fraught with a dear cargo, and some frosty
night a horseman, on a tragic errand, rattle with his whip
upon the green shutters of the inn at Burford. — STEVENSON:
A Gossip on Romance

ADVENTURE! The *Standard Dictionary* divides it, like
Gaul, into three parts, peculiarly interrelated, yet thinly
divisible from each other: — (1) A remarkable or hazardous experience; an unexpected or exciting occurrence.
(2) A hazardous or uncertain undertaking; a daring feat.
(3) The encountering of risks; daring and hazardous
enterprise.

And the writing of it has come to signify swift dramatic
action, having a spirited and triumphant finale.

But life in the Desert, — for that matter, life anywhere,
— does not advance to a whiplash conclusion. One may
not dismiss unwelcome characters simply because con-
venience or stark justice demands *Finis*. Despite taut
emotions and unsavory possibilities, they go on living
and muddling up the action; and the sun rises, and
to-morrow is another day. My personal experiences
among the Indians in the lonely places have not been

exactly hazardous or desperately daring from my point of view, indeed, not half so venturesome as nights I have spent in New York. One will have to accept these reminiscences as simply unusual and I hope not uninteresting happenings, with what of thrill they may inspire. Would you insist that I lug in ghosts or bandits? Should I stage a massacre? Perhaps I could contrive to have Youkeoma abduct the trader's daughter, and arrange a nick-of-time rescue by the cavalry. But Youkeoma was interested in ceremonies only, as he told me, and the trader had no daughter. I should therefore libel a sincere pagan and a bachelor business-man.

Now it strikes me that there is more of nervous drama in Colonel Scott's going alone into a half-hostile camp, facing down a band of sullen fellows, and coming out with obedience to his decisions. It strikes me, too, that in these desert camps that have known so little of discipline, with no force in the offing and no hope of one, is the real drama of an Agent's life. I can relate my kind of thrill, but there will be little of dramatic conclusions. Nothing of wild rides, and pursuits, and ambuscades; nothing of foiled villains, and certainly nothing of beautiful maidens in distress. This last the Indian Service does not invite, and if accidentally acquired does not long retain.

The nearest to that sort of adventure I ever came was in meeting the mail-hack one cold sunset, far from the Agency. It was driven by a half-frozen Mexican who could speak no English beyond: "Buenas dias, señor. Mucho frio. No savvy."

There was a pleasing young woman with him, who said she was a teacher, ordered to report to the Agent at Keams Cañon. Our meeting-place was about thirty miles from the last post-house, and quite ninety miles from the railroad. I can imagine how strange and timid one feels under such conditions. It had been a bleak day, and a keen night was coming on. My auto would reach the Agency hours before those two weary bronks could plod in; so I introduced myself, and said she would travel quicker to the Agency with me. She looked me over: dingy hat, rusty puttees, red nose, everything — and decided to remain with the voluble Mexican.

I can remember leaving Chin Lee one winter's night, black shadows on the snow-covered desert and a razor-edged wind coming straight out of that huge funnel, Cañon de Chelly, to go seventy-five miles to Kayenta, the most isolated post-office and trading-post in the United States. I had been bluffed into it by my friend, the Water-Witch, who wanted to save the morrow's daylight.

"Can you stand an all-night hike?" he asked, solicitously. "Sing out if you can't. There's a good bed here, and — "

"I'm game for it, if you are," I said, but without enthusiasm.

The engine of his emaciated Ford clucked, and the snow crunched under its wheels. For the first hour a brisk conversation kept us illuminated and fairly warm. Then it grew deadly cold, with that relentless, piercing cold to be experienced only at night in those cruelly bleak, windswept, desert wastes. I bit down on my pipe to prevent my teeth castanetting. I felt of my face to be sure it had not cracked off. And we rode on and on, paralleling the dim Black Mountain barricade. Finally, with bitter exasperation, the Witch called out: "Dammit all! ain't you cold?"

"Froze," I gasped.

"Well, there's a trading-post hiding in this side cañon,

if I can find the road to it. You'll never sing out. I give up. Let's make for camp before we both perish."

I uttered choking sounds of thanksgiving. And it drearily seemed, for a space, that he would not be able to find the trail. The snow was unbroken in the hills. Then we caught a gleam from the black, gave a hail, and found a cedar-fire welcome.

Those are Arizona adventures.

One may encounter them in boggy flats, or in blinding snowstorms; in seeking to cross a river in springtime without too much knowledge of the ford; in facing the hot sand's lash that stings as powdered glass; with exhausted horses and far from the town, on hearing the crunch of a drive-pinion twenty miles the wrong side of home; at nightfall; at midnight, noon, or dawn. The blush of morning on snow-encrusted cliffs, the wistful mysteries of summer twilight, the burnished glories of an autumn sunset, have no appeal then. Simple struggles with the elements and distances of the lonely Desert, when tired out, cold, hungry. They are the day's work, hard, exhausting work. And one does not record such things in Annual Reports.

But, since adventures are in demand, perhaps I can resurrect a thrill or two from the notebook. Long ago I listed them as scenery for stories, meaning to import a few interesting and even beautiful types as characters, for the honest-to-God, on-the-ground people steadily refused to become heroic. Relatively mild affairs these, with only two persons killed, two crippled up a bit, some little blood spilled, and lots of nervous imagining. My men were uneasy at the time, and I most scared of all.

If I had thrust these episodes on a New York editor, out of their order and true atmosphere, garnished with a

picaresque dressing, he might have praised them; but I
was not among those killed, and reflection urges that this
would probably make a difference to him. Aside from
having a thumb sprained when an angry Indian tried to
wrench it off my hand, I was not physically hurt; but my
nervous system was slightly warped each time, and I have
been reported on as an efficient, but very profane man.
Quite so. I will admit that I never took any saints along
on these trips.

And in every single one of these affairs, the enemy
triumphed. "The man or the hour had not yet come";
and while I have had mounted messengers of both sexes
come to me on both frosty and tepid nights, their errands,
after due investigation, and however irritating, could
not be classed as tragic; but there were times when "the
feeling of it had me to bed and up again" in a round of
anticipation and some little suspense, decidedly not so
pleasurable as romantic Stevenson found his.

One undertaking began with Limping Joe paying attention to Do-hahs-tahhe's wife. This was not appreciated
by either of them, and the husband first warned, and then
threw Limping Joe bodily out of his neighborhood. This
angered the potential home-wrecker, and he returned with
a light rifle. Do-hahs-tahhe was sacking corn in his field
close to his hogan. He saw Limping Joe approaching, and
while .22's are rabbit-guns, they sometimes go off when
least expected and injure people. Again Do-hahs-tahhe
flung himself on Limping Joe; he wrenched the rifle away
from him, threw out the single shell, and smashed the
stock over a stone. Observing then that he held only the
barrel, he whirled it around his head and let go of it.
It winged off, end over end, and down into the wash.

Limping Joe went down into the wash and found the gun. He examined the lock and saw that a shell would go into it. Pointing it in the air, he pulled the trigger. Bang! it was all right, even though it had no stock for the shoulder. Then Limping Joe put in another shell, stalked up the bank, and shot Do-hahs-tahhe through the lungs.

Therefore the Indian Agent had to forward one physician, one stenographer, one notary public, and a few police, promptly, hurriedly, to take the man's dying statement: the doctor to tell him he was dying, the stenographer to report him, and the notary to swear them all. The police meantime grabbed Limping Joe. Do-hahs-tahhe died in a few hours and Limping Joe sat in the guardhouse with gyves upon his wrists, also shackles securing his ankles, and a log-chain connecting the two contrivances. I did not intend that he should — and he did not — get away.

This was in Territorial days, and a Reservation criminal-case came, strangely enough, within the jurisdiction of the Territorial courts. I sent for the county sheriff, and he arrived with one huge deputy, both of them heavily armed.

"Why the arsenal?" I asked of the officer, who had a reputation for fearlessness.

"Well, I have had Indian prisoners taken from me before," he said.

Now there had been some little rumor of dissatisfaction among the relatives and friends of Limping Joe. They felt he should be tried by the Agent, quite as one who had purloined a sheep, and they expected that he would receive a mild type of punishment. Gossip had it that they would oppose his being removed from the Desert.

"I'll go with you to the Reservation line," I said to the

sheriff, "and this side of it, they will have to take him away from me."

"Very good," replied the officer, "because I would n't fight for him."

And I made up my mind that neither would I.

We started with the stars still bright in the sky, three o'clock of a morning, to cover the thirty-five miles to the line. The sheriff and deputy rode in a buckboard, the prisoner with them. An Indian boy drove my buggy, and I sat with a gun on the seat. Nothing happened. We did not see a Navajo on the trip. After lunching at the line, we parted with the officers, and prepared to return that same day. Seventy miles for the team would be a hard drive and would bring us in late at night; but this is in the day's work too.

All that afternoon the horses jogged homeward. The prisoner off my hands, I dropped the gun into a bag under the seat. It was getting on to dark when the team began wearily climbing the last long rise that separated us from the drop down into Keams Cañon. There was a fringe of cedars at the top, black as spectres against a dull red sky. The horses plodded nearer and nearer to the crest of the ridge. One could see the branches of the old trees now, as if etched on the sky's plate.

Then came a call, a Navajo cry. My boy pulled in the team with a sudden wrench. He had been watching the edge of the hill. And from the trees four or five men stepped quickly into the road. I made a swift clutch on the seat for the gun, and then realized that it could not be there. The bag had slipped back into the boot, and was mixed with halters, nose-bags, and the clutter of a desert buggy. There was a moment — it seemed a week — of tense chilliness, while they lingered in the dusk, as if waiting for us. One cannot wheel a buggy in a desert road. It was either stop or go on. Then they crossed into the cedars, and we heard them moving off, talking in Navajo. One began to sing. My Indian boy laughed as if relieved.

"The miners," he said.

And sure enough, they were my own coal-working gang that had quit the drift at five o'clock and had reached that point on their way home. But I had thought, and so had my driver, that friends of Limping Joe were about to greet us. It was just the right time in the evening, and just the right color in the sombre landscape; and they had stepped from the trees, half-waiting, in just that manner.

Limping Joe? The court treated him with customary severity. For this deliberate, cold-blooded murder he received the terrible sentence of three years in the penitentiary, and had quite six months off for good behavior. During his protracted absence I issued rations to his aged parents and, after quite a little correspondence, some of it acrid in tone, convinced my Washington critics that I had not persecuted the poor fellow.

The East contains very few officials having the courage of Roosevelt, who wrote, with respect to the Navajo particularly: —

These are as a whole good Indians . . . although some are very bad and should be handled rigorously. . . .

For the last quarter of a century the lawless individuals among them have done much more wrong (including murder) to the whites than has been done to them by lawless whites. The lawless Indians are the worst menace to the others among the Navajo and Utes; and very serious harm has been done by well-meaning Eastern philanthropists who have encouraged and protected these criminals.

IN THE TWIN-BUTTE COUNTRY

SILVERSMITH JIM: A TYPICAL NAVAJO

And Francis E. Leupp, one-time Commissioner of Indian Affairs, held this view: —

Agents and other Government officials, when of the best type, have done most good; and when not of the right type have done most evil; and they have never done any good at all when they have been afraid of the Indians or have hesitated relentlessly to punish Indian wrongdoers.

Apart from the administration period of these two men, few Indian Agents have expected to receive support in any effort thoroughly to punish Indian criminals in the Desert. The tone of the Indian Bureau this last decade has been largely one of compromise and apology: with superiors in office; to sentimentalists; with and to discontented or stupid or evil Indians who blocked progress. Annually, when seeking appropriations, it has apologized to Congress for asking, and then apologized most humbly when denied. Charged with the protection and welfare of incompetent human beings, one would think it dealt in wooden dolls. Inconsistent, and of little vision, wastefully parsimonious, ignoring sage advice, ready to compromise, it has been a poor source for justice and a sorry judge of men. Of timely intelligence it has demonstrated little, and of sincerity, less. To manœuvre in the winds of expediency, to trim sail for maintenance in office, to drift hopefully, has been its course and policy. The distant field has viewed such variable charts with suspicion and dismay.

Perhaps a parable may prove amusing.

"Colonel" Oldhouse, who had about reached the retirement age, suspected all new-fangled methods. Behind his desk rested an old hand-made army-chest, strapped and locked to withstand the strains and bruises of frontier travel. The Colonel dated from those days when the stage ran "to the States," and Santa Fe was an outpost of progress. In that chest reposed his warrants and accounts, neatly arranged, jacketed, and briefed. He could go to it in the dark and instantly find Voucher 137 for the second quarter of 1889.

"Colonel," said a very young man, "Why don't you order some files for your papers, with sliding drawers, and rods, and — "

The Colonel snorted.

"They're no good," he snapped; "the damned things are made by machinery!"

Exactly, Colonel; you have accurately described the ineffectiveness of a filing-case.

XXIII

THE RED BOOTLEGGERS

And I will make it felony to drink small beer. — *King Henry VI*

THE heart of the Enchanted Desert, consisting of the Hopi Reserve and a wide strip of Navajo country surrounding it as a frame, was not troubled by the liquor problem among its natives so long as the State of Arizona remained generously wet. The Hopi Indians have no use for liquor, and will not tolerate it. On one occasion men of the mesas, who were without authority to act as policemen, arrested and brought in a Navajo who had simply exhibited a suspicious bottle; a very singular thing for Hopi to do, since they are not bold, even when commissioned. For years Hopi and Navajo freighters packed Government stores from the railroad town of Holbrook, distant eighty miles from the Agency and nearly fifty of them outside the reservation, without engaging in sprees or bootlegging. The Navajo rather likes his beverages, and they do not improve him as a neighbor; but drunkenness was rare even among the Navajo in those days.

When the State went dry, the acquisition of liquor presented something of adventure to those who were naturally lawless. And it was not long before cargoes of cheering fluids began to arrive in the Navajo country from New Mexico. The town of Gallup became a point of interest for Indians who never before had visited it. Gallup is one hundred and five miles from the Hopi Agency, and of course contraband is not packed along highroads.

When the "special officers" of the Indian Liquor Service descended on Gallup, the Navajo organized relays to serve the back country; and the special officers did not follow into the lonesome places. One might be sure that at every Navajo gathering there would be boozing, and at points one hundred to one hundred and fifty miles from the source, and that same distance from special officers. The smugglers would hide the liquor beyond the great circle of campers, in the black of some thicket, and along in the early morning hours, when chance visitors had departed and watchers were tired out, the bibulous would appear in various stages of intoxication. They were then dangerous.

My police force consisted of eight Indians, half of them Navajo. This was the "army" granted me in 1911, with due regard for Colonel Scott's recommendation that I should have twenty-five men headed by a white officer. And in 1921, ten years after that first recommendation, Major-General Scott, retired, of the Board of Indian Commissioners, reviewed the Hopi-Navajo situation, and again reported: —

In 1882 an Executive Order set apart 2,472,320 acres (3863 square miles) of land for the Moqui Reservation, for the use and occupancy of the Hopi *and such other* Indians as the Secretary of the Interior might designate.

At that time someone with a ruler drew on a map a parallelogram which represented an area, approximately 75 by 55 miles, for a reservation, without the least regard to topographical and ethnological conditions, and misnamed it the "Moqui Reservation."

It is quite apparent that in 1882 the authorities in Washington either were densely ignorant of the situation in this country at that time, or were utterly indifferent to it; and by laying out the reservation with a desk ruler and an utter disregard of the welfare of the Hopi, they laid the foundations for trouble and suffering which have developed a situation that calls for remedial action by the Indian Office.

This whole land is semi-arid, and a large portion of it is absolute desert. The Navajo are aggressive and independent. There is no doubt that the majority of those on the Moqui Reserve have come in from all sides with a deliberate purpose of taking the grazing land which rightfully belongs to the Hopi. *When a Navajo sees a Hopi with anything he wants, he takes it*, and there is no recourse.

For years this preventable situation has continued. In 1911 I was sent by President Taft to Keams Cañon with troops, to enforce some regulations of the Indian Office. I then found the Navajo encroaching on Hopi land and mistreating the Hopi Indians. The Agent, at that time, was given but three police-men, too poorly paid to attract the right men with which to maintain order on a reservation having the area of an empire. I then recommended that he be given twenty-five well-paid policemen with a white chief. The number was increased to eight without change of compensation, which number has lately been reduced to six.

This statement is enough to show the absurdity of any expectation that the superintendent can keep order. The superintendent is powerless to maintain the dignity of his office, with the result that the authority and dignity of the Indian Office and of the United States are made a mock over a large section of Arizona.

You see, my successor was having his troubles too with the gentle feudists, and the Hopi were petitioning as usual. So the Office changed the name of the Reservation.

In addition to the eight men that had been granted me, several of the range employees were commissioned as special officers of the Indian Liquor Service. Perhaps I should say, "Deputy special-officers of the Service for the suppression of the liquor traffic among Indians." But what is a title among friends? And the commission was a splendid gratuity, carrying no extra compensation, whereas the employee so acting, in a true missionary spirit, simply risked his life. Few men care for this work, and fewer are zealous at it. Those who came into the regular Service as farmers or stockmen did not relish finding themselves drafted as policemen. It is dangerous work among such Indians as the Navajo, and the man, white or Indian, who accepts this duty expects assurance of consideration and backing should anything unpleasant occur. And in time they all heard of the Walter Runke case, plus the charming experiences of that Agent's faithful subordinates.

Several times my white deputies, aided by Indian police, made arrests in camps in the wee sma' hours, and had their prisoners taken from them. Several times they managed to deliver prisoners at the Agency, and the apology of a guardhouse failed to retain them. After I had the window-bars reënforced and the door double-grated, and chained a few worthies to the wall, the effect of punishment slightly improved. But I could do this only after having procured the guilty ones, and the hunting of them was becoming more and more dangerous. One night, between the hours of ten and two, I searched a number of Navajo camps in the north, seeking an escaped prisoner. This was probably a hazardous proceeding, for the innocent Indians felt aggrieved at the invasion of their privacy, and the guilty had the pleasure of outwitting me — a very easy performance.

When next a dance was advertised, I assembled the Indian police, the judges, and a dozen of the influential head-men or chiefs of the tribe. I counseled them all to assist in this campaign against liquor, which was ruining their young men; and this they promised to do. Especially were the older chiefs earnest about it. They did not wish the tribe to suffer discredit, with the strong probability of a few murders to boot. About twenty men departed to the place of the dance, all pledged to exert their very best grade of moral suasion, fatherly counsel, and peaceful penetration.

Two days later a squad of indignant head-men assembled in my office. They were evidently angry about something; and the spokesman talked plainly.

"We have failed," he said. "After midnight the drunkards began to appear, and dance and shout and annoy decent people. Several were arrested by the police, but they were supported by others, and the police could do nothing without fear of hurting someone. Then we old men undertook to shame them. They rose against us all, and drove us headlong from the camp — police, judges, chiefs. This matter places us in a shameful position before our people. We want you to write to Washington for soldiers. They have sent soldiers here before, and they can do so again. We need them. You tell Washington that."

But just at that time Washington had its hands full of typewriters, holding the Germans to strict accountability on paper; and one Villa was scouting along the Border.

My remaining hope was to trap the smugglers before they reached the scene of disposal. And following this method, it came about that One-eyed Dan and his partner, hailing from the Fort Defiance district, were arrested as they traveled north on my reservation. They had a trunk loaded with the most diabolical booze. It was in standard bottles, with all seals intact; but the bottoms had been plugged by an electric process, and the good stuff replaced with a concoction that suggested Battle-axe tobacco in a solution of nitric acid. Two drinks of this would cause a jack rabbit to assault a bobcat. And for this enthusiasm Navajo Indians would cheerfully pay thirty-five dollars the quart.

We lost little time in questioning these fellows. The Federal Court was in session at Prescott, Arizona. One-eyed Dan *et al.*, arrested at noon, were delivered at the Agency by two o'clock; and by three, autos were rolling with these gentry and witnesses and the evidence, toward the railroad. We would catch the night train, and make a swift job of it; one day peddling in the empire, the next in court and ready for sentence. Dan and his compadre were made comfortable in a back seat, handcuffed, and shackled together. A Navajo will not hesitate to leap from a car if free, and then it is either let him go or wing him. It does n't pay to wing him.

But we were delayed. One cannot make an average twenty miles per hour through that country, and it was close to six o'clock when we reached the Indian Wells trading-post, just across the reservation line. All through that district the Navajo are settled upon alternate sections of land governed by the Leupp Indian Agency, and it is not "reservation" of a solid block. The intervening sections are "railroad lands," bonus grants for building what is now the Santa Fe system. In this fashion the Government gave the first railway a very large part of the Southwest, a seemingly unimportant and nonproductive country at that time, and one could find Santa Fe titles forty miles either side of its tracks. The Indians knew nothing of these paper records, and roamed indiscriminately with their camps and sheep, wrangling about water with range cattlemen who had leased from the railroad, viewing with suspicion those few men who bought outright; and Washington found it — still finds it — "a very perplexing question."

The trading-post was closed, its owner at supper. But sitting on the stone doorstep was a dejected Navajo who appeared to have had a desperate and losing battle. His head, face, and shirt were covered with blood, some of which had dried; and some of the fresh he was still trying to staunch. Just then the trader appeared.

"Glad you arrived," he said, seeming relieved. "I was wondering what to do about this. I saw the whole affair. This man fought with two Navajo off there in the flat. They were through here several days ago, going to the railroad for liquor. Seems that they got back with it all right, and would n't give this chap his share. Anyway, they fought it out, beating him over the head with their forty-fives. I've been washing his scalp this last half-hour."

He could give the names of the two, and the location of their home camp.

"Just back in the hills," he said, waving. "Not more than two miles at most. They ought to be cinched."

"It's not my jurisdiction," I said. "Their Agent is fifty miles away, and one hundred miles roundabout the railroad."

"Time he gets here," said the trader, "booze and all will be gone, and may be another scrap or two; like as not, murder done."

"Have they been gathering for a sing?" I asked.

"No, nothing scheduled like that. They're running north into your country, peddling a little along the way."

Now it looked as if someone should do something without waiting for telegrams and a handful of printed tracts. I had One-eyed Dan already in hand, and three "special deputies" to assist in the capture of those who had trimmed the fellow on the doorstep. The injured man agreed to identify and to appear against them. We would bag the whole outfit, and stand four in court next day. The trail was warm, and the Leupp Agent could not hope to arrive before the next afternoon. And it was only two miles over the hill.

"We'll have some supper, and then get those fellows, if you" (meaning the trader) "will show the road."

"I sure will," he agreed.

After a meal, he led the way in his car, and we followed. Two miles over the hill! It is true we found one deserted camp. And then we went on and on. The orders were, silence, and lights out. The road into the Castle Butte country is winding, over little steep-pitched hills and down through narrow washes. When we had gone five miles, deep night had shut down, lighted only by a misty moon that rather obscured things in those twisted little vales and defiles. Suddenly the trader stopped his car.

"I believe that's one of them," he called.

Ahead of us showed a pony. Two of the deputies jumped out and ran forward, to find a man and a boy on the one horse. Off came the man, and the boy too. At the car he was identified as one of the assailants. The pony was turned loose to graze. The man joined One-eyed Dan _et al._ in the rear seat, another pair of handcuffs making the three secure in one squad.

But we had reckoned without the boy. He was about ten years old, and these things seemed to him as mysterious, not to say alarming. When he realized that strange men had chained up his kinsman, he raised a soul-stirring bawl to Heaven. It was no time or place for explanations, so we gagged him with a handkerchief and prepared to go on.

"How much farther?" I asked the guide.

"Just over the next hill."

"Well, this speedometer says we have come seven miles."

"From the next pitch we shall see the camp," he assured me, confidently.

"How many live there?"

"Two families."

And from the next rise we could see the light of a fire.

"It looks like a larger camp than that," I told him. "Are you sure there is no sing going on?"

"Not a sign of it these last several days. That fire's in the corral, just beyond their hogans."

"Then run all three cars fairly close to the gate of it. Keep these prisoners in the last one, back in the shadow, and don't make a show of guns. I'll go in and investigate. If you fellows hear a row, you can then come up."

The light of the fire grew brighter as we crept on, driving the cars as noiselessly as possible, and one learns to do that in the Desert. The corral was a large one, the logs set on end, and the firelight streamed through the crevices. One could not see inside until very close. About twenty yards from the gate or entrance we lined the cars, throwing the headlights on that opening. It is trying to face a brilliant auto-lamp, and those behind it have an advantage. I jumped from the step and went quickly forward, carrying a quirt.

In a strange country and among strange Indians, a gun may prove a dangerous weapon; but that does not prevent one from carrying a quirt having a loaded grip.

If anyone had caught the boy's cries or had heard our approach, there was no sign of it. Apparently there was no one to hear. The place seemed deserted. Outside the corral, one could see only a silent camp, untenanted, noiseless, painted by a great wave of brilliant light. No dogs started up. It was very strange, and decidedly unlike most Navajo camps.

At a brisk walk I went through the corral gate — to face fifty or more husky Navajo Indians, all males, crowded together, waiting. And each one of them eyed me as if to ask my business. They knew that I was not their Nahtahni.

There was no going back. I would have to chance their sober or drunken condition. I walked up to the fire, and asked, with as much unconcern as possible to muster: "Where is Bitani Bega?"

Silence — that sullen, contemptuous silence of the suspicious Navajo who has not come forward to greet one, and who will hide whatever he knows behind a mask of indifferent and stolid ignorance. I looked them over, wondering if they were all strangers to me. A colony of my Navajo lived in the southern line and traded at the Indian Wells post; but not a man of them could I see. Then, in all that crowd, I sighted an educated face. One learns to distinguish between the Navajo who has been to school and the one who has never had a hair-cut. The former has a keener expression, a brighter cast of countenance, though his hair may be once again uncared for. I walked up to him, and demanded: "Where did you go to school?"

He wavered for a moment, as if to deny his knowledge of English, and then answered: "At Leupp."

"Why did n't you speak up before? You know me?"

"Yes," he said. "I remember you at Leupp. I was a little boy then, and you went away. You are superintendent up here somewhere."

I felt easier now. But I did not care to have any one of them straggle outside, to learn that I had three Navajo handcuffed in my car, and one of them their own, to say nothing of a boy who had been gagged. Just then the trader and one of my deputies, who had waited long enough and were wondering what had happened to me, appeared in the gateway. I told them to stop there; and, as I expected, so long as they were there, no one of the crowd sought to go out.

"You can interpret for me," I said to the returned student. "I am looking for a man named Bitani Bega, who lives in this district, and who runs booze. He beat up another Navajo this afternoon at Indian Wells. I want to know where he is.'

The young Navajo rattled this off to the crowd.

"Ep-ten," they began to exclaim, in various tones, shaking their heads, meaning that this was entirely outside their knowledge.

"Do you see that fellow here?" I called to the trader, wondering what I should do if he did recognize him. But the trader shook his head.

At one end of the corral was a brush shelter or shed. Under it camp equipment was scattered: harness, boxes, kegs for water-carrying, and blanketed bundles.

"Tell them I am going to search the camp," I said.

"Search for what?" several asked.

"For liquor," and with no positive assurance that I would be permitted to continue long, I went about it. It was simply a display, to keep up appearances. Any quantity of liquor would have been cached outside, and as all present were sober, it was not likely that any had been brought in. My sole idea was to bluff them for a little, and then get away. I sincerely wanted to get away without fuss. Undoubtedly they had congregated for a drinking bout, and I had one of them, and the second bootlegger was probably watching from some hillside brush at that moment. Later in the night they would welcome him and his assortment of bottled trouble. They moved away from their belongings, and I failed to find any contraband in the various bales and kegs scattered under the shelter.

"You tell these men that I am going on to Leupp. If there is any boozing here, you may expect that Nahtahni will hear of it."

They received this in silence, but it was a silence that seemed to bode me no great blessing. The men at the gate swung the cars around to head away from there, and then I strolled out of the corral, carrying a belief that I had narrowly missed something. And if you do not grasp my emotion, if you think I was unnecessarily alarmed, I cannot hope to convince you or explain how one feels hostility and resentment among these desert people. I was not welcome in that camp, and very likely it was a good thing for me that I did not find Bitani Bega.

The road away from the camp was now better known to us, and we did not waste time. At the first camp we dropped the boy, and he scuttled away in the shadows, followed by a lecture in Navajo.

"How's the Cottonwood crossing?" someone asked the trader.

"It's all right, if you know where to hit it," he replied. "Go on down there and wait for me. I'll get my coat at the store, and a couple of shovels, and then pilot you

across. Don't attempt it without me. You'll get bogged,
sure."

He left us at the next turning, and we went on to the
crossing. There was no bridge in those days, and the
Cottonwood was a nasty place. At times one could go
straight across, and at other times he would do well to go
several miles up the wash to cross and return. We drove
on carefully and worked our way to the edge of a hum-
mocky place, and there was nothing to do but wait for
the trader's return. The night had grown clearer now;
the air was crisp and the stars bright.

I'll see if the engine needs any water," said one of
the men.

The three prisoners drowsed in the rear seat. We both
got out and leaned our rifles against a front fender. The
driver of the other car did the same. Having watered
the iron horses, we stepped off a few yards and stood
talking, when suddenly, one of the men threw up his hand
and called: "Listen!"

One can hear noises a long way in the open spaces, and
we had left the hills and were now in a great flat. On the
quiet air came the sound of many hoofs, drumming, racing
down on us. A quick scramble back to the cars and the
rifles. There was no crossing that wash without a guide.
We swung the cars broadside of the road, and turned off
the lights.

Of course, we thought the boy had returned, and
they were now about to rescue their captured neighbor.
Naturally they would seek us at the crossing. I threw the
rifle lever and a shell into the breech, and learned across
the engine. We would have the car between us.

The hoofs pounded nearer, a dozen or more ponies.

"Uptohulloa!" roared the big stockman, a word he

could fire like a broadside. They reined in, a group of shadowy horsemen.

"Where you going?" was pieced out from our smattering of Navajo. Then one of them rode forward, and we recognized a man from a camp below the wash.

"Going home," he said, simply.

We had no fault to find with this, and said so. Their ponies slowly and gingerly began crossing the bog, following a devious trail. Another thrill shattered. It is a land where nothing ever happens until, through misfortune or misunderstanding, the wholly unexpected occurs.

When our guide came up, we too crossed, and three hours later we reached the Holbrook jail. The deputy sheriff in charge said that all hotels were filled, and we were too tired to seek lodging elsewhere. What would do for the prisoners would be gratefully accepted by the posse. So we all slept that night behind the bars.

Very early I found a physician to examine and dress the wounds of our battered witness, and I telegraphed the Leupp Indian Agent for instructions as to the one prisoner from his Bidahoche province. He replied that he would come for the man. We went on to court with the liquor cases.[1] There One-eyed Dan and his partner pleaded guilty, and were sentenced to a rest of several months in

---

[1] Sections 2140 and 2141 of the United States Revised Statutes, together with later laws and amendments, empower Indian Agents and their properly commissioned deputies to search for, confiscate, and destroy intoxicating beverages within Indian country, to seize the means of transportation, to destroy stills, and to prosecute in the Federal Courts those persons who violate these statutes. Indian Agents and their "special deputies" are clothed by law with the authorities of United States Marshals and their deputies in the prosecution of this work. The possession of intoxicating liquors in the Indian country is prima facie evidence of unlawful introduction.

While the provisions of the National Prohibition Act limited these authorities for a period, the United States Supreme Court has held that the earlier laws enacted for the control of Indian country are not inconsistent with and were not repealed by the National Prohibition Act. To-day, an Indian Agent has practically all the original power with which to curb the liquor traffic within his jurisdiction.

jail; whence, having recuperated and made new plans, they returned to the back-country game with renewed spirits.

My colleague of the Leupp Agency managed things differently. The complainant and prisoner were taken to his headquarters, where he heard the case as Nahtahni, and sentenced the guilty to break rock for a considerable period. However, this was not nearly so impressive to the Indian as action in a foreign court, removed from the Indian country; but it is a pity that the circumstance of capture and the possibility of crime weigh so little when the Indian culprit is arraigned before those not conversant with his daily life.

XXIV

HELD FOR RANSOM

It is always a temptation to a rich and lazy nation,
　To puff and look important and to say:
"Though we know we should defeat you,
We have not the time to meet you.
　We will therefore pay you cash to go away."

And that is called paying the Dane-geld;
　But we've proved it again and again,
That if once you have paid him the Dane-geld
　You never get rid of the Dane.
　　　　　　　　　— *Songs from English History*

FOR seven long years I lived in a two-penny house at the Agency, the rooms of which were nine by twelve, and the floors not level. I decided to increase the size of it, so that three or four visitors might arrange themselves in one room without compelling their host to step outside. This necessitated removing several walls, and for months I slept in a draughty place, surrounded by broken plaster, piles of lumber, mortar-boards and paint-pots. If one wished to call, he scrambled up a long plank having cleats nailed to it, fell over the débris, and projected himself into my bedroom. It was literally all doorway, and it opened on the Desert.

One morning, about three A.M., I was aroused by a resounding crash. Some one called earnestly for Moungwi. I turned on a flashlight, and rescued an Indian policeman from a trap of metal-lathe and scaffolding. It was one of the Tewa who had ridden in.

"What's the trouble?" I asked him.

"There's a man shot in the Wepo Wash — Navajo; and they're holding a Hopi for it. Billa Chezzi says must kill him *pronto*. Come right away and stop it. Here's a letter."

The note he handed me had been hurriedly written by an Indian girl of the mesa, and she had been so filled with the necessity for my coming "to stop it" that she had failed to give all the facts. It appeared however that an unfortunate Hopi, held a prisoner by the Navajo of the North, was to be butchered by sundown; and the sun had gone down and was about to come up again.

I aroused the physician and the big stockman from their slumbers.

"We'll start at daylight, so get ready."

The stockman routed out the Navajo interpreter, and they began adjusting a Ford car, in the hope that it would hold together through a nervous experience.

Just at daybreak a range Navajo rode in with another note. This was from the redoubtable Ed, trading now in the Bakidbahotzne country of the central North, and who kept me advised from that distant station.

Billa Chezzi and his gang have a Hopi boy up here, and all last night they argued to kill him. I advised them to send for you. They are not in the best of humors. Seems that this Hopi boy shot a Navajo boy. Bring the doctor. The Navajo is not dead yet.

Now this looked a trifle better, but there was an ominous possibility in his last sentence. "The Navajo is not dead — yet."

There were four of us in the car: the physician, the stockman, the Indian interpreter, and myself. Several policemen clattered their way over the shorter trails, but I did not feel that they would help matters much. On reaching the First Mesa we learned that a Hopi lad named Lidge Palaquoto, the son of Pah-lah, a widow, and who was aged about fourteen years, had been out with sheep in the upper Wepo Wash. He had carried a .22 rabbit-gun. When he did not return at nightfall, search developed that he was in the hands of the Black Mountain Navajo. He had somehow and for some unknown reason shot a Navajo boy, about two years older than himself.

We would have to round the First Mesa and go through the Wepo Valley sand, but at that Henry's contrivance would make better time than the traditional bronk. In a novel, requiring at this stage a thrilling rescue, we should have rushed to the corrals, subdued several chilly and resisting horses, and consumed four hours pounding through sand and greasewood, to arrive with a clatter and amid dust and revolver smoke. We should have dashed down on them, spattered a volley, swept the lad from the ground in passing, plunged on, and disappeared in a blaze of glory. Yes, I have written that sort of nerve tonic. But we did n't do anything of the kind. We used a Ford. And despite all one's imagination and nervous energy, there is no glory in a Ford.

But in the more prosaic manner we could make the trip in two hours, without saddle-sores, carrying all the believed-necessary tools for any possible emergency. The doctor had his kit for his method of life-saving. There were two Winchester carbines, the stockman packed his cavalry-type .45, and I carried in a spring-sling under my left arm one of Mr. Colt's automatic specials. It did not invite attention there, hampered no one, and could be withdrawn in less than an hour's time. The Government officials at Washington consider these adjuncts altogether unnecessary, and often write words to that effect; and they are unnecessary in Washington, where the writing officials who frown on them are usually to be found at desks, nursing plans for future campaigns. This affair was not billed for Washington. It did not concern auto traffic. It was to be staged in the upper Wepo Wash, and Ed's note had stated that Billa Chezzi stood peevishly at the head of his gang. One should keep in mind that the Navajo go armed. There would be plenty of forty-fives and a few heavy rifles in that crowd. I had prevented their procuring ammunition from the licensed traders of the reservation, but no one prevented their procuring it off the reservation, from unregulated traders and in the railroad towns. Both Federal and Arizona State law decree against the furnishing of either arms or ammunition to Indians, and despite numerous murders in the Navajo country, these laws have been the deadest of defunct letters.

Perhaps, trending along the lines of recent admonitions, we should have carried an outfit for the making of tea, together with several hymnbooks. However, I had other ideas on this subject. I recalled how this favored son of the Desert, to wit, Billa Chezzi, had held up Hubbell the trader, threatening him with a rifle, until disarmed, overpowered, and chained to a post. How he had started a war against a former superintendent. How another Arizona pioneer had been forced to beat Billa nearly to death in defense of his own life. This last affair had occurred at Fort Defiance. And, of course, to be fair to the chief, he had been drunk on all occasions; but could I be sure of his sobriety on this one?

When the car swung around the point of the First Mesa, I counseled the doctor thus: —

"Ed seems to think this Navajo boy will not live. Let us hope he is alive when we get there. You examine him and, at first opportunity, without inviting excitement, tell me about how long he will last. I shall have just that much time in which to settle things. I may need it."

"Suppose he dies?" said the doctor.

"I am hoping he will not die until I have made arrangements. If he kicks in before that, I don't know just what will happen."

And this did not appear to ease the physician's mind.

Half an hour later we saw them, a large party of Indians in the central flat. Some of them were mounted, but for the most part they had turned their ponies loose to graze and were grouped in a throng on foot. It would be there among them, probably haranguing, that I should find old Billa Chezzi, alias Crooked Fingers, with a black silk handkerchief swathed about his head, the perfect picture of a desert bandit. Old, wrinkled, and yellow-toothed, with bleary eyes that narrowed when he became sullen, Billa Chezzi was not the pleasantest of the Navajo chiefs.

"When we get there," I said to the stockman, "look around for that Hopi boy. If you see a Hopi boy, and you have an opportunity, put him in the car; and then you stay with him."

"What then?" he asked.

"Well, if they want him that badly, compel them to climb into the car and take him out of it."

"Do you want me to bean one of those fellows, if they try that?"

"No — that would'n't help any. Simply compel them to take him away from you by force. I'm afraid you will not have the chance. Keep your gun on the seat, but don't use it."

NELSON OYAPING: TEWA
CHIEF OF POLICE

BILLA CHEZZI: CHIEF OF
THE NORTHERN NAVAJO

"You mean — just let them see that it's present?"

"Exactly. But don't make the mistake of pointing it at any one of them, even if he does clamber in."

With the Navajo on his native heath, idle gun-play is a very dangerous experiment, and may prove a grievous mistake. If one draws a gun, the Navajo expects that it will be used. He too has one in his belt, the Government being too pacific to object. There are no delicate preliminaries, such as the usual invitation to elevate the hands and behave. The Navajo reasons simply that a gun will explode in his face anyway, and he hopes to beat one to it. It is not an exhibition of his courage or judgment; nothing more or less than ignorant fatalism. While few Indians suicide, often a moody Navajo will announce that he is about to die, and perhaps, if the genii work upon him strongly enough, he may step toward the event. It is all right, though, and creates no comment or offense to have a somnolent gun in plain sight. The Navajo is used to weapons and the gesture is not one of potential threat.

About sixty yards from the group of Indians we found a shelter at the roadside. It had been hastily constructed — cottonwood poles, with a blanket across them to afford a little shade. The doctor stooped and crawled in to view his patient. Several elders of the family were there, besides the mother and father of the boy, and I shook hands with them. In a few moments the stockman was missed, but when next I looked toward the car he had returned there. Beside him perched a little Hopi boy.

"I've got him," he called to me.

That part of it was finished nicely, but the question of keeping him was yet to be decided. Just then the physician crawled out from the shelter with no joy on his face.

"Bad," he said. "Shot straight down through the top

of the skull. Looks as if he was fired on from above. He may live an hour — not longer than that."

Now from the direction of the mesas the Hopi were gathering. We had passed a few of them on the road, trudging along determinedly. For the first time in my experience with them, they were going doggedly into the debatable country for a council with the old enemy, and with a view to resisting him if necessary. It looked as if there would be a fight, unless somebody weakened.

"They are not going to kill Lidge," announced one sturdy fellow as we passed him.

"Keep quiet about that," I cautioned him. "Let me talk with those fellows."

So, when I walked toward the group of Navajo, I realized that Hopi were coming up and making an equally sullen group behind me. The Navajo crowd parted and old Billa Chezzi stepped out of it. He had a light rifle in his hand, and a woeful expression on his aged face. He put his arm around me and besought me as his younger brother. And then tears, large, globular tears, coursed down the ragged furrows of his cheeks, as he told me of the senseless crime that had been committed against them. A small boy wickedly shot down, an innocent slaughtered, a wanton killing. And so they must have blood for this thing: an eye for an eye, — though he had no knowledge of the sacred Books. That was the old law in the Desert. And he did not let go of the rifle. As he wept copiously on my shoulder, I reached down and took hold of the gun, too. Then we talked along sympathetic lines, each holding tenaciously to the weapon. I understood that it was the evidence in the case.

When he went further into his recital, through the interpreter, he came to mentioning the gun's part, and it was necessary for me to examine it closely. He did not want to give it up at first. But he finally yielded it. I opened the breech, and was glad to find it empty. Then I took it by the barrel, grounded the stock in the sand, and he never got hold of it after that. Somehow, I felt a little easier in having it to myself. In a measure, he had surrendered a bit of his problem into my hands.

And we talked. Finally we sat down on the ground and a number of his band with us, the rest crowded up, standing. Now I had expected that Ed would come up. He was the best interpreter in the Navajo country, and not afraid of them. It was plain that the sympathies of my Indian interpreter were not with the Hopi in this argument. Aside from the impending death of the boy, here was another real danger, and one that most Agents are forced to suffer. Indians cannot be rushed to a decision. They must have their talk out, and through talking always weaken their grievances. But untrustworthy interpretation has caused more than one man's death. "I will fix it up for you," silently decides the ignorant mouthpiece, thus fastening his poor intentions on the one who will have to accept responsibility in the end. And sometimes he fixes it entirely too well. Seldom it is that he interprets the full value of the discourse. He avoids completely translating unpleasant orders, for that might involve him among his people; and when the break comes he will surely prove a traitor, and may be found largely responsible for the break. His sympathies well-up when least expected, and the emotions of my interpreter in this affair had begun to display partizanship.

Finally there came a welcome call, and Mr. Thomas E. Thacker, otherwise known as "Ed," a square trader and a straight talker, rode up.

"They were at it all last night at the store," he said.
"They had the boy there and, whether or no, they were for
killing him. I told them they would have to reckon with
you first, and next with Washington, and not to start
anything they maybe could n't finish. How's the other
boy?"

"The doctor gave him an hour to live, and half of that
is gone."

"Make a deal then, before they savvy it," advised Ed.
"The squaw will let out a yowl when he dies."

That was what I had feared. With my back to that
little shelter, I had lived in dread of the Navajo mother's
wild wail.

"But, Citcili," said Billa Chezzi, for the thirteenth time,
"what will this poor woman do without her son? She
will have no boy at home. The sheep will go untended,
and — "

And for the fourteenth time I told him that matters of
this kind must be settled at Washington, that far-away
indefinite place where so few things are ever settled.
Washington, to the Indian, has the force of a legend. It
is one of the four Corner-Posts, the city of the Dalai Lama.
The soldiers came from there when the Navajo were
herded to the Bosque Redondo in '63, and Billa Chezzi
could remember that, if his cohort of sons and neighbors
could not.

"Well then, she must keep the Hopi boy," he decided.
"He cannot go back to his people any more. She must
have a son."

When I glanced at the car I noted that four or five
husky Indians would be leaning against it, talking with the
stockman. He had taken the Hopi boy between his knees.
I was afraid something foolish might occur, and went back.

"They have been over here four times now," he said; "But they have n't quite got up the nerve to start anything."

At least fifty Hopi Indians had gathered; they stood apart, watching and waiting.

"Have you men any money with you, cash?" I asked them.

The Hopi can always be counted on to have something for a rainy day, and it was very likely to storm.

"I've got five dollars," said one.

"Get what you can from the others. One hundred will not be too much." And then to others who were stockmen: "Have you fellows any cattle in this wash?"

"Our cattle are off there," pointing.

"It's this way," I explained. "We can't fight that gang. The boy will die soon. I'll have to buy them off. How many steers can I have from your several bunches?"

This was quite in line with the Hopi method of dealing with the aggressive Navajo, who had oppressed them so long. They held a rapid discussion and came to quick decision.

"What you need for it," said the spokesman.

"Understand: I don't think Washington will approve of our being held up, and I will have you repaid, if that is possible."

He nodded.

"Take some of the boys and round up those cattle. I may likely require seven or eight two-year-olds."

By this time too they had collected a wad of bills. I went back to the Navajo and began talking again.

"Let us understand this," I told Billa Chezzi. "This shooting was not like a fight between two men, enemies. These were boys — children. They may have been playing together. It was an accident. Of course, that is a careless boy, and Washington does n't want him loose in this country. Sooner or later, he would likely hurt someone else. And I will send him to a place where he cannot hurt any more people. We have such places for bad boys."

"But what will this poor woman do for a son?" he whined.

"You will have to find her a son from among the Navajo. She would n't want a Hopi boy. Every time she looked at him she would think of this happening and be sad. That would n't do. This is what I will do for the father and mother: I will get money from these Hopi, and what is lacking I will pay in cattle."

There was a consultation among them. Some grumbled, but I knew that most of them would regard cattle as better property than a Hopi lad who would have to be watched. They saw too that the Hopi stockmen were busy rounding up the herd. Then they talked a bit with the trader, who was a man of good advices. Ed spoke to me: —

"They want to know if you will stay with the wounded boy until he dies — you and the doctor; and then will you have him buried?"

"Yes, we will attend to that."

"And they want to know if you will pay them now, to-day?"

"Just as soon as the steers are cut out from the bunch."

Then I drew out the money. They eyed it covetously. We agreed on approximately five hundred dollars in cash and stock at the current prices. A dozen Navajo rode off to assist in cutting out the animals, and I sent a Hopi to make the count. The crowd began dwindling away.

A NAVAJO BOY WHO HAS NEVER BEEN TO
ANY SCHOOL

Something had been settled, and they wished to be off before Death stalked across the plain. The Navajo have an awesome fear of the dead; but they would rally again at the mourning feast.

Just then the woman raised her wail, — a long, quavering cry.

I have related before in this chronicle that the Navajo shun funerals. We buried the lad in the sand-dunes close by, and carried Lidge off to the Agency, giving notice to his mother, en route. A short time after this I sent him to a non-reservation school. It would be well for him to be out of the Desert for a few years, — five would be none too many, — otherwise, he might be found along the trail some morning, gone to join that other lad he had so strangely hurt.

It was not possible to get from Lidge a connected story of the shooting. It is my opinion that the Navajo boy rode up, saw the gun, and wanted it. "When a Navajo sees a Hopi with anything he wants, he takes it." Lidge was on foot. No doubt the Navajo boy threw himself off his pony and came around under the horse's neck, stooping. Lidge, more in fright and dismay than in anger, let him have it in the skull.

I prepared a report of this affair for Washington. The details were recited, and I referred to many reports of Navajo aggression, with the Hopi always helpless and never supported. Now, in effect at least, they had made their Agent stand and deliver. When last they had tried something of this kind, against Agent Reuben Perry of the Navajo Agency, who was caught in the Chin Lee country and held prisoner for several days, Commissioner Francis E. Leupp had taken prompt, decisive action. I could not plead an exactly similar case, for only the Hopi had lost. But it seemed to me that an effort should be made to recover, to impress a realization of law on these insolent tribesmen.

I waited patiently. In 1911, with troops on the reservation, it had required four months to consider a similar injustice, and by that time the soldiers were gone; and later, with respect to the restricted range over which the Hopi and Navajo wrangled, the Office had concluded, as a mild corrective, that "this is a very perplexing question."

But less time was lost on this occasion. The answer was brief, pointed, final. It was written on a half-sheet, for paper was being saved to reduce the national debt.

DEAR MR. CRANE:

Your report of —— date received, relating the facts in the case of a Hopi boy named Lidge, who shot a Navajo of about the same age.

Your action in this matter is approved.

Cordially yours,

———

XXV

WANTED AT COURT

When the coster's finished jumping on his mother,
He loves to lie a-basking in the sun;
Ah! take one consideration with another —
The policeman's lot is not a happy one.
                                    —*The Pirates of Penzance*

In Keams Cañon, the Moqui — now the Hopi — Agency is built on terraces. The highroad to anywhere and everywhere passes through this cañon on the lowest level, and all the visiting world and its wife must pass in review before the Agent's office and his home. The grounds were once barren of trees and shrubbery, and there had been a time, in the season of swift midsummer rains, when several shallow arroyos would flood the place. Off the main cañon are bays or alcoves, and a quite large one immediately behind the buildings of the plant. Its stream-bed would, once or twice a summer, throw a yellow foamy river into the highroad, and carry away tons of cinder ballasting that had to be renewed. This had been tolerated for years, when all necessary to correct it was to cut a straight channel for the annual flood, raise the highroad-level, and bridge the point of crossing.

This bridge, having a wooden floor, became my signal of traffic. A belated freight-team would rumble across it, telling of supplies; the weary stride of a buggy pair would herald that the doctor or the stockman had reached home and would soon report. Seldom did it announce anything after ten o'clock. Then the cañon was an enchanted place, bathed in summer moonlight or ghastly sheeted in the winter snow, quiet, sleeping. When a horseman crossed that bridge in the late night or early morning hours, it was either an Indian drifting homeward, belated, half asleep, or a messenger to the Agent. A swift driving canter, and I waited for the slipping of moccasins along a cement walk and the rattle of a quirt on my door; I was about to say, my shutters.

Now and then the message would have a tragic possibility in it: the physician wanted, quickly; or the news of a plague among the people. One would expect the police to pack the most disturbing announcements; but, strange to relate, in the two cases bordering nearest tragedy the messengers were women.

One, an employee of the field, came late at night to tell that Indians proposed to break quarantine and remove patients from a temporary hospital. This was during one of the plagues; and the Hopi suffer many, due to their congested and unsanitary mode of living. The mesa villages welcome every infection. A man should have borne this message, but the woman had slipped away as the one least likely to be missed, and round about the trails and roads, twenty-five miles, came for police. The reservation had no telephone at that time. The swift pace of the pony across the bridge aroused me. Next I heard rapid steps on the walk, then someone ascending the verandah steps. But for a wire screen, the front door stood open.

"What is it?" I asked.

No answer.

"Who is that?"

Silence.

My hand slipped over to the automatic. Threats had
been made against me by Navajo. In 1916 they techni-
cally murdered me, and the press carried the story because
of the Indian flavor. I had the unusual experience of
reading my obituary in many papers, and might have felt
puffed up about it had I not recognized a tone of regret
when the rumor was exploded. Now I knew there was
someone on the porch, and if the someone had a good
excuse for being there, why not announce it. Just as I
prepared to send a shot across it, out of the silence came a
faint gasping, as if the person sought to speak and could
not. The woman was suffering from bronchitis, and had
lost her voice in that cool ride across the desert. And
she might have lost her voice entirely at the end of it.

The second instance happened earlier on a summer
evening. This time someone was riding fast — faster than
an Indian goes unless something of moment has occurred.
I found an Indian girl at the door. She was a returned
student who had reported to me a short time before,
home from a non-reservation school. She had gone back
to her people's camp. I had not recommended that, for
her people were among those who sometimes made
trouble. Years before, this one member of a large family
had been sent to school. After three years she had returned and had been again sent away. It was the only
thing to do for her. In dress, training, and standpoint
she had become an alien. When she came home again,
she had ceased to be a savage. I had warned her not to
visit the camps.

"Stay at this school for your vacation. Let your people
come here to see you. They will come."

But she felt that she should go to her mother and
sisters.

"Well?" I asked her.

"The men had whiskey," she told me. "And they did n't want me there. They were afraid I would tell you. And I said I would tell you, if they did not stop drinking. So they beat me, and they beat my sister too."

"Who beat you?"

"Hoske Nehol Gode."

"And who is that? I don't recall that name?"

"He is my cousin."

I took her to the hospital and the physician reported that she was badly bruised up. It appeared that she had been given quite a trouncing by the worthy cousin. The name was strange to me. Perhaps, I thought, he comes from the Fort Defiance country.

Now it happened that a trading-post had been robbed only a short time before. The fellow who conducted it was not in my good graces, he having sought to evade the livestock-buying regulations. I had confiscated his purchases and closed his place of business. The Indians knew that this gentleman had lost official standing; so, while he was absent, seeking a means of reopening,—and this means seeking political influence sufficient to overawe and intimidate the Agent through pressure at Washington, — a band of native rascals looted his store. It was my duty to punish these thieves too, if I could find them. The police recovered most of the goods, but of course foodstuffs and silver trinkets were never returned. It was believed by the Indian officers who investigated that this robbery could be fastened on one Guy, his brother Jay, and perhaps others of their gang. These men had been to school long enough to acquire English names. They headed a crew of a dozen or more bad eggs, gamblers, whiskey-runners, general mischief-makers, who defied and worried the decent Navajo and troubled those police who did not protect them.

But I did not connect either Jay or Guy with Hoske Nehol Gode. Who would? There is little hope of making an accurate census of the nomadic Navajo; and whenever one does succeed, he will have the joy of recording three to five names for each adult. The Navajo, in speaking of or to one another, do not use given names. Too many of their titles mean infirmities or weaknesses. Some of their names are not delicate; and by this I mean that they are coarse enough to offend Navajo. One learns in talking with them through interpreters, to say "this man," or "that man," and to leave the name of him alone. Many of them establish their identity by relationship. Instead of saying "I am the Man with the Broken Nose," he may call himself "Curly-Hair's Brother-in-Law." And therefore, when an official goes looking for an obscure member of the tribe, seeking him under his real name, he is apt to meet and talk with Curly-Hair's Brother-in-Law, or Victor Hugo, if the man has been to school and had a literary teacher, to learn finally that Curly-Hair's relative by marriage, the brilliant French poet, and the Man with the Broken Nose, are all one and the same person. This game of hare and hounds is often humorous, unless it chances to be dangerous.

Now it also happened that I was preparing a number of cases for presenting to the Federal Court. Trips from the remote desert to court are troublesome and expensive, so one likes to assemble them in batches and thus clear the docket. I was gathering Hopi and Navajo witnesses, and chanced to need as one the wife of "the Ghost." How was I to know that the Ghost's wife was a sister of the returned student? This woman knew something of the robbery.

I did not connect the two incidents. And I did not know that there was still another sister, practically a twin in appearance of the one wanted. That morning I learned that the apparition's better half was weaving a blanket down the cañon. The Ghost's wife did n't want to go to court, and assured me that the person I needed would be found at the camp where the returned student had met with her beating. By going there I could kill two birds with one stone — procure the wife of the Ghost, and the sister of the student who had suffered also. I did wound two birds, all right; for at that camp I encountered both Guy and Hoske Nehol Gode.

If I have not confused matters, it will be recalled that I wanted Guy for burglary, and Hoske Nehol Gode for assaulting two women. Now Guy and Hoske Nehol Gode were one and the same person. Guy did not know that I suspected him of looting the trader's store, but he perfectly well knew that I might be looking for him to answer the assault-charge.

There were three of us — a Tewa policeman, the big stockman, and myself. We found the camp a short distance off the main road to Gallup, back in the trees. It held several women, four or five young fellows who promptly departed, and one large, heavy-set man who looked twenty-five years in age, and who was perhaps thirty-five. The Navajo men do not show their true ages until long past thirty. It is difficult to gauge their years until the lines begin to set in their faces.

Among the women I recognized a duplicate of the Cañon weaver. Assuming that this was the person who knew something of the robbery, I began to question her, using the policeman as interpreter. The Tewa Indians usually speak three languages: their own and Hopi and Navajo.

The big fellow at the fire pricked up his ears. He feared that she would tell of the beating, for she was the sister who had been beaten; and lo, here she was being questioned concerning the blankets he had removed from the trading-post. I have no doubt that this caused him great uneasiness, and soon he began to evidence his disapproval of my questions, claiming that the woman knew nothing about the affair of the robbery. Several times he interrupted, asking: "Why you want to know that?"

I had no intention of disturbing this sullen fellow, but when he interrupted again, I told him to hold his peace. I turned to the old woman of the outfit.

"Do you know where Hoske Nehol Gode is?"

Neither she nor any one of them knew. The man at the fire sneered and seemed amused. I suspected that he would know something.

"What is your name?" I asked him.

Of the two evils, he chose the one he thought I knew less about.

"Guy," he said.

Now did I not want Guy for burglary, although I had not been seeking him? This was too good an opportunity to be missed.

"Well, I have been looking for you, Guy," I told him. "You will go back to the Agency with us."

The resistance of an Indian is always negative. He stood up, and started to move off, out of the camp. I therefore of necessity had to move out of the camp with him, for I had him by the shirt-collar. This fellow must have weighed two hundred pounds of well-knit muscle, and he was in perfect fighting trim from roping and handling and riding rough ponies, and generally leading an Indian's life in the open. At my best Arizona weight, aside from determination and official authority, I tipped the beam at one hundred and eighteen pounds. He walked off with me just as a range bull would depart with a sixteen-pound Boston terrier hanging to his muzzle.

The Indian police are always slow to come into action, so Guy had carried me about fifteen yards before the Tewa added his handicap by pinioning the Navajo's arms from behind. To rid one's self of an opponent like that, it is necessary to toss him completely over one's head; and this the Navajo desperately endeavored to do; but the Tewa held to him tenaciously and between us Guy — alias Hoske Nehol Gode — was seriously inconvenienced. He stopped moving out of the camp, and began to plough up dirt in circles, viciously seeking to rid himself of the policeman, who, like an Old Man of the Sea, perched between his shoulder blades. Then the stockman, who had been at the car, arrived to assist; and once they had him well fastened, I drew a pair of handcuffs from my pocket, and slung one of them across Guy's wrist. It locked down, but he objected to our arranging the other cuff where it belonged. In the meantime, however, he was not standing still. The four of us were slipping, side-stepping, puffing, and straining about. The Tewa did not dare loose his hold of the Navajo's arms, and his elbow grip prevented us from forcing his wrists together. Officers in a different service would have adopted different methods; but we were of the Indian Service, and had probably followed the wrong course as it was. We should have reasoned with him, and recited a bedtime story.

Now, in this melee, Guy secured a nice twisting grip on my thumb; and I received instant notice that he meant to wrench that thumb off my hand.

"Break his hold, quick!" I called out.

Promptly from the stockman's belt swung a forty-five, and smash, down it came across Guy's hand. And very promptly too he released his hold.

Until this time there had been no sound from him, other than his gasping breath and the noise of struggle. At the blow, he raised a call for help and, like an infuriated animal, he threshed about and threw us with him. The dust arose and the chips that carpet a camp flew. The Tewa swung from side to side; but the Tewa did not let him go.

There was a noise in the fringe of little cedars around us, and several Navajo appeared. And they advanced. And just then the stockman dropped his gun.

It fell in the dirt under our feet, and down swung this wild bull of the pampas, the Tewa balancing between his shoulders, to reach the weapon. One moment Guy's feet were on the gun, holding it down, and next the stockman's foot would scuffle to scrape it aside. With the stockman bent down for it, the Navajo would be clawing at his neck or kicking at his face. It was a furious scramble, and if he ever reached that automatic gun it was ready to explode.

The sight of the gun, too, seemed to anger and justify those others who had come up. It seemed probable to me that someone of the party would be hurt, and I preferred it to be a Navajo. So I stepped back out of the fuss, drew my gun, and warned those newcomers to keep their distance. They halted at the camp's edge.

"Why don't you smash that animal?" I called.

The haymaker that Hoske Nehol Gode then received in the face would have staggered Dempsey. It straightened him up, but very much to my surprise, it did not fell him. The shock, however, caused him to reel off the gun, and promptly the stockman recovered it.

"Knock him down the next time."

And smash went the forty-five over Guy's head. But he did not drop. A Navajo of the back-country dresses his hair in a thick mattress across his scalp. Blood began to stream down his face. He let out a wild cry that he was being killed, a call for the women to help him. The night before they had sent a messenger for protection from this bully; but now they responded to his aid. They came forward, ready to claw us; and just what was the ethical thing to do then, I am not prepared to state.

"Turn him loose!" I called to the policeman.

"He may have a gun!" said the stockman.

"Then we will have to shoot him," I said; "Turn him loose."

The Tewa released his hold, and Guy, wearing one bracelet, made a rush out of the camp. He wanted no more of fighting, but it was evident that the place was unhealthy for us. We could hear him crashing through the brush, while we proceeded to the car. The women followed to the edge of the timber and shrilled their threats. It was probable that Guy would find a weapon; so we lost no time in vacating that section of the Desert.

Later in the day the leader of the clan came to see me.

"I have told Guy," he said, "to make no more trouble."

"You may return and tell him something more than that," I replied. "Tell him to be very careful not to enter this cañon, for I mean to kill him if he does."

That was the last I saw of Guy for several years. He kept to the back-country, after his hand and head had healed, and avoided the Agency. He filed off the handcuff. Navajo are expert at that. He was not prosecuted for beating the women, nor for the burglary. You see, three days after this affair I asked the United States District

Attorney for an indictment on these charges, and a bench warrant was promised to assure his arrest by the United States Marshal. The Marshal asked me what success he might expect to have in procuring this belligerent, and I related our experience.

"He is one of a gang, and it may be necessary to arrest several of those fellows. I would n't come alone. Of course, you may deputize some of my employees, but they do not care for that work. And if you ask me the easiest and most effective way to serve those warrants, I would say with a squad of uniformed men from Fort Apache. They were playing ball in Holbrook when I passed through. The Navajo bad-man respects a soldier, and he does n't respect anything else. He will not be awed by your badge of office. He does n't know what it means."

Evidently the Marshal transmitted my suggestion to his superiors at Washington, for at once, by telegraph, I was challenged by the Commissioner of Indian Affairs, who demanded *an explanation of my call for troops!* The United States Marshal never appeared on the reservation. Guy and his assistant thieves and bullies are still at large, and I suppose they beat women and loot stores whenever the spirit moves them.

XXVI

HOPI ANNALS

But chiefly I write of Life and Death, and men and women,
and Love and Fate, according to the measure of my ability.
--Kipling to Gobind

THE Hopi people are bound up in clanships, rituals, and
ceremonies. Herbert E. Gregory, in his remarkable volume of statistics, entitled *The Navajo Country*, has this to
say of them: —

These people have maintained themselves and preserved their
race from extinction in a singularly unfriendly environment.
With incredible skill they have practised the art of conserva-
tion of water, and that the mind of the race is intent on this
one problem is shown by the organization of the clans and
the elaborate ceremonies devised to enlist the coöperation of
unseen Powers which are believed to control the rainfall.
Endless toil and endless prayer, both directed to increase and
to preserve the precious water, constitute the life of the Hopi.

We find in their desert cairns of rock something different
from an ordinary monument to mark land or to point a
road, having in them special gifts of feathers or painted
sticks.   That certain clans may never be without the
feathers of the eagle, these birds are captured young and
reared in cages or at the ends of chains on the housetops.
A curious sight to see: a captive eagle, baleful of eye,
morose, sullen, posed at the edge of a roof, a brooding,
vicious prisoner with beak and talons like razors, a

A HOPI RANGE-RIDER

BLUE CAÑON: A STUDY IN BLUE-AND-WHITE

dangerous thing to approach carelessly. These birds must be reared unharmed, therefore the nests are robbed of the young. A wounded or crippled sacrifice will not be accepted; for, aside from being the source of feathers, it is said that eagles are smothered to death in certain ceremonies.

In distant places, the far-away headlands of the Butte country and the sky-drifting mountains, it is said the Hopi have altars. There is one, a young Hopi told me, atop "Sist-ter-vung-ter-we," or "one that is farthest west," in the long line of volcanic piles bordering their southern boundary. And once I received a handful of round, painted sticks, a miniature faggot, from the distant Apache Reservation, with an inquiry from that Agent as to their meaning.

"Yes," said a Hopi, "they are from the Rain altar down there. The Hopi go to those places at times. I have no doubt you could find some in the San Francisco Mountains, if you knew where to look."

Prayer-sticks, tied in little bundles, offered to the gods. And reflect for a moment. The Apache was an enemy, a most bitter and sinister enemy. The most southerly and westerly ruins of Hopi civilization are to be found along the Rio del Lino, or Flax River, as the Little Colorado was named by the Spanish. Their dawn settlements are far to the north, in hidden cañons close to the Utah line; and it is not likely that their eastern pueblos, those of the Hopi proper, were ever beyond the upper reaches of the Jedito Wash country. But these prayer-sticks are found far beyond those limits. They suggest religious pilgrimages into enemy provinces. Perhaps the early Hopi accepted even this dangerous means of placating his deities. Primitive knowledge would have located the sources of rain in the western range, where the San Francisco peaks lift their snow-capped heads, and in the White Mountains of the Apache country. The Navajo fastened his legends to that highest desert elevation, Navajo Mountain, and it is not likely the Hopi ventured there. But his Rain gods, those powerful to relieve the aridity of his country and ensure against famine, dwelt in mountains somewhere, and therefore, trembling perhaps, muttering incantations, he went to them.

Anything that is strange, and possibly potent, has been absorbed into their embroidered religion. The clans like to procure colored glass. They make much of tortoise shells, and other things speaking of the sea. President Roosevelt was petitioned by them to forward a jar of sea-water. They have — or had — a Parrot clan, a fantastic touch reminiscent of some lonely friar who had a mission garden and in it kept his pets.

Close to their homes are many shrines that excite the curiosity of tourists and that sometimes get visitors into trouble. Once a couple of the overly curious were thrashed with whips by Hopi of the Chimopovi district — for which the guilty were severely punished by the Agent then in charge. But more than one Agent has ordered busybodies to replace bahoos and gifts taken from such places. While I had a hand in this, and finally stopped the plundering of old graves, and once prevented the sale and removal of an entire Hopi altar, still I must admit that I never caught a tourist or a "scratcher" pillaging a newly made grave.

Most of the clans must have been intermingled in so small a population. We have Youkeoma's statement that there is a Ghost clan, subdivided into a Ghost-and-Bird clan. A more intelligent member of the tribe once en-

A HOPI SHRINE

A HOPI WEAVER OF CEREMONIAL
ROBES

A KATCHINA DANCE
Showing the elaborate masks used by the Hopi

deavored to recall for me the numerous fraternities of his people. He said: "The Sun, Salt, Crow, and Ant clans are dead. There are no more of those people. The Parrot clan now has but one member, a woman. The Bear clan is the largest, and next come the Sand and Snake clans. There are the Spider and Evergreen clans. Some of them go in groups, so we have the Bear, Spider, and Evergreen clans associated, as is the Rabbit clan with the Tobacco clan. We have the Eagle, the Horn, the Fire, and the Flute clan; the Antelope, the Lizard, and the Corn clan." And when that group of progressive head-men petitioned Washington in 1886 for a school, they signed themselves as leaders of the Mountain-sheep clan, the Coyote and Badger clans, the Rain, the Reed, and the Katchina clans. But one of these men is living to-day — Honani, of Chimopovi, always one of the friendlies. The most interesting and impressive of them, Shupula, father of the chief Snake priest, died July 4, 1916, a benign old man whose features are preserved in a splendid piece of modeling by Mr. Emri Kopte, the sculptor who has lived for many years among the Hopi Indians.

Next to these phases of his religion are the red pages of his life-calendar. The Hopi is born to a heritage of toil in an unfriendly environment, and perhaps to misunderstanding and small sympathy; but the poetry of his life begins at once. The paternal grandmother acts as his nurse. After bathing the child she anoints it with wood ashes, that he may have a smooth body. The mother is supposed not to let the sun shine on her for the period of twenty days, at the end of which time the child is named. Only the women of the husband's family are present at this ceremony. They bring a blanket of Hopi weave, and a bowl of sacred water to place before the mother. They wash her hair with this water. Each of these godmothers brings an ear of corn as an offering. They dip the corn in the water and stroke the head of the infant four times, making at the same time a wish for its health and happiness. Each of them suggests a name. The child will belong to the mother's clan, but will be named for something denoting the father's clan. If the father happens to be a member of the Sand clan, his children will be named for things common to the desert sand.

On the twenty-first day after the birth these women have assembled and washed the mother's hair. This is before sunrise: they are a dawn-loving people. Then the grandmother takes the infant in one arm and the mother by the hand. Imagine that little ceremony upon the craggy mesa-top in the gray chill of the desert morning, high in the thin air, overlooking all the dim sleeping valleys. They step to the mesa edge to view the rising sun. Sacred meal, mixed with corn-pollen, is strewn on the air. Then, as that mellow light flames the farthest east, radiating from the hearts of all the people, gilding Yucca Point and the Terrace of the Winds, plashing warmly the cold walls of the mesa fortress, the grandmother speaks the name she has selected from those suggested for the child.

If the child be a girl, she will receive another name on reaching maturity, when her hair will be washed and arranged in the symbolic whorls as a sign of womanhood. If a boy, he will receive another name at a certain ceremony entitling him to wear a mask and to dance. These names then last through life.

One can understand from this little baptismal scene how my friend of the Second Mesa, Ta-las-we-huma, got his name. It must have been a beautiful sunrise, and the little fellow must have been well-favored in the sight of his

HOPI MOTHER IN GALA DRESS, WITH HER CHILD

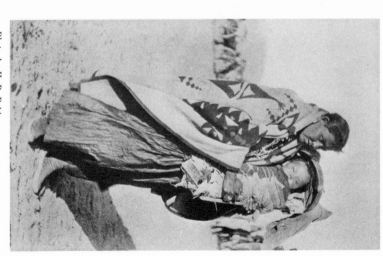

Photo. by H. R. Robinson

NAVAJO MOTHER, WITH A CHILD IN ITS CRADLE

sponsors; for his name may be translated, "Glow of the Rising Sun."

The Hopi do not name their children with the frank vulgarity that so often is found among the Navajo and other tribes. Many of their titles are pure poetry. We have Lo-may-ump-tewa — something Going Straight and Good, as an arrow — and Se-you-ma — one who Carries a Flower. Then there are many names such as we commonly associate with Indians: Sah-mee or Green Corn, and Qua-ku-ku, or Eagle Claws.

The Hopi maiden is most frequently given a tender name, and she is often a pretty little thing deserving it. We find Tawa-mana, or Girl of the Sun, and Pole-mana and Pole-see, meaning Butterfly Girl and Butterfly Flowers (buttercups).

They are equally tasteful in naming places. I have already mentioned Huh-kwat-we, the Terrace of the Winds. Of their closer and more intimate places we find Ta-wah-pah Spring, the Spring of the Sun, at one time a most precious waterhole, however roiled and muddy. And Pah-lots-quabbie, the "place where we get red paint for the face," a point of particular interest to the women who wish to preserve their complexions. Despite their copper-colored skins, the intense rays of the desert sunlight cause them to take measures for protection. Much of Indian face-painting is cosmetic, and not for the brilliant color-scheme that a tourist connects with war-parties and potential scalpings.

Many of their names are difficult to translate in a word or two, since they most often describe things fully. The desert Indian is not a word-maker, and for unfamiliar objects he does not create nouns. There is Dah-vuph-cho-mah: this spot white men call the Hill of the Water-Witch, for it is where the Water Development chief has his home, shops, and office. He calls it a "camp." Camp or not, it is a haven of welcome for rare souls, including itinerant artists, poets, and depressed Indian Agents. A disappointed candidate for the much-coveted mayoralty of Polacca, probably actuated by bitterness, once dubbed this prominence Pisgah. The Hopi named it, long before the mystery of well-rigs and peach-tree wands was known, Dah-vuph-cho-mah: "the place where we dry rabbit-skins for the quilts." Quite simple, is it not?

The Hopi once made many robes of rabbit-skins. It was necessary to bury the pelts in the sand before removal to the mesa-top, a ceremonial matter; and Dah-vuph-cho-mah was the place to do it. The skins were then rolled into ropes, thick and soft, and sewed together. I last saw these coverings at Hotevilla, where so many traditions are preserved.

And this suggests the methods of rabbit-hunting. The Hopi does not seek bunny with .22 rifle, or bow and arrow, or snares. Actually he drops the swift creature with the Hopi rabbit-stick or boomerang, a curved piece of mountain-oak that these Indians throw skillfully. But the answer to the inquiring tourist is — "He runs the rabbit down." The Hopi are fleet of foot, and of course our touring friend devours this explanation literally. Hopi rabbit-hunts are joyous community-affairs, and they do run the rabbit down. They encircle a very large area of desert valley, all runners, all bearing rabbit-sticks. Then they begin contracting the circle. As the rabbits flee before one advancing line of beaters, they are turned back by other lines. From every bush, it seems, Hopi are bobbing up, with menacing blows and wild cries. The game is thus run down and killed when tiring. Patient

burros bear home the spoils. I have seen these beasts
covered with dead rabbits, while afar in the plain still
arose the merry shouts of the running hunters.

The language of the Tewa is composed of shorter terms.

"What do you call these?" I asked, showing some local
beans.

"We call them 'tdo.'"

"What does that mean?"

"It means 'beans.' When a Tewa means beans, he says
'beans.' But when a Hopi speaks of these, he says:
'Kotcha-cha-chi-morzree,' 'the beans that are soft when
boiled a long time.'" So he described them first, when
experimenting with their cooking, and he has never seen
fit to shorten his nomenclature.

Compared with the stalwart Sioux or the equally tall
and vigorous Navajo of the mountains, men of the horses,
the Hopi are at first glance a little people. This has
brought them some sympathy from those who seize on
superficial appearances. The mature Hopi has a thick
figure, not inclined to fatness, but with barrel-like lungs
and a sturdy back. He would make a fine wrestler. As
he has accepted things of civilization via the trader, and
absorbed so much from his neighbor, the Navajo, his
costume is not radically different to-day. The curious
dresses of the olden-time, of buckskin, cloth of native
weave, and feathers, such as may be seen in the Harvey
collection at Albuquerque, have disappeared from the
mesas and to the younger generation are unknown. A
shirt of velveteen, loose trousers of some light cloth,
often pure white, moccasins of red-stained buckskin and
his own peculiar design, a handkerchief twisted about his
head, these form his costume. Most of his ornaments are
bought of the Navajo, save that an occasional Hopi silver-

smith will hammer the metal into Hopi patterns, such as butterflies and snakes with turquoise eyes. When you see these forms, they are Hopi. The Navajo does not use them.

But in this dress of the men the resemblance to the nomad ceases. The true Hopi is marked by his short stature, his broader and radically different physiognomy, and especially by the dressing of his hair. The Navajo is usually a sloven with his hair. Do not get too close to him. The Navajo draws his hair tightly back from the brow, and catches it in a knot or a queue at the back of his head. And there is little difference between the men and their women. The Hopi wears the bang and the straight bobbed effect that came out of Egypt. When it is possible, he takes scrupulous care of his mane. Hair-washing is an important feature of all ceremonies. He was the first bobbed American.

To-day this effect will be found among the orthodox only. The younger men, home from schools, have adopted the comb and shears as they drift away from many fetishes. But hair-cutting has produced some serious wrangles with the Hopi. Long ago an Agent zealously interpreted a Washington order to mean that all Indians, not only those in schools, should be made to cut their hair in white man's fashion — as if this would produce civilization overnight. To the elders of the tribe this was a terrible heresy, and they resisted very naturally. It is too bad that orders cannot be transmitted in the form of blue-prints.

The women of the tribe are the strongholds of conservatism. I recall holding a council of mixed sexes, the talk relating to some form of community improvement along modern lines. And when it was over, I asked my interpreter: —

A NEW SON OF THE DESERT
One who has been to school and who runs his own cattle

Photo. by George L. Leaming
HOPI GIRLS ARRAYED FOR A DANCE

"Do you believe they understood?"

"The men, of course," he replied, emphatically; "but do you think it possible to get that stuff through a Hopi woman's head? Epten. The men will try to carry out your wishes; but they are in for a very unpleasant time of it with their women. A Hopi woman! She is like a piece of sandrock. The winds wear it away, but it will take many years."

The younger women, who have had schooling, wear the gingham and calico dresses they have learned to make and launder, and the field matrons assist them in renewing these garments. But the old ones, and the students of middle-age, are most likely to be found wearing the ancient Hopi weaves. A dress may be of thick cloth caught at one shoulder, leaving the opposite arm bare, belted at the waist with a woven sash, the wearer's legs and feet bare most of the time, unless for some special journey she dons the woman's wrapping and shoe of buckskin. She grows thick and fat, her countenance rounding into a broad, complacent face that can smile pleasantly or become stolidly impervious as the mood strikes her. Once married, her hair is parted and hangs down her back in thick plaits. Her hands are thick and coarsened from hard labor, the making of pottery, and especially from the baking of piki bread.

This baking is done on a red-hot stone over the fire. The Hopi woman sits before it, at her side a pan of batter, sometimes colored red or blue. She dips her hand into the batter and smears it deftly over the hot stone. Before it has burned and curled, she wipes over it a second layer. This last cooks perfectly in a thin wafer, quite like tissue-paper, crinkled and brittle. This she peels off and places in a pile of such sheets. All day she does this, often until her palm is perfectly cooked with the bread. The sheets are then rolled, again resembling a packet of tissue, quite like those we used to buy at Christmas time for decorations. A dozen of these rolls, and the Hopi man will take the trail, fully provided with provender.

Some rather reject the thought of eating piki bread, but I have sampled Indian foods more than once, and with different results. An old Navajo shemah can broil mutton ribs and prepare a pot of coffee over a hogan fire in such a way that one who has had a hard trip, — and more of it to come, — thinks them delicious. And piki bread is not half bad, although rather flat in taste, and gritty, for the sand will intrude; and I suppose if one accepted it as a steady diet his teeth would be worn down in time, like those of the older Hopi. As for the cooked hand, one should gratefully accept and eat piki without being too curious as to its making. The proof of the pudding is in the eating.

Next in the Hopi life-calendar appears the urgent necessity for marriage. The happy man has very little to do with this affair. The bride-elect — self-elected — and her mother, a wily dowager who has contrived a large part of the proceedings, decide most of these things for themselves. I cannot say how early negotiations have been opened by the aunts and uncles of both signatories, but of course they have been consulted. At any rate, on a day the girl and her mother pay a visit to the eligible young man's home, and tender his parents a present of piki bread and cornmeal on a woven-reed plaque. Most Southwest tribes use a wedding-basket symbol; the Navajo import from another tribe a wedding basket of definite design, and will use no other. If the boy's parents accept

these presents and replace them with a portion of mutton
on the same plaque, they have signified their consent to
the union. If there has been dissension between the
Montagues and Capulets and a plague on both houses,
so to speak, the disdaining parents give this piki and meal
to others, signifying their lack of interest in mere for-
eigners, and these receiving diplomats break the sad news
that a perfectly good offer has been declined.

But if the present is accepted, the uncles of the bride-
elect gather at her home to advise her concerning the
duties of a good wife, and at an appointed time the girl,
accompanied by her parents and close relatives, headed
by the one who named her, proceed to the home of the
groom's parents for a feast. This gathering is held at
night, and when they depart the bride remains. She
spends four nights in her husband's people's home, doing
the housework for the whole family. Very early in the
morning she begins the corn-grinding, to pay for her
husband. During these four days there is a ceremony of
hair-washing, and her hair is given a peculiar cut to
mark her as a married woman. Ever after she wears it so.
And during these four days the boy's uncles bring in
cotton for her wedding-robe. They are paid for it in
meal, and they depart to the kiva to weave it. While at
this weaving, they are fed by the girl's family. At the
end of the four days the robe is finished. The uncles
heap a wealth of advice on the groom before he departs
from the home of his birth. Then the bride dons the white
robe and goes with her husband to the home of her own
parents; that is to say, she is accompanied by her husband.
If he has had any ideas of a home of his own, away from
the precincts of mother-in-law, he has not announced them,
and apparently discretion is the better part of valor.

In this manner a young lady has gone to the home of a desirable young man, proposed for him, married him, partially paid for him, decked herself with apparel manufactured by his people, and then led him to her home in triumph.

There is nothing new under the sun. Vamping was reduced to a precise science by the Hopi many centuries before the pueblo de Los Angeles was dreamed of.

"And — hark! As I live, again the villagers!"

All this has not been enough to establish cordial relationship between the families. There must be something in the nature of a riotous shivaree. These folk who have captured our darling boy must not be permitted to crow too loud. So the mother of the groom, his influential aunts and other female relatives, especially those whose temperaments will lend verve to the affair, proceed to the rival house. They go upon an errand of mock-seriousness that may assume proportions. They will say unpleasant things in loud voices, especially for the benefit of the neighbors, to the effect that this bride has numerous and glaring defects, and that, if the truth be told, perhaps their paragon has not acquired the most beautiful and gracious of the village maidens.

The women of the bride's household reply in kind, their language not always the most decorous. Personal references are made, involving the cleanliness and habits of both parties, and a friendly fight is on. These ladies proceed to sling mud, — at first verbally, and then actually, — real mud, over the house and each other. The bride and her mother will have to have a vigorous housecleaning after this, and fresh plastering on the interior walls. Perhaps that is the idea of it — to make them furbish the domicile.

The masculine element is conspicuous by its utter absence. The men know better than to appear. Like white men on house-cleaning day, they seek the highest roof or the lowest cellar, along with their disconsolate dogs. Woe betide any absent-minded one who strays within the field. Both parties are likely to turn on him with more than words and mud. It is not likely that the men will dare come home until after sunset, when, no doubt, their attention will be distracted by recitals of the affair, and the condition of the home will cause them much grief.

A friendly, if undignified, roughhouse, to show the world that these two families, now having common interests, can endure the most unpleasant conditions and survive.

And would you imagine that the groom is ever to have a home of his very own, with a fireside, and slippers, and everything? Not unless he has his Agent behind him and bravely kicks over the sacred traditions, risking ostracism possibly and at least a great deal of home-town misery. Just how long Jacob will serve that family for Rachel, I am not aware; and unlike Jacob, he serves after having been snared. He draws and transports the water, if he has a wagon; he cuts the wood and attends the field; he wrangles horses, herds cattle, and helps manicure the sheep. He is owned by this old mother who directed her daughter's attention toward him.

To be fair, sometimes the girl has fancied him for herself, without too much urging of family; and I recall asking more than one diffident groom, when about to publish banns: —

"Do you really, of yourself, wish to marry this woman?"

"Well, sir — she wants me to marry her."

In delicate matters of this kind, the Hopi young man is pleasantly agreeable and strives to please.

And I succeeded in getting very few of them to take another point of view. There were several determined Romeos who had selected girls for themselves, who paid court despite all family disapproval, and who finally won out in their suits. But they were shrewdly wise to fortify themselves in Governmental positions: interpreters, policemen, laborers, or assistants, otherwise they would likely have been ostracized and come close to starvation. Having joined the Moungwi's official family, however, and being endowed with monthly salary "fresh and fresh," they could assert a bit of independence, could demand immunity from the bitterest of traditions; and I suppose they made much of their closeness to the Big Chief. Most Indians do. "I will tell my white uncle" has throttled many a threatened unpleasantness.

Then too, they were regarded by those less fortunate as rich men, having, besides a monthly surety, certain perquisites and a supposed subtle influence in foreign affairs.

"This Moungwi speaks to Washington by papers and the singing wires; and do you not know, stupid one, that I often talk with him?"

Their family visitors and retainers increased and were many. Not an enviable position, a place at court, despite its reflected importance and privilege. And the fall thereof when, Fate decreeing, the Moungwi with loud words dismissed one of these believed favorites! A return to the kiva influences was not a happy experience. Sanctuary had not been copied or absorbed from those early Spaniards and their holy friars. Indian ridicule and Indian persecution can be very cruel.

Few of the young men have the wherewithal to build a home or to buy one, either at the mesa or in the valley, so they are tied for years to this feudal family-system, waiting to inherit from their elders.

Even when one is so fortunate, so energetic, or so rash as to throw aside the traditions, he simply accepts bondage without mother-in-law, since no part of the house nor anything he brings to it, other than his personal belongings, may be claimed by him. The woman owns and rules the home, and this includes the children and the harvest. The children are of the mother's clan. The man may disport himself, gaily dressed and agile as a panther, in the ceremonies; he may be a leader in the hunt; he may declaim in the kiva; but his authority ceases at the threshold of the Hopi home.

For has not this woman, during the first year of her married life, ground from one to two thousand pounds of corn meal in payment for her man and her wedding dress? She has, indeed. And since she has purchased him, she has the right to divorce him. He may slave in the hot fields and the sand-blows, running to and from the patches, hoe on shoulder, to charm a crop of corn. He has planted with ceremony — so many grains for the hot wind, so many for the field rat, so many for the katchina, and so many for himself; but once he has harvested it, and packed the Hopi share to the home cellar, his ponies may starve for the lack of a hatful of grain if his wife is not generous. One thing with another, I think the Hopi male has a rather tough time of it. Sometimes he grows a bit fretful and proceeds to push his wife about, rarely going so far as to box her jaws, which she very often thoroughly deserves and earns. Then, if she still likes him, she appeals amid tears to the Agent, with view to having him reprimanded and, unless it be crop-time, jailed. But if she does not care for him overmuch,

having, as related of an Ethiopian matron, "entirely lost
her taste for that man," she abruptly divorces him.

This action calls for no assemblage of the family circle
or of chieftains, no personal complaint, no service of notice, as one might imagine. Friend husband returns at
evening from the sheep-camp or cornfield, probably
crooning an old kiva hymn, at peace with all the Desert
and its demons, to find his saddlegear, his cow-rope, and
his other shirt on the doorstep. The decree is thus handed
down, recorded, and confirmed. There is no appeal. He
is out. He hoists his few belongings on his back and
departs away from there.

If a young man, he will likely return to the parental
roof; if not, he becomes a solitary and a wanderer for a
season, roosting about where nightfall catches him, to be
found later in company with some divorced woman or
widow, cheerfully toiling to harvest corn for children not
his own. When this thing has been repeated a number of
times, and throughout a whole tribe, the Agent's job of
keeping vital statistics of clarity begins to loom into proportions. A Hopi genealogical record resembles a war-
map. The keeping of it becomes abstract science, having
both biological and anthropological phases.

I have known Hopi men of middle age who long maintained a fatherly interest in their children after such a
social cataclysm; but they were not many, most of them
growing careless of any and all responsibility; and I have
found women as the heads of households to which — to
adjust the records — I had to assign four husbands, all
living and none present.

But to return to the Hopi wedding. After the four days
spent in the home of her husband's people, and her triumphant return with the captive to the house of her

HOPI WEDDING COSTUME

mother, the bride is supposed to deny herself the pleasure of all Hopi revelry and ceremony until the next Neman Katchina Dance. This occurs about a fortnight prior to the Snake Dance of August, and is an appeal for rain and harvest fruition. Then she arrays herself once more in the pure white robe, and appears for a few moments at the ceremony. This is to be her last bid for public attention and the bride's centre of the stage, before settling down to a life of toil certainly, the rearing of many children probably, and perhaps a number of alliances. But it matters not how troubled her life, how peaceful, pure, how hectic; this first marriage is the only one to be distinguished by a ceremony and a symbol. This is the last time she wears the robe — save one. When next we see her in its white folds, she, having fulfilled the monotonous duties of a true Hopi or having, like Emma Bovary, tested all of life's experiences, is waiting, peacefully uncaring, to be carried to her last bed in the shadow of the great, immutable mesa.

My introduction to the importance of the wedding robe came about through an effort to eliminate the evil power of the tribe's old women. The weddings were arranged entirely too early, and operated to defy both Arizona State Law and Service regulation. It was a foxy method and held to with savage determination. An appeal to the Bureau would have brought only the hopeless decision that a tribal marriage had been declared a legal marriage by great Eastern Solons bent on pushing Orientals into Occidental grooves. Often too, young people were forced into these marriages. And the results were highly pleasing to the Hopi elders, and four-fold: Rachel's mother procured labor in the form of Jacob. Jacob's family received the ton of corn meal that Rachel would grind. Certainly

Rachel, and often both contracting parties, were prevented from attending the schools, as the old Hopi earnestly desired; and Hopi traditions as to fruition were completely satisfied.

There was an even more serious result. This grinding of corn meal early and late, crouched over the stone metate, ended in the young mother's losing her first-born. At one time there was no Hopi woman at the First Mesa whose first-born child was living.

So, as Moungwi, I gave them fair warning that these things must stop. They did not stop. An Indian, of whatever tribe, will always chance a test. They are a great people for stolid experiments. My first idea of punishment was, the child-wife to the boarding-school, the groom and his father to the Agency jail.

"But," these male unfortunates finally convinced me, "you are punishing the wrong persons. We men have had nothing to do with the matter. Get the old women."

And when this was done there were lamentations and floods of tears. One old virago nearly washed me from her home. It was a wet season at the mesa. And the virus worked about as successfully as a local philosopher of the Hopi described another's conversion to Christianity *via* baptism.

"First time they get him, just like vaccinate him — no take. He backsliding now — dance all time — old Hopi again. But next time they get him baptized, mebbeso it take all right — mebbeso."

Not all of my efforts produced success.

You may ask, Why not secure the girl in school before this untoward happening? The younger children of the Hopi all attend day schools, located close to their homes, and often a girl will reach maturity before the matrons

have knowledge of a marriage scheme. With the child-wife
in the boarding-school, caught during those first four days,
there was no procession to mamma's house, no corn-
grinding, no attendance of the Katchina dance, and no
robe. The joy had been taken out of life. There was
mourning in both camps; for, as Jacob was in jail, there
was no water-hauling, no woodcutting, no unpaid laboring
in the field. It was a very sad state of affairs, tribally, and
apparently this strange Moungwi had little sympathy for
the human race, — at least the Hopi division of it, and its
urge to perpetuate itself.

One day, about two years after the imposition of such a
sentence, I met an old man at a distant mesa who asked
for a talk.

"His daughter is home now," said the interpreter, "and
he wants your permission to have her robe woven."

"Robe — you mean a wedding robe?"

"Yes. You recall she had no tribal ceremony; and it is
like this: When the white people marry, they have a ring.
The white robe is our ring. If she dies, there will be no
robe to bury her in."

Such is the stupidity of the alien when he seeks to rule
the so-called heathen. My method was justified to protect
the weak and the young, but I had cast out sentiment.

> It may be they shall give me greater ease
> Than your cold Christ and tangled Trinities.

Quite so many Lispeths. I promptly gave permission for
the weaving of a robe, and I hope she has had no use for it,
nor will have, these many years.

The mid-West moralist may interpolate a question here.
Without their own service, did you permit them to go unmarried? This had little in it of the material compared

with that robe episode. But as Moungwi, a commissioned Head of the people, vested also with the authority of the State of Arizona, I would solemnize a legal ceremony if events had proved one necessary and the parties had attained a legal age. I never married a woman to a scoundrel. But I have married four couples in one morning, issuing first the State license as a deputized clerk of the court, solemnizing the ceremony as a magistrate, blessing the bride, and immediately thereafter summoning into open court the groom and all other guilty persons for trial on a charge of child-prostitution. This method was drastic, and very wearing on one who had other things to engage his attention. And it was not a very cheering family-event. But it finally produced obedience. There came a time when the Hopi would consult the Agency records as to their children's ages, and would inquire about school terms, and what Moungwi thought about it, before framing-up family alliances.

The happiest of the Hopi marriages were those following my permission to schoolboys and girls to arrange their own courting, sometimes at the school, thus breaking down old mesa-lines. Boys of the First Mesa married Hotevilla girls: a thing that would never have been tolerated by the parents on either side. Close as are the mesas, housing the one people, they might as well be separate provinces. Seldom will a First Mesa marry an Oraibi, for instance, and vice versa. A local form of derision among the Hopi is to mock the differences in pronunciation and intonation of their common language. Oraibi is less than thirty miles from Walpi, and yet an Oraibi is a being recognizing a different civilization.

When last I visited Phœnix, I entered a shop to make a purchase. A fine-looking Hopi came forward and greeted me. We talked about the folks at home, of his summer visit to the mesas, who had died and who had married.

"Now let me see," I parleyed, for it is hard to remember all individuals of a tribe. "You are married — what is your wife's name?"

"Why, you know her; she was Youkeoma's grand-daughter."

"Sure enough — Viola — the one who hid in the wagon and ran away to school at Phœnix, for fear I would send her back to Hotevilla."

Birth and baptism; marriage and divorce; many dances; a lifetime of endless toil and endless prayer; many harvests, rich and meagre. Then comes the time when he has planted his last crop, or she has finished the last of household labors. Something happens to end things, and to serve summons to the Judgment Seat, that lonely prominence overlooking the Oraibi-Dinnebito Washes in the west. The tireless feet will no longer cover the steep trails to the pueblo on the heights; the mesa and the valley will know them no more. Death, as to us all, comes as a surprise. There is a sad wailing that is soon hushed.

A woman of the family prepares the body for burial and washes the hair. Then someone is nominated to sit with the dead, to express the common grief. When first I heard of this, he was described as "the one who has to be angry with the dead." But the explanation was somewhat distorted. The person who has this duty does talk to the dead, saying: —

"Oh! why did you leave us? Were you angry with us, that you have gone away never to return? We are left here, lonely. What was it we did to make you angry with us — that you have left us. . ."

If death occurs in the night, the burial is early the next morning. No food is eaten. The body is arranged for burial in a sitting position. A corn-planting stick is placed so as to project above its head. Then the father or nearest male relative carries the body to the sand-mounds below the mesa where adults are interred and buries it. Young children have shallow graves in another place, for it is believed that their spirits are weak, too weak to struggle through deeper soil.

Then the father returns to the home, procures food that he carries to the grave in a ceremonial bowl, and leaves it there. One finds these bowls, broken, in the sand; and of course it is expected that they will not be disturbed. Above the graves of children one may find weathered toys and the remnants of a doll.

Returning to the house a second time, he gathers all the mourning ones around a common bowl of food, and they break their fast.

A simple life, simply ended.

These people succumb quickly to disease. Their mode of living invites infection and spreads contagion. They suffer epidemics periodically, and these are like the plagues of Egypt. Measles is a scourge; they have known small-pox many times; the Spanish influenza decimated them. But while these are swift and virulent enemies, they may be fought vigorously and checked at last. There is one disease as fateful as themselves, stealthy, insidious, that cannot be mastered. The white man ensnared by it finds in the Desert a place of refuge, of hope; but the Hopi refuge has not been found.

There is among my photographs one of a Hopi girl wearing the tribal dress, her hair in whorls, a wistful expression on her face. I will not tell you that this is an

Photo. by Emri Kopte

A HOPI BEAUTY
The dressing of the hair in these peculiar whorls (or squash-blossoms) requires
hours of the mother's time. It is the symbol of womanhood.

Indian princess, for there are no Indian "princesses" outside vaudeville. She is simply Stella, of the First Mesa. When she was not more than six years old, I found her on the mesa-top, very dirty and ill-nourished, an orphan, a waif, being passed around from one family to another. I packed her off to the Cañon boarding-school, and almost immediately thereafter, upon advice of the physician, to a sanatorium. When I next saw her there, she was a contented little girl, very pretty, with a red bow of ribbon in her dark hair and a taste for chocolates in her mouth. And then more years rolled away, and again I visited the place. This time she had grown swiftly into young womanhood. She had suffered a relapse and was in bed.

The physician in charge accompanied me through the wards, for a number of my Hopi were there, and finally we stopped for a little chat with Stella. She still had a taste for candy, and so informed me. This being "uncle" to several thousands has its responsibilities.

"She has been here a long time," I said when we came away.

"Yes — an uneven case, erratic chart; and that sort seldom make a complete recovery. By the way, did you notice anything peculiar in her expression?"

"Well," I replied, "she was a very pretty little child, and she has n't quite lost all that. There is something wistfully patient about her — a half-smiling sadness — "

"The very thing," said the doctor. "I wondered if you would notice it. The Mona Lisa look: Fishberg mentions it. Stella is a perfect example."

But when I last visited the mesa Stella had a home in which to welcome me. She had tired of the long years at the sanatorium, and they were many; she had returned, as they all endeavor, to her people on the mesa-top; and she still liked candy, and she still had that placid, melancholy expression.[1] I have sought to rescue many Hopi from that dread disease, with varying success, but she is the only Gioconda I have found among the Indians.

[1] This facies has been recognized by the laity, and the folklore of Europe abounds in sayings about the facial expression of the consumptive. Writers of fiction and painters have also considered it "interesting," and make great use of it in their productions. Many of the classical and modern painters have depicted this cast of countenance, showing the false euphoria of the smiling, tranquilly bright, yet melancholy eyes of the consumptive, which are perhaps best seen in Leonardo da Vinci's La Gioconda — a picture of a phthisical face superior to any description that can be given of it."
—Fishberg: *Pulmonary Tuberculosis*

L'Envoi

By a curious irony of fate, the places to which we are sent
when health deserts us are often singularly beautiful.
—STEVENSON: *Ordered South*

"KEAMS CANON!" A commonplace name, because a trading rover had made it home. Tom Keams has gone roving into shadowy lands. "Lu-kah-des-chin," the place of the reeds, is the Navajo name. For nearly three hundred days of the year it possesses the finest climate in the world, air like wine, filtered clean and sweet through ten thousand square miles of unpolluted wilderness.

In those few remaining days are the contrasts. An odd change, at the close of a sunlit winter day, to have the sky suddenly go drab and dull, promising a bleak night, and then the added silence of the falling snow. Stealthily the storm would come upon us, whirling crisp dry flakes, weaving a magic veil to drape white all the cliffs. A new hush in the Desert. And at morning, a crystal landscape, glittering like an old-time Christmas card.

Chattering birds in springtime, pausing for a little from their travels, gossiping of Mexico and strange Southern lands. They rejoice in this oasis. The filmy gray of the cottonwoods lends them a screen; already the swelling buds are pale green against the colder tones of the Cañon walls. A last patch of snow on a north ledge suddenly seems to slip, and is gone; and where it was shows the newest bloom, a tiny bit of desert scarlet.

Now the rains, — little showers and furious deluges, — the cliffs washing clean as they soak as sponges. The arroyo roars and boils its sudden surprising current, and each alcove of the high rocks springs its miniature silvery waterfall. Then the rare aroma of wet cedars and a thirsty soil, all parched things drinking as gluttons; while above, in a twilight sky, appear rainbows, katchinas of the heavens.

Can you wonder that tramps and painters, cowpunchers and poets, return to this Empire of Enchantment? It is one of those fanciful "other places," one of the last having an horizon.

> The place we're in is always *here*,
> The other place is *there*.

I have had something more to say of my Navajo friends, their ways and ceremonies; of the curious, shy, and altogether lovable Indian children and their schools; of that strange medley from the Civil Service grab-bag, the employees; of quarantines, and wars against disease; of the curse of the medicine-men; of the baronial traders and their frontier systems; of Indian art and industry; and too, something more of the Desert itself, its great cañons and monster monuments, the mammoth jewels of the Empire; and of those crumbling ruins in the North, beyond the rim of the Black Mountain, long-lost cities of the dead, picturing the futility of men and the vastness of desert time. But the book closes. The story of an empire cannot be compressed into one volume.

In August 1919 I received orders to take charge of the Pueblo Indians of New Mexico, those dreamy towns along the Rio Grande, in the land of the Spanish bells. My headquarters would be at Albuquerque, but a few miles from where Coronado made his winter camp in 1540, on that long hike to Quivera. It was not until I made this announcement that I fully knew my host of desert friends. The staff gave me a farewell dinner, of course, and there was speechmaking and a lot of neighborly merriment that several times jangled off the key. You see, I had been there a long time, and whatever my faults and deficiencies, they knew them. As I have written earlier, it is hard to change czars.

The people of the Desert are seldom effusive or voluble. They rode in, pairs and groups of them, to wish me good luck and to say good-bye. The Hopi tried to express his regret; the Navajo stood about diffidently for a little, and then shook hands without an effort at a word, and rode away. Those who knew me best brought little presents of rare value to one who knew their history — a basket, a painted piece of pottery, an old ceremonial bow. One of them, who liked me well enough, could not come; so he asked a missionary to write exactly as he dictated.

DEAR MR. CRANE,—

Because I have heard that you are about to leave us I am thinking about you, and I am sorry. You have been good to us. You are a good chief.

You have helped us with our horses, cattle, and sheep more than any other chief we have had. You have helped us greatly in sickness, and I am sorry that you are going to leave us.

I hope to see you before you go, but perhaps I will not get a chance to see you. I am glad you gave me a work to do, and I have patched up a number of quarrels, have brought the people together and made their troubles right.

I am sure I will not forget you. No matter where you go, I will remember you. The people love you.

Because I think I will not get to see you before you go, I wanted to say these things to you. You have always been kind to me.

My wish for you is that you have strength and gladness.

JUDGE HOOKER

My relief, a special officer who would await the appointment of my successor, asked me to supervise that August Snake Dance. So a day or two before leaving my post I was once more policing the Walpi ledge among the rattlesnakes. Then I left the "provinces of the Mohoce or Mohoqui," and the Indian Agency I had either built or reconstructed. It was not the barren, cheerless place I had receipted for. It had been my home in those long, silent, desert years, and I had come to know every rock, every bush, every tree, or so it seemed; and where once I had thought to effect escape in a feeling of rare relief, that was not exactly my emotion. I looked back and saw the Agency as a little town asleep in the ancient, mellowed cañon, dreaming under turquoise skies. Some last Indian waved a farewell. Then the car turned one of the desert "corners," and while I was not going beyond the Enchanted Empire, — for the mystic country of the Pueblos is only another wonderful province, — yet I had left its heart, and its simplest, kindest people.

A long time after that, I heard this story. One of the interpreters, who for years had been my voice, moped around the Agency for days, gloomy, half sullen. He had been a merry fellow.

"What's wrong with you, Quat-che — sick?" asked an employee.

The Indian looked surprised, and seemed to think for a reason.

"I am unhappy," he said, finally. "Sometimes I listen — and I miss the boss's footsteps."

A Note About This Index

The Navajo and Hopi spelling used by the author has been retained in this index. Though it does not always follow current usage it is close enough to offer no real problems.

Wm. H. Farrington, Santa Fe, N.M.

Abbott, Sarah E.—234; at Hote-
    villa, 145; threatened by
    Youkeoma, 184-185
Abeita, Pablo (Isleta)—219
Allòtment Acts—206-207
Arizona—marriage laws, 221-222
Awatobi (ruins)—102; mission
    destroyed, 103; village
    destroyed, 104

Bacabi, Ariz.—196
Bacabi Canyon, Ariz.—87
Beck-a-shay Thlani
    (Navajo)—28,66,69,77,78
Benavides, Fray Alonzo—103
Biddahoche Plains, Ariz.—62
Billa Chezzi, "Crooked
    Fingers" (Navajo)—123,
    125,158,313,315-323

Bitani (Navajo)—123
Bitani Bega (Navajo)—306-307
bootlegging—297-311
Bureau of Indian Affairs—
    established, 217; first
    commissioner, 217; trans-
    ferred to Dept. of Interior,
    219; see also Indian Service
Burton, Charles E.—213

Campbell, Gov.   —248
Cardenas, Don Garcia Lopez
    de—103,240
Carlisle Indian School—152,154
Carson, Col. Kit—on management
    of Indians, 118-119
Castle Butte Station,
    Ariz.—55,58-59
"Charlie" (Indian trader)—225

Chepaulovi, Ariz.—196
Chimney Butte, Ariz.—58
Chimpovi, Ariz.—150,151,
173-174, 196
clans (Hopi) see Hopi
Indians—Clans
Clezzi Thlani (Navajo)—138
Collins, Ralph
(sub agent)—148-149,213
Coronado, Francisco
Vasquez de—102,240
Courts of Indian Offenses—132-
135; established, 219
coyote ("Mi-he")—90
Coyote Springs, Ariz.—57
Crane, Leo—leaves Washington,
1910, 19; first agency, 21-29;
offered Moqui (Hopi) Agency,
97; takes agency, 101-112;
Sioux agent, 208-209, 218;
camera fees, 251-252; and
Lidge Palaquoto, 214-324;
erroneous murder report,
327; becomes Pueblo
agent, 362
Curtis, Natalie—86

Dinnebito Wash—143
Do-ahs-tahhe (Navajo)—291-292
Dolls-Grind-Corn Dance
(Hopi)—276-282

Ed, interpreter see Thacker,
Thomas E..
Espejo, Antonio de—103
Espeleta, Fray Joseph de—
killed, 103,145

factors (Indian agents)—216-217
Fewkes, Dr. Jesse
Walter—cited, 268
Figueroa, Fray Jose de
—killed, 103
First Mesa—196,204,234
Fishberg,   , "Pulmonary
Tuberculosis"—cited, 360

Gallup, N.M.—297
"Ghost's" wife (Navajo)—329-330
government loans (see Hopi
Indians—government loans)
Greeley, Horace (Hopi)—131-134
Gregory, Herbert E., "The
Navajo Country"—cited, 336
Griffin, Cyrus—216
Guy (Navajo) see
Hoske Nehol Gode

Hano (Tewa), Ariz.—founded, 136

Hauke Mesa, Ariz.—101
Hayden, Carl—248
Honani (Hopi)—210,339
Hooker Hongave
(judge)—132-134,363
Hopi (Moqui) Indians—79; in
Pueblo Rebellion, 103-104;
as police, 136; physical
characteristics, 146,343;
and Indian Service, 148-155;
and Col. Scott, 159-180;
creation myth, 163-167; children and schools, 152-180;
characteristics, 190-207;
history, 196-199; population
figures, 198; compared to
Jews, 198-199; relations with
Navajos, 200-201, 298-299,
312-324; trading habits,
224-225; in World War I,
226-237; and Liberty Bonds,
228-237; government loans
("reimbursables"), 237-238;
photographs of ceremonies,
251-255; Snake Dance, 201,
205,244,245,248-251,260-274,
276; Dolls-Grind-Corn Dance,
276-282; and liquor, 297;
religion, 336-339; clans, 338-
339; naming ceremonies, 339-
341; personal names, 341;
place names, 341-342; rabbit
hunting, 342; dress, 343-345;
marriage customs, 346-357;
divorce, 351-352; burial customs, 357-358; disease, 358-360
Hopi (Moqui) Reservation—79,
98-99, 196-207
Hoske Nehol Gode
(Navajo)—328-335
Hoske Yega "Old Mike"
(Navajo)—137-138
Hostin Chien Bega, "Bull-
Neck" (Navajo)—139
Hostin Nez "Tall Man"
(Navajo)—123-125,132,133,134,158
Hostin Nez Bega Number 4
(Navajo)—125
Hotevilla, Ariz.—142-145,196;
establishment 87,166-167;
children and schools, 152-180
Hubbell, John Lorenzo—148,248,
269,270,315
Huh-kwat-we (Terrace of the
Winds)—283
Humphrey, David—216
Hunt, Gov.   —248

Indian Agents—3-6; duties, 114-

118,220; history, 215-223
Indian Liquor Service—298-311
Indian police see police (Indian)
Indian Service—waste and in-
    efficiency, 108-109; inventory
    system, 108-111; and politics,
    119-121; history, 215-223;
    and Indian criminals, 295;
    see also Bureau of Indian
    Affairs
Indian Wells, Ariz.—101,185,302

Jay (Navajo)—328-329
Jedito Wash—102
Jews—compared to Hopi, 198-199
"Judgement Seat" (mesa)—92

Keams, Tom—211,361
Keams Canyon—293,361
Keams Canyon Agency, Ariz.—
    106-112; first school, 148,
    210-211, school dispute, 155-
    180; established, 211; hospital,
    214
Kewanimptewa (Hopi)—87,125
Kopte, Emri—339

Leaming, Mr.   —236-237
Leupp, Francis E.—323; and
    Hopis, 150-151; cited on
    Navajos, 295
Leupp, Indian Agency—302
Liberty Bonds—sales to
    Indians, 228-237
Lidge Palaquoto (Hopi)—314-324
Limping Joe (Navajo)—291-294
Lincoln, Benjamin—216
Lo-lo-lo-mi (Hopi chief)—148
Lone Cottonwood
    Springs, Ariz.—57
Lu-kah-des-chin (Keams
    Canyon)—361

Machongnovi, Ariz.—196
medicine man (Navajo)—71-73
"Mi-he" see coyote
miscegenation see Arizona—
    Marriage laws
Moencopi, Ariz.—88
Mohoce see Hopi
Mohoqui see Hopi
Monument Point, Ariz.—84
Moqui—definition, 195-196;
    see also Hopi
Moqui Buttes, Ariz.—63
Murchison, Kenneth F., "The
    Evolution of the Indian Agent,"
    —220; cited, 221

Navajo Indians—death and burial
    customs, 126-129; as police,
    137; relations with Hopi, 200-
    201,298-299,312-324; trading
    habits, 224-225; Roosevelt on,
    294; and liquor, 297-311,328;
    personal names, 329
Navajo Mountain—144
"Nultsose"—definition, 67

One-eyed Dan (bootlegger)—
    301-302,304,310
Oraibi, Ariz.—86,196; factions,
    87-88; description, 90-93;
    invaded by U.S. troops, 1890,
    .148-149; invaded by U.S. troops,
    1894, 149-150; smallpox, 1898,
    150
Oraibi Wash, Ariz.—84-85
Oyaping Nelson (Tewa police-
    man)—176-177

Padilla, Fray Juan de—102-103
Pah-lah (Hopi)—314
Painted Desert—101,196,241
Pavatea, Tom—234-237
Perry, Reuben—323
Pesh-la-kai Etsetti—78
photography—at ceremonies,
    251-255
piki bread—345-346
police (Indian)—135,298-300
Porras (priest at Tusayan)—
    poisoned, 103
prayer sticks (Hopi)—337

Rabbit-ear Butte—101
railroad lands—302-303
Rainbow Canyon—9,10
Rattlesnake Butte, Ariz.—57
Red Mesa, Ariz.—84
"reimbursables" see Hopi
    Indians—government loans
Roberts, Mr.   —65-77
Robinson, Herbert F.—cited, 268
Rodgers, Mary Y.—185,234
Roosevelt, Pres. Theodore—118;
    cited on Navajos, 294

"Sack-hair" ("Boss," "the
    Chief")—24-29; 30,36-39,48-49,
    78-79,94-96
Sackaletztewa (Hopi)—173-174,
    176-177
Sageny Litsoi (Navajo)—138
Sandia Indians—104
Sandoval decision—217
Santa Maria, Fray Agustin—
    killed, 103

Scar Chin (Navajo)—123
Scott, Col. Hugh L.—135,156,
 270; at Keams Canyon, 159-180;
 at Hotevilla, 161-180; and
 Youkeoma, 162-180,189; cited,
 298-299
Second Mesa—196,230,231,234
Senagathe, "Wanderer"
 (Navajo)—123
Seton, Ernest Thompson—205-207
Shelton, Mr.   —253
Shupula (Hopi)—339
Shupula, Harry—202,210
Silversmith Jim (Navajo)—123
Sioux Indians—208-209,218
Sitchumnovi, Ariz.—196
Smith, Mr.   —56,58-59,61
Snake Dance (Hopi)—201,205,
 244,245,248-251,260-274,276;
 washing of the snakes, 269-274
Squash Blossom Butte, Ariz.—63
squaw dance—65-77
Stella (Hopi)—359-360

Taddytin (Navajo)—139-140
Taft, Pres. William H.—104
Tewa, Ariz.—196
Tewa Indians—in Hopi service,
 136-137; as police, 137,139,176
Tewaquaptewa (Hopi)—86-87
Thacker, Thomas E. "Ed"—
 72-73,313-323
Third Mesa—196

Tolani Lakes, Ariz.—84
tourists—240-259
Tovar, Pedro de—85,
 102,103,240
Trader system—established, 216
Truxillo, Fray Joseph de—
 killed, 103
Tusayan—102,196

Vargas Zapata y Lujan Ponce
 de Leon y Contreras,
 Diego de—103

Walpi, Ariz.—196,202-204,262
Washington, Pres. George—
 appoints Indian
 commissioners, 216
Wepo Wash—313-315
Whispering Bill—123
White Cone—101
witchcraft—130-131
Womack, A.H.—212,234

Yellow-Horse (Navajo)—123
Youkeoma (Hopi)—86-87,142,
 181-190,213; to Washington,
 104-105; imprisoned, 145;
 and Col. Scott, 162-180,189;
 founds Hotevilla, 167; threatens
 Miss Abbott, 184-185; imprisoned at Keams Canyon, 186-
 189; released, 189

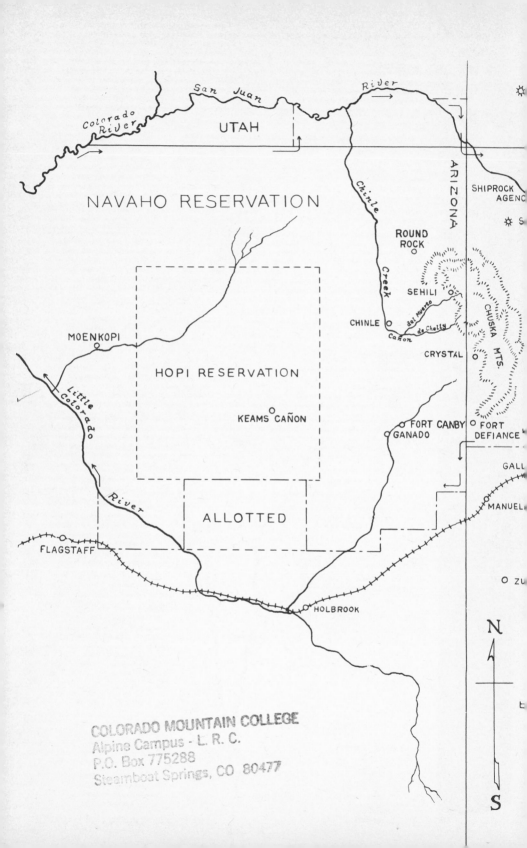

NAVAHO RESERVATION

UTAH

ARIZONA

San Juan *River*

Colorado River

River

SHIPROCK AGENC

S

ROUND ROCK ○

Chinle Creek

SEHILI ○

CHUSKA MTS.

CHINLE ○

del Muerto

Cañon de Chelly

CRYSTAL ○

MOENKOPI ○

Little Colorado

HOPI RESERVATION

KEAMS CAÑON ○

○ FORT CANBY
GANADO ○

○ FORT DEFIANCE

GALL

River

ALLOTTED

MANUEL

FLAGSTAFF ○

○ ZU

○ HOLBROOK

N

S